THE BRITISH HORROR FILM

THE BRITISH HORROR FILM

FROM THE SILENT TO THE MULTIPLEX

IAN FRYER

FONTHILL

Fonthill Media Language Policy

Fonthill Media publishes in the international English language market. One language edition is published worldwide. As there are minor differences in spelling and presentation, especially with regard to American English and British English, a policy is necessary to define which form of English to use. The Fonthill Policy is to use the form of English native to the author. Ian Fryer was born in Blackpool and educated in Leeds; therefore British English has been adopted in this publication.

Fonthill Media Limited
Fonthill Media LLC
www.fonthill.media
books@fonthill.media

First published in the United Kingdom and the United States of America 2017
Reprinted 2021

British Library Cataloguing in Publication Data:
A catalogue record for this book is available from the British Library

Copyright © Ian Fryer 2017, 2021

ISBN 978-1-78155-641-2

The right of Ian Fryer to be identified as the author of this work has been asserted by him in accordance with the Copyright, Designs and Patents Act 1988.

All rights reserved. No part of this publication may be reproduced, stored in a retrieval system or transmitted in any form or by any means, electronic, mechanical, photocopying, recording or otherwise, without prior permission in writing from Fonthill Media Limited

Typeset in 10pt on 13pt Sabon
Printed and bound in England

This book is dedicated to all the people who have helped and inspired me along the way, especially the following:

Jay Slater, the world's most patient and understanding editor, along with Alan, George, and Josh at Fonthill Media.

Jackie, my partner, who has had to watch a lot of very strange movies over the past couple of years, only occasionally asking 'Why are we watching this, again?'

David and Simon, for helping to keep me hydrated and reminding me that there is a world beyond old movies.

Mike Jones, for being just amazing while I have been snowed under working on this book.

Ziva the dog, for giving me an excuse to occasionally get out from behind various screens and see the outside world.

Finally, Arthur Crabtree, the best film director ever to emerge from Shipley, West Yorkshire. Seeing his incredible Fiend without a Face *via a chattering 8-mm film projector some thirty years ago was my first clue that there was a world of incredible little-known films outside the mainstream.*

Foreword

Looking back over the years, I feel so lucky at having lived through a time when it was always possible to see new horror films on a big cinema screen and to share the experience with an audience. I can still remember the collective response to shock moments when watching Hitchcock's *Psycho* for the very first time and feeling the tension build in the audience while watching Jack Clayton's *The Innocents*.

However, I can also remember being a teenager in 1950s Britain and just how frustrating it was to be a horror fan at that time. The frustration being caused by the shortage of horror films and how to see them if they were available. There were two main reasons for this situation: firstly, I was too young to see X-rated films; and secondly, the two major cinema circuits were reluctant to book horror films due to their 'family audience' policy. To make things even worse, the wonderful American horror comics were banned. Therefore, the only way to see any kind of horror film was the occasional screening of older films such as Universal's *Frankenstein*, Lugosi's *Dracula*, and the amazing *King Kong* by the more adventurous independent cinemas. It was on a Sunday 'one-day only' showing at a small Classic cinema that I managed to see the 1946 film *The Beast with Five Fingers*, which starred the wonderfully creepy Peter Lorre. It tells of a revengeful severed hand that strangles people, and there is one scene in which Lorre nails the hand to a block of wood in order to keep it under his control, but, in the dead of night, the hand pulls itself off the nail. The scene stayed in my mind for a long time after. I was hooked and I wanted to see more.

It was May 1957 when *The Curse of Frankenstein* opened in London to mixed reviews and astonishing box-office success; it was also to be the first in a long line of gothic horror films from Hammer. It could be said that 1957 was the beginning, or at least the rebirth, of horror films in Britain. It was certainly the beginning for me. Even though I was still legally too young for X-rated films, I was tall for my age and somehow I managed to avoid the theatre attendant's watchful eye, and during the following period, I was able to see many of the great horror and science-fiction films of the '50s. I had always loved the big fast rides of the fairground and, through horror films, I discovered that as part of an audience you could experience the same sensation of tense anticipation and fear, all in the safety of a darkened cinema. I was already determined to become a film director and now I knew I wanted to control the roller coaster ride.

My wish came true when I had the good fortune to direct my own horror films in the 1970s; undoubtedly the golden decade for British horror, particularly for British independent horror films. This was a time when, almost every month, two or three new horror films would be showing at a cinema near you.

There may not be as many horror films seen at cinemas now as there were in the 1970s, but with all the new alternative ways to watch films and with an ever-growing number of festivals devoted to the genre, the British horror film can still reach its audience and there will always be the film that stands out from the crowd and will get the attention it deserves. This brings me to *The British Horror Film from the Silent to the Multiplex*, Ian Fryer's in-depth study of the horror film in all its forms. It investigates all aspects of the genre and the elements that defined the British horror film, tracing its roots back to the English gothic novels of the nineteenth century. Informative and entertaining, I have no doubt this excellent book will become an essential reference for all fans of the British horror film.

Norman J. Warren
London
May 2017

Acknowledgements

The following books have been especially helpful in my research: *The Hammer Story* by Marcus Hearn and Alan Barnes (Titan Books, London, 1997); *English Gothic: Classic Horror Cinema 1897–2015* by Jonathan Rigby (Signum Books, England, 2015); *Christopher Lee: The Authorised Screen History* by Jonathan Rigby (Reynolds and Hearn, London, 2001); *The Peter Cushing Companion* by David Miller (Reynolds and Hearn, London, 2000); *Vincent Price: The Art of Fear* by Denis Meikle (Reynold and Hearn, London, 2003); *Boris Karloff: More than a Monster* by Stephen Jacobs (Tomahawk Press, Sheffield, 2010); *Hammer Films: The Bray Studios Years* by Wayne Kinsey (Reynolds and Hearn, London, 2002); *Beasts in the Cellar: The Exploitation Film Career of Tony Tenser* by John Hamilton (FAB Press, Godalming, Surrey, 2005); *Censored: The Story of Film Censorship in Britain* by Tom Dewe Matthews (Chatto and Windus, 1994); and *Gothic Literature* by Andrew Smith (Edinburgh University Press, 2007).

Professor John Bowden's work on Romantic and gothic Victorian literature on the British Library website was also extremely useful: www.bl.uk/romantics-and-victorians/articles/gothic-motifs

CONTENTS

Foreword   7
Acknowledgements   9
Introduction: Snapshots of Horror   13

1	Birth Pains: British Horror Pre-Cinema	15
2	From the Silents to the Thirties	19
3	Forties Gothic	31
4	Hammer Films 1946–56: Before the Horrors	42
5	Hammer Films 1957–70: The Rise of the Gothic	53
6	Amicus Productions: Milton Subotsky and Max Rosenberg	106
7	Tony Tenser and Michael Klinger: Two Guys from Another Part of Town	127
8	Pete Walker: Suburban Horrors	144
9	Norman J. Warren: Horrors from Beyond	155
10	The Haunting of Harry Bromley Davenport	160
11	Eurohorrors: Italy, Germany, and Spain	162
12	American-British Gothic Horror	166
13	*The Omen*: Hollywood from Bust to Boom	170
14	Art Horror and the New Screen Violence	174
15	The Fall of the House of Hammer: 1971–79	178
16	The 1980s: Raising Hell	186
17	The 1990s: New Blood, New Mediums	199
18	The 2000s: Homemade Horrors and Zombies on the Run	208

Endnotes   221
Bibliography   223

Introduction
Snapshots of Horror

Tod Slaughter as Sweeney Todd, eyes bright, leering and twirling his moustache as he prepares to send another victim through the trapdoor of his barber shop. Michael Redgrave as Maxwell Frere, in his hospital bed with staring eyes and fixed grin as we realise his personality has been taken over by his ventriloquist's dummy Hugo. Christopher Lee as Count Dracula, teeth bared and eyes bloodshot as his animal nature is revealed. Matthew Hopkins, his face a grim mask of murder as he watches a beautiful young woman being burned at the stake. Dorothy Yates, apparently a sweet old Scottish lady, was revealed as a deranged, psychotic murderer, advancing towards her next victim, power drill in her hands. Frank Cotton solving a puzzle box, but on opening it, hooks and chains appear from the walls and tear his body to pieces. Jim waking up in hospital to find not only the hospital deserted, but, apparently, the whole of Central London.

All these are snapshots from the long history of the British horror film, a genre that emerged from the shadows of the American and German film industries to become the country's national genre of popular film. So natural was the fit between horror and the European sensibility that when Universal Pictures began making their legendary series of horror pictures in the 1930s they turned to a German visual style and British actors. In the post-war landscape of film, the only convincing way to put a gun in the hands of an Englishman was via the limiting form of the war movie, putting British film production at an automatic disadvantage against American products.

The horror film had its roots in the literary and artistic styles that were deeply embedded in the British psyche. Therefore, when Hammer Films—thus far a small independent studio producing B-pictures for the British and American markets—took on the world with the one-two punch of *The Curse of Frankenstein* and *Dracula* in 1956 and 1957 respectively, there was finally a type of British film that could provide the excitement and physical action audiences craved. This represented the horror genre returning to its natural home and flourishing.

In the horror film, Britain found its national genre of film, able to express in popular form important and complex ideas about Britain's past and present. While doing so, Hammer also proved that British film producers could take on the best the world had to offer, beginning a process by which, for a while at least, it appeared that the entire American film industry had moved to London's Wardour Street. When the British film industry came close to expiring in the '70s, for a while the horror film stood, the only type of film still able to attract funding and audiences. Since then, the British horror film has metamorphosed and returned, roughly once every decade, returning in rude health and a different form to prey on our deepest, darkest fears.

In *The British Horror Film from the Silent to the Multiplex*, I tell the story of the British horror film from silent days to the present. The aim has been to describe what took place (no small feat considering the length of time the book covers) and most of the horror movies produced in Britain, while also presenting a healthy slice of opinion. Discussing film history should be fun, and hopefully I have been able to communicate some of my enthusiasm for the subject and the sheer fun I have had discussing the films. Please accept my apologies in advance if I do not like one of your favourite films, particularly if it is *The Devil Rides Out*—I tried, I really did.

Now read on and join me on misty moors, in doom-laden castles, in laboratories creating nameless horrors, and inside the mind of a certain sweet old Scottish lady carrying a power drill. The horror starts here.

Ian Fryer
Bradford, West Yorkshire
May 2017

1
Birth Pains: British Horror Pre-Cinema

The Home of Horror

Much of this book is concerned with British horror films made in the post-war era, especially the body of work made from 1956 onwards, the year in which Hammer Films shocked the world with its hugely successful *The Curse of Frankenstein*. The particular set of circumstances that led to a small B-picture studio becoming the most consistently successful in Britain over a period of at least ten years are covered later in this book, but looking back, it was only natural that horror films should be produced in Britain. To discover why, we need to look back to the literary roots of the gothic horror genre itself.

The original Goths were a Germanic tribe who settled throughout Europe between the third and fifth centuries AD who helped to bring down the Roman Empire in Western Europe. The term gothic as we understand it today and its importance in the history of the horror genre comes not from there, but instead from an artistic movement known as the Gothic Revival. Spanning the early eighteenth to the late nineteenth centuries, the Gothic Revival covered several disciplines, most importantly architecture and literature. In architecture, the Gothic Revival style rose from the status of rebellious upstart—beloved of the wealthy and artistic—to being such a mainstream symbol of the power of the British establishment that Britain's Houses of Parliament were designed in this style in 1840 by Charles Barry after the previous structure was destroyed by fire.

In a way, this was appropriate for a structure that wished, despite the modernity of its construction, to suggest to onlookers a link to the past—that this was an ancient seat of power and its rulers wielded its authority by ancient right. Neither was especially true, but the whole point of the Gothic Revival style was to present a theatrical representation of the past. The style was popularised in Britain by the writer, art collector, and politician Horace

Walpole, Earl of Orford. Purchasing a house, Strawberry Hill, Walpole set about converting it over the next thirty years into a gothic fantasia, reflecting his artistic tastes and fascination with medieval history. Even in Walpole's lifetime, Strawberry Hill, by now resembling an impressive white castle, was a tourist attraction, its interior packed with impressive-looking, cheerfully historically inaccurate detail.

In the heightened atmosphere of Strawberry Hill, inspired by a particularly vivid dream, Walpole wrote what is generally acknowledged to be the first gothic novel, *The Castle of Otranto*, first published in 1764. In the spirit of historical fakery that inspired Strawberry Hill, the novel was in its first edition claimed to be from a rediscovered and translated manuscript originally printed in Naples in 1529, telling a story yet more ancient. The utterly strange story is of Manfred, Lord of the Castle of Otranto, whose son is killed on his wedding day when a huge metal helmet falls on him. Driven half mad by this turn of events and by the prospect of the end of his family line, Manfred resolves to marry his son's intended bride, much against the wishes of the lady herself, not to mention his own wife. The appeal of *The Castle of Otranto* is in its atmosphere, events taking place in a skilfully described world of gloomy battlements and dungeons infested with an air of madness.

Other writers were inspired by Walpole's example, though it was not until the 1790s that the genre began to truly take shape with critical mass of popular writers who developed the key themes, settings, and character types that others would return to time and again. Ann Radcliffe began a series of gothic novels with *The Castles of Athlin and Dunbayne* in 1789, following this with the hugely successful *A Sicilian Romance* the following year. By 1794 and *The Mysteries of Udolpho*, Radcliffe was attracting huge advances for her work. So popular was her work that Jane Austen wrote *Northanger Abbey* as a comic satire on Radcliffe, explicitly naming many of the popular gothic novels of the time that Austen read. Unlike other eighteenth-century gothic novelists such as Walpole and Matthew Lewis—whose highly popular *The Monk: A Romance* was published in 1796—Radcliffe tended to give her stories rational explanations for the apparently supernatural events that took place. What she helped to establish was the figure of the brooding, aristocratic villain residing in an ancient castle, which served as a template for characters as diverse as Charlotte Brontë's Mr Rochester in her 1847 novel *Jane Eyre* and Count Dracula in Bram Stoker's 1897 *Dracula*.

A second wave of gothic novels appeared in the nineteenth century, including gothic influenced romances such as the aforementioned *Jane Eyre* and two highly influential works written as a result of a literary competition between Mary Shelley, her future husband, Percy Shelley, Lord Byron, and John Polidori to see which could write the best horror story. Mary Shelley's *Frankenstein: or The Modern Prometheus* clearly won, and it has been one of the most influential books on the history of the horror genre. Springing from the same competition was Dr John Polidori's *The Vampyre*, the first modern appearance of the vampire in fiction. Adapting the image of the notorious Romantic libertine Lord Byron for his protagonist Lord Ruthven, Polidori helped to fix the character traits of the vampire in the popular imagination.

Not all gothic stories in this period were located within the horror genre, most notable are Charlotte Brontë's *Jane Eyre* and her sister, Emily's, *Wuthering Heights*, both of which were published in 1847 and saw gothic themes entering mainstream literature. Gothic horror became increasingly popular in Britain through the work of two Irish writers most famous for vampire stories, Joseph Sheridan Le Fanu, author of *Carmilla* (the story of a female vampire), and Bram Stoker. Stoker, of course, was the author of the most famous vampire story of all—*Dracula*.

This was popular literature and not aimed at literary respectability, but even these were not the most populist of horror literature. The figure of the vampire fixed in the imagination by Polidori was introduced to a much wider audience via the medium of cheap 'Penny Dreadful' publications presenting serials including *Varney the Vampire*. This was written by James Malcolm Rymer beginning in 1845 and was published over a period of two years in epic length—the practice was for unpopular serials to be quickly curtailed and popular ones to be extended. *Varney the Vampire* was extended to the point of tedious unreadability over 232 chapters, but contains sequences of well-constructed horror that remain effective today.

Gothic Themes and Imagery

Bram Stoker's *Dracula* can be seen today to distil many of the ongoing themes and images of the gothic genre. The genre tended to have periods of popularity during times of uncertainty, such as during the French Revolution in the late eighteenth century—which caused the fear of a wave of similar uprisings across Europe—and the Industrial Revolution—changing relations between genders and classes and upsetting long-held certainties. As well as the fascination with the medieval world that lay at the heart of the original wave of gothic writers such as Walpole, we see a tension between the ancient and modern, which is very typical of gothic fiction.

In *Dracula*, young lawyer Jonathan Harker is moved from the modern world in Britain, a great industrial power at the heart of a huge empire, to imprisonment in the archaic society of Transylvania. Van Helsing battles Dracula armed with ancient knowledge, but the heroes of the novel are armed with the most modern of communications technology in what is a violent conflict between the old and the new. It is also very easy to read into

Dracula a degree of social comment on European aristocracy, literally sucking the lifeblood from the ordinary people they oppress. It is interesting to note that the novel was written by an Irishman—in the late nineteenth-century atmosphere of revolutionary ferment, an English author might have been more likely to find a threat to the aristocratic classes as horrifying, rather than siding with those who wish to destroy the Count.

Another key theme explored by Dracula is that of differing states of being. Count Dracula is both human and animal, while at the same time neither, in just the same way that a werewolf is neither human nor beast. Frankenstein's monster is neither dead nor alive in the traditional sense, in exactly the same way that ghosts are in some way between these two states. Robert Louis Stevenson's novella *The Strange Case of Dr Jekyll and Mr Hyde*, published in 1886, concerns someone who transitions between two different states of being, one rational and one savage and animalistic, examining the idea that we carry within us both conditions at the same time.

Gothic literature came at a point in time when politics and philosophy were exploring the idea that relations between people, including class and gender, were not fixed. It provided a space to talk about subjects that mainstream literature tended to shy away from thanks to the distancing device of the supernatural and uncanny.

Writers associated with the Romantic movement such as Coleridge, Shelley, and Byron were attracted to gothic literature in its earlier forms as a way to explore how the irrational and supernatural could be used to comment on real life experience. The tensions between the rational and irrational in gothic writing can be seen to stem from a central philosophical debate of the eighteenth Century. Enlightenment thinking represented a system of beliefs extolling the virtues of rationality and of the observable world. This represented a challenge to traditional religious thinking, and in reaction to this, the Romantic movement argued that human experience could not be completely explained by science. A key concept of Romanticism was the sublime—that quality of greatness that cannot be explained by rational means. The sublime could also be associated with feelings of terror as this was the most powerful emotion most people might experience.

2
From the Silents to the Thirties

Silent Screams

Gothic horror was reaching a peak of popularity during the period in which cinema was developing from a scientific curiosity to a viable form of mass entertainment, offering visual opportunities that were quickly taken up by early film directors. The earliest filmmakers worked with what we today might term horror themes in two ways: firstly, they adapted popular stage melodramas from the only recently passed Victorian era such as *Maria Marten or The Murder in the Red Barn*, based on a real-life 1927 murder case. The story quickly passed to the status of legend, being told in sensational fashion in books, cheap 'Penny Dreadful' magazines, and by travelling 'barnstorming' theatre companies. With the primitive film technology available and the still undeveloped visual grammar of the medium, it made a lot of sense for pioneer filmmakers to choose subjects and stories that audiences would already be familiar with. Thus, *Maria Marten* had been filmed at least five times before Tod Slaughter starred in the 1935 sound version, while *It's Never Too Late to Mend*, another melodrama later filmed with Slaughter, had been filmed in 1913, 1917, and 1922.

Some British producers in this early era attempted something more ambitious than pointing a camera at stage actors miming their way through melodramas, more in the fashion of the famous work of George Méliès, who was producing early science fiction fantasies that stretched the trick photography then available to the limit. Such titles included *The Haunted Curiosity Shop* (1901), in which a mummy transforms on screen into a skeleton. Subjects relating to ancient Egypt became popular subjects for film productions after the discovery of King Tutankhamun's tomb by Howard Carter's expedition in 1907. This strand of horror included director Will Barker's *The Beetle* (1919), based on Richard March's 1897 gothic story,

Barker having in 1916 made a film version of Oscar Wilde's *The Picture of Dorian Gray*.

As film grew in popularity during the 1920s, growing into a truly mass entertainment medium, British producers began to suffer in comparison to the material being imported from America and Germany. The horror hits of the 1920s, which achieved major popularity and are remembered today, are not the work of Will Barker or his contemporary Cecil Hepworth, the latter having set up studios in Walton-on-Thames that outlasted his 1923 bankruptcy and were active until 1961. It was difficult for the underfunded British production sector to compete with the huge productions of American studios. This was especially true of the work of Lon Chaney, the foremost star of horror films and hugely talented both as an actor and a make-up artist, leading to his being popularly known as 'The Man of a Thousand Faces'. Chaney's status as a legend of silent horror rests on three films, the first two of which were what production company Universal described as Super Productions, being of a far greater scale than the normal run of films that made up its release schedule at the time. Chaney's Quasimodo in *The Hunchback of Notre Dame* (1923) and his title role in *The Phantom of the Opera* (1925) shocked audiences with the elaborate and physically demanding make-up effects Chaney utilised to alter his appearance. Moving to MGM, he starred as the vampiric Professor Burke in *London After Midnight* (1927) for director Tod Browning, and stills of his staring eyes, jagged teeth, and top hat have tantalised film scholars for decades since the only known copy of the film was destroyed in a fire in 1967.

The country most renowned internationally for the artistic quality of its films in the silent era was not America however, but Germany, where the deep shadows and distorted perspectives of German Expressionist filmmaking gave horror cinema its lasting visual signature. Robert Wiene's *The Cabinet of Dr. Caligari* (1919) was one of the earliest and most visually extreme examples of this style, starring a young Conrad Veidt as Cesare the Sonambulist, and proved hugely influential. In 1923, another horror film still widely seen today was released, *Nosferatu, a Symphony of Horror*. Directed by F. W. Murnau and starring in the title role the mysterious and possibly pseudonymous Max Schreck, *Nosferatu* was an uncredited filming of Bram Stoker's *Dracula*, which set the style for future cinematic versions of the tale. We are very fortunate that the film remains available for viewing as the Bram Stoker estate won a court case over the unauthorised use of the Dracula story and all copies were ordered destroyed. Highly influential on future horror film production were *Der Golem* (1920) and Fritz Lang's huge science fiction epic *Metropolis* (1926), both of which can be seen stylistically and thematically as precursors to James Whale's later Frankenstein films.

So renowned were German film production techniques that Britain's brightest young film director, Alfred Hitchcock, was sent to Germany to study production methods. Hitchcock directed his first two films, *The Pleasure Garden* (1925) and *The Mountain Eagle* (1926), in studios in Munich, scoring his first popular hit the following year with his Jack the Ripper thriller *The Lodger*, which bears many of the visual hallmarks of the German Expressionist style.

The Sound Era

Despite the great success of the Lon Chaney films, horror as a genre did not achieve mass popularity until the sound era, when Universal had enormous success with its film versions of *Dracula* and *Frankenstein*, both of which were first released in 1931. While Tod Browning's direction of the former proved rather pedestrian, British director James Whale proved a sensation with his handling of *Frankenstein* and its sequel *The Bride of Frankenstein*. Many British actors had made the trip to Hollywood to take advantage of the opportunities offered by American studios desperate for stage-trained actors with clear voices, thus the Universal cycle of horror films of the 1930s and '40s was strongly populated by British performers.

Dracula was cast with the actor who had played the title role on Broadway, Bela Lugosi's thick Hungarian accent at least having the advantage of being genuinely from the region in which the story is set. *Frankenstein* saw Whale populate his mythical middle-Europe with a large number of English actors, including his friend Colin Clive in the lead role of Henry Frankenstein and, as the monster, a gaunt actor who had been in films since 1919, usually at the bottom half of the cast list. At the age of forty-four, the dark-skinned, angular-featured Boris Karloff had grown into his unusual looks and had recently made a big impact both on stage and film in the prison drama *The Criminal Code*. Despite his stage name, Karloff had no known Slavic heritage and was born in London in 1887 as William Henry Pratt. His role in *Frankenstein* would make him a star for the rest of his life.

A large expatriate community of British performers grew up in Hollywood, many of whom made an impact in horror films including Basil Rathbone (South African born but raised in Britain), Lionel Atwill, Ernest Thesiger (splendid as Dr Pretorius in *The Bride of Frankenstein*), and George Zucco (who brought a touch of villainous class to seemingly every single horror B-picture Hollywood produced in the 1940s). This meant that Hollywood's horror output of the 1930s had a distinctly British feel to it, as did associated films such as Universal's 1939–46 *Sherlock Holmes* series starring Basil Rathbone and Nigel Bruce, which often utilised horror's visual motifs.

This provided a unique opportunity: genres such as Westerns or gangster pictures were highly popular with British audiences, but deep American associations made them almost impossible for British producers to emulate. The development of the horror as a film genre made it possible to make British pictures, which might not be too far removed from the highly popular Hollywood product. One way in which this was achieved was by importing the two biggest stars the American horror film had produced since the death of Lon Chaney in 1930: Boris Karloff and Bela Lugosi.

Boris's Return Home

The colossal success of the Universal cycle of horror pictures sparked the production of a limited amount of horror film production in Britain. It helped that the two most iconic stars produced by these films were occasionally willing to take the trans-Atlantic sea voyage from America: Boris Karloff because he was English and still had a large family in the UK, being the youngest of nine brothers; Bela Lugosi because his Hollywood career was in dire straits.

Karloff was first to make the trip in 1933 to star in *The Ghoul*, for Gaumont British. Based on a play by Dr Frank King, this was directed at Lime Grove studios by T. Hayes Hunter, an American director who had formerly worked for Samuel Goldwyn before moving to Britain in 1927. The striking photography in the shadowy German Expressionist style was by the expatriate Austrian cinematographer Günther Krampf. This adds up to a film that has more visual flair than the rest of Britain's horror output of the 1930s put together.

Karloff plays a dying Egyptologist who purchases at great expense a jewel known as The Eternal Light, which legend has it, can grant the secret of immortality. A number of people turn up to try to get back the jewel, which has been stolen from Egypt, but Karloff promises that if it is taken from him, he will return from the dead and kill.

The Ghoul was thought to be a lost film for many years until a damaged, subtitled 16-mm print appeared, which did not exactly show the film off to its best advantage. Subsequently, a pristine copy was found in a film vault, which means that this oddity can now be viewed in absolutely beautiful quality. What this reveals is a film that looks terrific, but which has some problems. There is a great cast, headed by Karloff, but also including his *Bride of Frankenstein* cast-mate Ernest Thesiger, Cedric Hardwicke, and, making his film debut, Ralph Richardson. On the minus side, juvenile lead Anthony Bushell (later to become a useful actor-director) is poor, rushing his dialogue and coming across as a bumptious ass.

The screenplay takes almost nothing from the original play, instead borrowing heavily from Karloff's then-recent Universal hits, particularly *The Mummy* and *The Old Dark House*. It also suffers from Karloff not being in the action enough, his character apparently dying, leading to a long middle section in which the pace of the film flags badly. Thankfully, he returns from the dead in scenes that fully utilise the actor's talent for mime and unique, gaunt physiognomy. Karloff's return in desiccated, murderous form enlivens the proceedings considerably, but the film then insists on giving everything a rational explanation.

Despite the best efforts of all concerned to make *The Ghoul* after the fashion of the Universal horror pictures, the film failed to duplicate the roaring success of those films and fell into a long period of obscurity. Three years later, Karloff returned to Britain, again for Gaumont British, to make *The Man Who Changed His Mind*. While this was not as overtly stylish as *The Ghoul*, it is a far more entertaining and witty film as well as being a very polished production.

Karloff plays Dr Laurience, who has invented a device to electronically transfer personalities from one body to another. Press magnate Lord Haslewood (the excellent Frank Cellier) agrees to fund Laurience's work, but withdraws his support after the scientific community mock his claims at a meeting to unveil his discovery. After Haslewood announces that his work is to be suppressed and destroyed, Laurience swaps the press magnate's mind with that of his crippled, acerbic assistant Clayton (Donald Calthorp, who extracts great fun out of the part).

In a highly unusual development for a Karloff movie, the show is stolen from Boris, in this case by Frank Cellier in what amounts to a dual role. As the pompous, self-promoting Haslewood, Cellier completely changes his performance as his mind is swapped. What follows is pure comedy, which is a wonderful surprise just as the film appears to be headed in the direction of heavy drama. Things get slightly more serious when Haslewood learns from his son (John Loder) that he has a serious heart condition. His own original body having died, Haslewood/Clayton wants to swap bodies with Loder so he can have a healthy body and inherit Haslewood's fortune, while Laurience wants to swap bodies with Loder so he can marry his assistant, Dr Wyatt.

Dr Wyatt is played by Anna Lee, who in real life was married to the film's director, Robert Stevenson. The pair later made their careers in Hollywood, where Stevenson spent many highly successful years directing feature films for Walt Disney. Lee makes for a highly appealing heroine, proving strong and capable, with a boyfriend who is there to be kidnapped and rescued, which makes a refreshing change from cinematic norms. As the boyfriend, John Loder is bright and funny, and was soon on his way to Hollywood in search of wider opportunities.

Boris Karloff stayed on to make one further British film in 1936. *Juggernaut* was a quickie made by Wardour Films, a subsidiary of ABPC, at Twickenham Studios. This time, Karloff plays Dr Sartorious, who is in poor health and, desperate for funds for his research, agrees for £20,000 to poison a wealthy man on behalf of his younger, unfaithful wife on the pretext of acting as his doctor. Naturally, the plan goes wrong, but my goodness it is hard to care one way or another in a film so statically directed and stiffly acted that even the presence of the great Karloff cannot sufficiently enliven things.

Vampire Over Welwyn Garden City

By one of those odd coincidences, which history is littered with, the company that tempted Bela Lugosi, Hungarian star of American horror pictures, to first appear in a British picture was none other than Hammer Films. Hammer at this point was far from being the thriving concern it became in post-war years, being instead a small company making cheap 'Quota Quickies' formed by William Hinds, who was more commonly known by the stage name he used as a music hall comedian—Will Hammer. This name he lent to the film production company he set up with, among others, James Elder Wills, and in 1935, Hammer and a new partner, Enrique Carreras, formed a film distribution concern, Exclusive Films. For most of its long life, Hammer Films would be something of a family affair and the sons of Hammer, Elder Wills, and Carreras would be intimately concerned in its future course.

For a brief period in the mid-1930s, Hammer Films attempted to produce more ambitious feature films, making *The Mystery of the Marie Celeste* with Bela Lugosi in 1935 and *Song of Freedom* in 1936 with the American singing star Paul Robeson. The experiment with larger scale film production proved a brief one and soon Hammer Films was wound up, the company concentrating instead on its more profitable Exclusive Films distribution arm for the next decade. Catapulted to instant fame as Dracula, Lugosi proved difficult to cast successfully and despite occasional high-profile roles in films such as Tod Browning's *Mark of the Vampire* (1935), he was on the cusp of a serious career slump, working for tiny fees on films such as Cameo Pictures' *Murder by Television* when Hammer's offer arrived.

The Mystery of the Marie Celeste offers an explanation for the legendary case of a ship found adrift with no crew on board. Here, the owners of the *Marie Celeste* need a new crew in a hurry and hire the local bar owner, a powerful figure in the locale, to find the required personnel. Lugosi turns up, having spent six years on board a ship called *The Black Dog* after being shanghaied, and despite being a shambling wreck, he is hired as bosun of the *Marie Celeste*. The first mate of the ship, it turns out, is the very man who shanghaied Lugosi six years previously and has done the same to half of the *Marie Celeste*'s new crew, with the captain's full knowledge. One by one, the crew start to disappear, some of them clearly murdered, with the dwindling band of survivors starting turn on each other.

The Mystery of the Marie Celeste was shot at Nettlefold Studios, Walton-on-Thames, by American writer-director Denison Clift, whose last film as director this would be. Sadly, the only surviving version of the film seems to be of its American release, retitled *Phantom Ship* and edited by some eighteen minutes. Although Lugosi is by far the best-known actor in the cast, it is interesting to note the presence of Dennis Hoey, who would later move to America where he would play Inspector Lestrade alongside Basil Rathbone's Sherlock Holmes. Lugosi's performance is broad and stagy, as is the whole production, but he shows real star quality, especially compared to the rest of the cast. He also gets a magnificent speech in which he describes what he suffered on his previous ship, including being flogged and lowered into the sea where a shark ate one of his arms. While some cast members are rather stiff, several performers lower down the cast list do have the genuine look of old sea dogs, especially J. Edward Pierce as the muscular, tattooed Harbens.

By now fifty-seven years of age and looking more like a kindly old uncle than a terrifying horror star, Lugosi was convinced to return to England in 1939 to star in *The Dark Eyes of London*. The year 1939 would go down in history as the absolute peak year of quality for Hollywood studio system—highlights including *Gone with the Wind*, *The Wizard of Oz*, *Stagecoach*, and *The Hound of the Baskervilles*. Even the career of Bela Lugosi took an upswing after the actor had barely worked for the previous two years, Universal having cast him as the malevolent shepherd Ygor in *Son of Frankenstein*. This was director Roland V. Lee's triumphant revival of the Universal horror tradition, which kept Lugosi in work either as Ygor or as Frankenstein's monster for the next few years, and led to another good role in 1939 in director Ernst Lubitsch's *Ninotchka*, in which Greta Garbo displayed an unexpected talent for comedy.

Bela's name only appeared above the title in films he made for poverty row studios, such as Monogram and Producers Releasing Corporation (PRC), the latter being renowned as the cheapest producers in Hollywood. Actors appearing in PRC movies were either new to the business or most definitely on the slide. An offer to appear in an English film, complete with an Atlantic cruise to and from the British Isles, must have appeared a tempting offer. Shooting on *The Dark Eyes of London* took place at Welwyn Studios in Welwyn Garden City, which Associated British Picture Corporation used as an overflow studio for their main production facility at Elstree Studios. The film was produced by John Argyle Film Productions, but Argyle was closely associated with ABPC—in an ironic situation that would be repeated occasionally in later years, ABPC could not release the film in its own cinemas as it attracted a 'H' certificate from the British Board of Film Censorship, which meant that none of the major chains would book it.

While *The Dark Eyes of London* was released in the UK via smaller, independent cinemas, it was picked up for distribution by Monogram in

America. Though the film was based on a novel by Edgar Wallace, still one of the most famous writers in the English-speaking world seven years after his death in 1932, he was known for his thrillers and detective stories. For Monogram, the selling point was Lugosi, so the film was retitled *The Human Monster* for its 1940 US release.

The Dark Eyes of London is certainly better produced that the average shoestring-budgeted effort Monogram produced, and the company must have been overjoyed to be handling a higher-class picture featuring one of its regular stars. The film is nicely photographed by Bryan Langley on some convincing, large-scale sets, and director Walter Summers handles the action nimbly, though even at around seventy-five minutes, the film is a tad long. As already noted, the film is based on a novel by Edgar Wallace, which was later filmed in entertainingly lurid style as *Die toten Augen von London (The Dead Eyes of London)* in West Germany in 1961. This British version is almost entirely a detective picture with a few horror bells and whistles added as Scotland Yard investigate a series of corpses found in the Thames. We learn almost immediately that the person responsible for the deaths is Dr Orloff (Lugosi), a doctor barred from working in the medical profession due to his being 'brilliant but unstable'. Instead, Orloff is working in London as an insurance broker while also sponsoring the Dearborn Home for the Blind. He has developed a money making scheme by which he insures people with no relatives, then has them bumped off and pockets the insurance cash himself. To carry out the killings, he uses one of the inmates of the blind home, the hulking, spectacularly ugly, and animalistic Jake (Wilfred Walter). His scheme begins to unravel when he kills a man who turns out to have a daughter who stands to inherit his money (Norwegian glamour puss Greta Gynt).

The film is somewhat let down by a dull leading man, Hugh Williams, playing the Scotland Yard detective on the trail of Orloff. This is a pity as the film is otherwise quite bright and well done, showing us a detailed and convincing look at police work—the concentration on forensic procedure in the script by John Argyle, Patrick Kirwan, and Walter Summers is fascinating and ahead of its time. Bela Lugosi gives a stilted and unsubtle performance, at times hamming quite outrageously. The horror contained in the picture mainly comes from blind murderer Jake and from Lugosi's climactic death drowning in mud, which is really quite horrible for a British film of the era.

There is some evidence on screen that *The Dark Eyes of London* was made with at least one eye on the export market, the film opening with a shot of Tower Bridge, and saddling Detective Williams with Lieutenant O'Reilly (Edmon Ryan) on loan from the Chicago Police Department. O'Reilly provides comic asides of the 'What goes on in this crazy country of yours?' variety in-between offering to beat up subjects and firing the pistol he has somehow been allowed to carry.

Bela Lugosi was to return to England once more to make a film in 1952, by which point, the Universal series had ended and the poverty row studios he had relied on to keep a roof over his head were closing down operations. Despite being seventy years of age and in increasingly poor health, Bela returned to his signature role of Count Dracula for a theatre tour, which included a series of engagements in the British provinces. The tour was a financial failure and Lugosi found himself without the money to return home. A deal was quickly made for Lugosi to star in a film in order to raise the required funds, *Mother Riley Meets the Vampire* (1952), written by Val Valentine and co-produced and directed by John Gilling, who would later direct a series of excellent horror pictures for Hammer.

The story was a continuation of the long and mirth-free Old Mother Riley comedy film series, which had ended the previous year on the divorce of comedy drag performer Arthur Lucan from his wife and stage partner Kitty McShane. This time, owing to a mix-up in the delivery of two crates, Mother Riley receives a radio-controlled robot and becomes mixed up with a fugitive mad scientist known as The Vampire.

Like the majority of horror comedies, *Mother Riley Meets the Vampire* is neither funny enough (nor indeed funny at all, hardly unusual for a Mother Riley film) nor scary enough. It is not without points of interest, though, and is surprisingly watchable under the circumstances, largely thanks to a talented cast giving their all. It really is surprising what a cast could be assembled for a low budget British comedy in 1952: Hattie Jacques shows up as one of Mrs Riley's shop customers and takes part in a musical number (it is hard to describe this as a musical, containing as it does only the one song), while a single scene in a police station features noted character actor Laurence Naismith and Alexander Gauge—soon to be internationally famous as Friar Tuck in the TV series *The Adventures of Robin Hood*—both uncredited as the local constabulary. An unlikely scene stealer is Judith Furse as Bela Lugosi's assistant Freda, who plays her underwritten part with a curious yearning in her eyes and a distinctive, deep-voiced European accent.

While not succeeding in its own right, *Mother Riley Meets the Vampire* does offer an interesting snapshot of the state of the horror genre in 1952. What is clearly demonstrated is that the horror iconography created by Universal Studios in the 1930s was not only regarded as no longer frightening, but was seen as downright comedic, a process that began in 1948 when Universal themselves produced *Abbott and Costello Meet Frankenstein*. The film also demonstrates that, despite future Hammer director John Gilling's use of shadowy lighting, the dominant movie genre at this point in the 1950s was not gothic horror, but science fiction. Both SF and horror iconography are traded on as Bela Lugosi's Professor Von Housen is known as The Vampire by the press and apparently identifies as such, sleeping in a coffin in full evening dress, but the film makes it clear that this is a delusion and that he is actually a mad scientist. His inventions include a machine that can make time run backwards and a radio-controlled robot (a prop that would turn up as late as a 1966 in an episode of *The Avengers*), an army of which Von Housen plans to use in order to take over the world.

Although *Mother Riley Meets the Vampire* was a strange, bizarre, and slightly sad end to Bela Lugosi's British film career, it did serve several purposes. The film made its way to America, retitled *Vampire over London*, which helped to extend the career of the ailing Lugosi, though his next stop was making films with Edward D. Wood Jr, who would become known, slightly unfairly, as the worst film director in history after his *Plan 9 from Outer Space* (1959) became a posthumous cult classic. It also became by far the most widely seen of the fifteen Old Mother Riley films thanks to the participation of Lugosi, helping keep alive memories of one of the most popular acts from British and Irish variety theatre.

Tod Slaughter: The British Barnstormer

British cinema production of the 1930s tended to fatally lack a certain degree of showmanship in the acting department. While the American stage could produce leading men like James Cagney and Humphrey Bogart, too many of their British equivalents were of the tight-jawed, uncharismatic like of Anthony Bushell and Hugh Williams, as described above. There was one star of British film, however, to whom the overrated British acting virtues of restraint and a stiff upper lip were alien concepts. Britain's greatest home-grown star of horror films was the unique figure of actor-manager Tod Slaughter, whose chosen metier of the Victorian-era melodrama was absolutely perfect for his richly hammy, no hold barred style of acting.

Slaughter was born Norman Carter Slaughter in Newcastle upon Tyne, and initially used the stage name N. Carter Slaughter. In 1924, he took over the Elephant and Castle Theatre, which took its name from the working-class area of South London in which it was situated. Staying for three memorable years, Slaughter and his repertory company developed their signature style of reviving popular blood and thunder plays from the Victorian era, attracting large audiences, many of whom would have been able to remember these shows from their original versions. Now known as Tod Slaughter, his company left the Elephant and Castle in December 1927 at the end of a long run of *Maria Marten or The Murder at the Red Barn*.

By the early 1930s, Slaughter had found a berth on the West End stage and scored a major success in 1931 playing Long John Silver in *Treasure Island* to matinee audiences and starring in *The Crimes of Burke and Hare* in the play by Gladys Hastings for the evening crowd. The great success of these performances pointed the way to his future career, which in the West End included Slaughter and Company of Barnstormers performing in plays such as *Sweeney Todd, the Demon Barber of Fleet Street*, as well as nostalgic sketch shows such as *The Music Hall of Yesterday*.

Slaughter had by now become a nationally famous figure, appearing in BBC Radio adaptations of his repertoire and provincial theatre tours. Producer George King signed him up to a film contract and a series of vigorous, low-budget horror melodramas were produced over the next five years at Sound City Studios, which eventually changed its name to Shepperton Studios. This began with Slaughter's old theatrical favourite *Maria Marten or The Murder at the Red Barn*, helmed by actor-director Milton Rosmer. King himself then took over directing Slaughter's films, starting with a new version of *Sweeney Todd, the Demon Barber of Fleet Street*, which came complete with a very odd comedic opening and closing sequence set in a modern barber shop. The role of Sweeney Todd was that which Slaughter was born to play, and if the production values of the film were somewhat slapdash, he attacked the title role of the barber whose customers wound up as pie filling with such moustache-twirling relish that the audience was swept along.

In the same year came *The Crime of Stephen Hawke*, again directed by King, which rang a few changes by being an original work in the style of melodramas Slaughter had made his name with. This time, Slaughter was cast as that most despised figure of the Victorian working classes, a moneylender. Being a Tod Slaughter movie, this one leads an even more dastardly double-life as a serial killer known as The Spinebreaker. David MacDonald, whose extremely variable career was to hit a bizarre sort of peak in 1954 with *Devil Girl from Mars*, directed the next film in the series, *It's Never Too Late to Mend*, based on a popular 1856 novel by Charles Reade that Slaughter had performed at the Elephant and Castle theatre in the 1920s, which had previously been filmed in 1913, 1917, and 1922. This was one of two Tod Slaughter films released in 1937, the other being an adaptation of Tom Taylor's 1863 play *The Ticket of Leave Man*, which saw George King return to the director's chair. Taylor's place in history was not sealed by this play, but instead by his *Our American Cousin*, which was the play Abraham Lincoln was watching on the night of his assassination. This is not Slaughter's best work, and it is mainly notable for the outrageously false facial whiskers worn by the male members of the film's cast.

King and Slaughter next tried something different in the form of a contemporary detective mystery, *Sexton Blake and the Hooded Terror*, which does not really sit within the run of Slaughter's horror melodramas. Slaughter's character of crime lord Michael Larron does trade on the actor's villainous image, and the character of Sexton Blake, a sort of Sherlock Holmes copy, had been in print since 1893, beginning an amazingly long run of original adventures that continued until 1969. Returning to more familiar material, the King–Slaughter partnership came up in 1939 with their most horror-themed work to date, *The Face at the Window*. This was based on a play by Brooke Warren that had been filmed three times previously, the last version being in 1932 starring Raymond Massey.

The timing of this switch to a more boldly horrific direction is interesting. Official disapproval of the horror genre by the British Board of Film Classification had reached such a pitch by 1935 that Hollywood studios significantly reduced their production of such films. By 1939, though, a hugely successful American re-release of *Dracula* and *Frankenstein* convinced Universal to reactivate their horror film series. The result, Roland V. Lee's expensive and stylish *Son of Frankenstein*, starring Basil Rathbone as the title character, was a box office triumph, which began a second cycle of Universal horror pictures. Horror was popular at the box office once more, and the Tod Slaughter films found distribution deals in the US.

With *The Face at the Window* and in the follow-up, *Crimes at the Dark House*, a 1940 adaptation of Wilkie Collins' famous proto-detective novel *The Woman in White*, Slaughter's films achieved a real increase in quality, emulating the vim and vigour of the best Hollywood product. This made it an even greater shame that the King–Slaughter film series ended just at this point when they were reaching their peak. Slaughter and his persona were as popular as ever, but the British Government disapproved of horror film production in time of war. When Slaughter returned to film production in 1946, it was in greatly reduced circumstances. His moment had passed, but as we shall see later, he did at least try until the very end to recreate his past glories.

3
Forties Gothic

Gainsborough and the 'Women's Picture'

The apparently sudden reappearance of the gothic horror genre with *The Curse of Frankenstein* in 1957 did not come out of nowhere. Despite the unpromising conditions for the development of any distinctively British school of horror movies existing in the 1940s, some of the groundwork for what was to come later was laid by both the British popular cinema of the 1940s and by the B-movie sector.

Most notably, a pre-horror genre of gothic romances and melodramas was wildly popular with wartime movie audiences inspired and led by the success of a series of costume dramas made by Gainsborough Studios. This cycle of pictures began in 1943 with *The Man in Grey* and was largely based on novels (now largely forgotten) by female novelists, with the aim of making films targeted squarely at women. With a large proportion of the cinema-going male population having been drafted into the armed forces, women, now a major part of the working population with unprecedented independence and disposable income, were a vital part of the cinema audience.

The peak in popularity of this type of film as the dominant genre at the British box office came in 1946. Gainsborough's *The Wicked Lady* proved the most popular film of the year, just ahead of the modern dress psychological drama *The Seventh Veil*, produced independently by Sydney Box. The latter borrowed not only its leading man, James Mason, from Gainsborough, but also much of its atmosphere and storytelling style.

The Gainsborough melodramas made popular stars of not only the leading actresses in these films, such as Margaret Lockwood and Patricia Roc, but also of the male leads, particularly James Mason and Stewart Granger, despite their often-secondary role in the narrative. The dominant male figures in these films harked back to the Byronic archetype of 'mad, bad and dangerous to know', often menacing the female protagonist. A vital factor in the appeal of these films is that the main characters driving the narrative are female—to this day surprisingly unusual in popular cinema.

Most film narratives are presented through the 'male gaze' (I do not present this as an original thought; it is a cornerstone of the understanding of film and gender), told through a male point of view and with female characters often presented as a mysterious, unknowable 'other'. The Gainsborough school of melodrama, like the contemporaneous 'women's films' from America starring actresses such as Bette Davis and Joan Crawford—both of whom would eventually come to England to make horror films—often present women who have their choice of men. These are, however, often unknowable, mysterious men with hidden motives. The female leads are seen as being powerful, but the men are attractive, saturnine, and dangerous. They are the sex symbols in these films.

Thus, Zachary Scott features as the superficially attractive, unfaithful husband of Joan Crawford in her Oscar-winning, career-defining *Mildred Pierce* (1945), in a very similar manner to James Mason's distant, cruel Lord Rohan in *The Man in Grey*, who only marries Clarissa Marr because he requires an heir. In neither film is the errant husband seen as being the only romantic alternative open to the female protagonist—these are women with choices in life, even if they sometimes make disastrously wrong ones.

The dualistic image of attractive, but cruel masculinity is brought to the fore in the trailer for *The Man in Grey*, which ends with a powerful image of James Mason, riding crop in hand, menacingly approaching a prone, terrified Margaret Lockwood. The stark sexuality of this sequence is hard to avoid, and indeed, a glowering Mason with crop in hand also featured on the film's poster artwork. It does not take a huge leap of the imagination to transpose the wrathful Mason with Christopher Lee's Count Dracula gliding towards another terrified, but aroused female victim a decade later.

Gainsborough Studios, in its 1943–49 costume melodrama period, can be seen to have some interesting parallels with the later success of Hammer Films: in both cases, an already existing studio unexpectedly found huge success that they were able to reproduce, creating a genre in the process with which they would be popularly identified with, despite their continuing to produce other types of film and in spite of the entrance of others into the same field.[1] In both cases, ending the successful cycle of films would spell doom for the studios' continued existence.

The Gainsborough series of gothic melodramas introduced a set of images, character types, and an approximate period setting (although the most popular Gainsborough films' Regency setting tended to be set somewhat earlier than that Hammer favoured), which would have remained familiar to audiences in the mid-to-late 1950s and ready to be reimagined and repurposed by Hammer with *The Curse of Frankenstein*.

The 1940s did present some movies with horrific or supernatural themes, despite various obstacles being put in the way of the production of such films. The major cinema chains, particularly Rank, which in 1941 increased its film exhibition holdings in Britain via its purchase of the Gaumont-British group of cinemas, had a policy of only showing films with a 'U' or 'A' certificate. These would help to capture the vital family audience, an absolutely key demographic in the pre-television days when film was the pre-eminent form of entertainment outside of the home. As John Davis, Rank's fearsome chairman, commented: 'fundamentally a film production is intended to satisfy the demand for family entertainment'.[2] 'H' certificate films were most definitely off the menu.

This did open up some opportunities for producers at the low-budget end of the market, making films that would be offered to smaller chains and independent cinemas. Very occasionally, the independent sector would be gifted with a major studio production, such as Associated British's 1942 film *The Night Has Eyes*, written and directed by Leslie Arliss and starring the up-and-coming British star of the moment, James Mason. The pair would score a huge hit the following year at Gainsborough with the aforementioned *The Man in Grey*. A psychological thriller in which Mason's traumatised, reclusive Spanish Civil War veteran is suspected, not least by himself, of being a dangerously unbalanced murderer, *The Night Has Eyes* was a handsome production with some genuinely unsettling scenes. Originally granted an 'A' certificate, the BBFC had a rethink and recertificated the film as 'H'. This was something of an embarrassment for Associated British, which had produced the film and were now unable to screen it in their own ABC cinema chain or sell it on to one of the other big chains, such as Granada or Odeon. This illustrated the limits of the 'H' certificate to cover the range of cinematic styles being produced even in the 1940s, and it proved a boon to the independent cinema sector, which gained what turned out to be one of the most popular British films of 1942.

Changes in Tastes and 'The Great Purge'

The Second World War had a profound effect on popular tastes in literature and film on both sides of the Atlantic. In America, dark melodramas, often made on low budgets and with an edge of violent despair about them, became popular, reflecting how the certainties of the pre-war era had been stripped away and the psyche of the fighting men (this was a very male type of filmmaking) had been damaged and brutalised. Their shadowy photography took visual cues from the same German Expressionist style that had produced the striking visuals of *The Cabinet of Dr. Caligari*. These films were not regarded by their makers as being any sort of coherent genre, but they proved enormously influential, with Hammer films (at this point mainly producing films under the banner of Exclusive) adopting the style for many of the thrillers they made during the 1950s. In post-war France, audiences were able, in a very short time span, to see several years' worth of Hollywood product made while their country was under Nazi occupation. A group of ambitious young critics from the magazine *Cahiers du Cinema* could clearly see the difference in tone between the post-war films and what had come before and dubbed the new style Film Noir, after the cheap *Serie Noir* crime novels popular in France.

The Film Noir were highly influenced by writers such as Dashiell Hammett and Raymond Chandler with backgrounds in pulp crime magazines of the pre-war era, such as *Black Mask*. These were tough stories for their era, but were made to look like mild compared to the massively successful Mike Hammer novels written by Mickey Spillane.

Spillane was an ex-fighter pilot who had joined the Army Air Corps the day after the Japanese attack on Pearl Harbor that brought America into the war. If his books lacked the literary aspirations of Hammett and Chandler's novels, he was still a highly skilled writer producing work that was hardboiled and brutal to an unprecedented degree. Also unprecedented was the success of the novels; the first Mike Hammer story, *I, The Jury*, first published in 1947, sold 6½ million copies in the US alone.

The Spillane novels were popular in post-war Britain—if you could find them. Supplies of American books were restricted due to the UK Government's desire to restrict the flow of dollars out of the country. In their place came a boom in *faux* American hardboiled novels written by British authors, usually under a suitably American-sounding penname, often printed by small publishers using whatever paper stock they were able to scrounge up. The most famous of these was James Hadley Chase's *No Orchids for Miss Blandish*, a fearsomely salacious and violent story about the kidnapping and sexual abuse of a wealthy heiress first published in 1939 that became a publishing phenomenon. The success of the fake Americana of James Hadley Chase and the even more pulp-influenced Hank Janson books (sold largely on the strength of titles such as *Broads Don't Scare Easy* and *When Dames Get Tough* and wonderful cover art by Reginald Heade) showed that there was a big market in Britain for more frankly told material than was being produced by 'respectable' book publishers and film producers.

So popular was *No Orchids for Miss Blandish* that, in 1942, the material was adapted into a West End play, and eventually into a highly controversial film released in 1948. The film bowdlerises Chase's original material to a large extent, as the British Board of Film Censors made it clear that the initial version of the script would never be passed for screening. The leering, sex maniac kidnapper Slim of the original story was transformed into a

Bogartesque gangster played by minor American star Jack LaRue, who even bore something of a resemblance to Humphrey Bogart. The resulting film, with attempts at American accents of varying degrees of accuracy by British character actors, was still remarkably brutal by the standards of either British or Hollywood film production of 1948. Not surprisingly, the film was made by independent company Tudor-Alliance for Renown film distributors—the majors would never have touched such material.

While this approach certainly proved profitable in many cases for independent publishers and film companies, it did have its limits. When the film of *No Orchids* was passed uncut with an 'A' certificate, there was a storm of controversy, which resulted in the chief censor having to issue an apology while many local councils outright refused to allow the film to be screened in their area. The film's writer-director St John Legh Clowes never directed again before his early death in 1951 at the age of forty-four, only writing one other script, for the horror comedy *Things Happen at Night*, released in the same year as *No Orchids*.

The makers of *No Orchids for Miss Blandish* could count themselves lucky that their efforts were merely condemned in the press and suppressed in some regions of Britain. Reg Carter and Julius Reiter, the publishers of the Hank Janson books, were sent to trial in 1954 for the publication of obscene libels. Their trial bore many similarities to the 1960 prosecution of Penguin Books over their publication of D. H. Lawrence's *Lady Chatterley's Lover*.

Officialdom's atmosphere of censorious prudery seemed out of step with the times by 1960, but crucially, the publishers of popular literature could not call upon the support of the liberal establishment. Carter and Reiter were both sent to prison, while the writer of most of the Janson novels, Stephen Frances, escaped jail in part due to his having moved to Spain, where he remained for the rest of his life.[3]

The legal persecution of the publishers of pulp crime novels, which today read as very mild stuff, seems absurd today, but it was not an isolated phenomenon and was part of a much larger picture. In the summer of 1951, two members of what later became known as the Cambridge Spy Ring, Kim Philby and Guy Burgess, defected to Moscow. Both had been double agents, working for Britain's security service, but for many years, they had been passing vital secrets to the Soviet Union. Burgess and one of the other members of the spy ring, Anthony Blunt, were homosexuals. Until 1967, homosexual acts were illegal in Great Britain, punishable by prison terms, which made being actively gay fraught with the danger of blackmail.

In October 1951, Clement Atlee's post-war Labour Party Government was replaced by a Conservative administration led by Winston Churchill. The new government was convinced by America's FBI that homosexuality represented a major security risk and needed to be supressed with the full weight of the law. Figures such as Home Secretary David Maxwell Fyfe and Sir Theobald Mathew, Director of Public Prosecutions, were responsible for what has become known as 'The Great Purge', which reached a peak during 1953 and 1954. The resulting wave of prosecutions for homosexual acts ruined many lives, including Alan Turing, whose work at Bletchley Park breaking German codes helped the Allies win the war. To avoid a prison sentence, Turing agreed to be injected with female hormones to supress his sexual desires. The effects of this treatment contributed to his eventual suicide.

The legal authorities extended their purge against homosexuality to a general 'war on vice', during which much that had been tolerated during the war years was suddenly cracked down upon with a heavy hand. Not only was the gay subculture and prostitution subjected to official repression, but a moral crackdown on art and literature was instigated, which reached absurd lengths: not only were the Hank Janson novels supressed, but the creator of saucy seaside postcards of Donald McGill was prosecuted under the Obscene Publications Act 1857. McGill, who was almost eighty years old at the time, escaped prison, but many postcard companies were driven into bankruptcy.

The moral crackdown of the mid-1950s was a tragedy for many ordinary people who were just trying to live their lives, as well as being a repressive force holding back the development of British film culture. The pointlessness of the enterprise is highlighted by the fact that within three years of this irrational wave of repression, Hammer films made British cinema a byword for new standards of horror and explicit violence.

Matters of Life and Death

Despite the legal and policy obstacles placed in the way of genre, films did emerge with horror and supernatural themes: prestigious A-pictures and bottom of the bill Quota Quickies and everything in between. Two of the former came from the rather unexpected source of Ealing Studios. Before the war, the company was best known for its popular comedies aimed at working-class audiences. These featured stars such as George Formby, the northern actor and comic song specialist who Ealing turned into a hugely popular national figure after he had proved his box office appeal on a regional level with a series of low-budgeted films made for Mancunian Films. Ealing had similar comedy successes with Lancastrian singer Gracie Fields and Will Hay, who delighted audiences with his line of slightly crooked schoolmasters. While their comedy successes continued during the Second World War, the conflict saw Ealing branch out into a series of documentary style war films.

By 1944, the tide of the war had turned and it became increasingly clear that the Allied forces would prevail. This meant that producers could look beyond the propaganda effort towards what type of films they would like to make in the future. Ealing head Michael Balcon was keen for the studio to attempt new styles and prove to both audiences and to the studio's new proprietors, The Rank Organisation, what its filmmakers were capable of. *The Halfway House* is a fascinating synthesis of wartime propaganda themes, supernatural elements, and the multiple-story portmanteau style that would become popular later in the decade, and by the 1960s, it would become a staple of the horror genre.

In Basil Dearden's film, a disparate group of strangers, each of whose lives had been affected by the war, meet at the eponymous Halfway House, a hotel situated in idyllic Welsh countryside, run by ghostly (real life) father and daughter Mervyn and Glynis Johns. We see each of their stories before they reached the house and how their stay at the ghostly inn gave them the opportunity to re-evaluate their lives and (in some cases) contribute to the war effort. Thus, a divorcing couple are reunited, a retired sea captain faces his fears and perceived disgrace to return to the navy, and a black marketer ready to sell out to the Nazis prepares to turn himself in to the authorities. The latter provides the film's most amusing scenes, as the crooked businessman fires an associate because the man is too honest, which goes against his scrupulous business principals.

Ealing's follow-up was released on 4 September 1945, two days after the Japanese authorities signed the surrender document officially ending the Second World War. *Dead of Night* makes no mention whatsoever of the war, a subject about which the British public were, after six years, thoroughly weary. The results became the most feted and influential horror film of the entire decade. The film builds on the supernatural elements that worked so well in *The Halfway House* and makes even more of the short story format. Here, architect Mervyn Johns visits a client at a farmhouse, only to find that he remembers being there before in a recurring nightmare. Each of the guests in the farmhouse tells a supernatural story, while Johns' nightmare becomes a linking sequence tying the whole narrative together. The stories cover a variety of moods, from high comedy to the blackest horror, while two came from famous writers, E. F. Benson and H. G. Wells. *The Golfing Story* was a droll golf yarn in which Basil Radford and Naunton Wayne (whose movie comedy partnership was established in Hitchcock's 1938 success *The Lady Vanishes*) play golfing friends, one of whom haunts the other after his death for committing the ultimate sporting crime—cheating. Two stories in particular, written by John Baines, made *Dead of Night* stand out: *The Haunted Mirror* featured Ralph Michael brought to the edge of madness after his fiancée Googie Withers buys a haunted mirror that reflects the room it formerly hung in, in which was committed a murder. The outstanding story by far was *The Ventriloquist's Dummy*, in which Michael Redgrave, giving a mesmerising performance quite ahead of its time, plays ventriloquist Maxwell Frere, who becomes controlled by the personality of his dummy. So memorable and effective was this story that it formed the basis of William Goldman's novel *Magic*, and Richard Attenborough's 1978 film adaptation, for which Goldman also wrote the script. *Dead of Night*'s much shorter telling remains the definitive version of the tale.

It should not be surprising that the latter part of the war years and the period following should see a strain of supernatural-themed drama emerging. This was a period in which people were faced with their own mortality and that of their loved ones. The aftermath of the First World War saw popular sentiment looking towards the supernatural as a way of coping with the overwhelming grief of a death toll, which affected every family in the land. The result in the late teens and into the twenties was an upsurge in interest in spiritualism, with charlatans and frauds preying on a large and vulnerable public.

During and after the Second World War, thoughts of life after death were largely confined to popular fiction and it is possible to see a link between not only Ealing's *The Halfway House* and *Dead of Night*, but also Michael Powell and Emeric Pressburgers's *A Matter of Life and Death*, which was released on 1 November 1946. While it is impossible to categorise this as a horror film, it does take on some of the same themes as *The Halfway House*. The idea of life beyond death, in the form of heaven, is addressed in a very witty manner in the context of the huge loss of life caused by the armed conflict. David Niven's bomber pilot is rescued and brought back to life by the power of love (and also by the sort of clerical error wartime audiences would have been all too familiar with). While *The Halfway House* and *A Matter of Life and Death* share this common theme of the living finding redemption through contact with the spirit world, *Dead of Night* has no truck with such notions. There is no redemption for Maxwell Frere's tortured ventriloquist, just madness and possession.

Almost impossible to categorise by genre was *The Queen of Spades*, directed by Thorold Dickinson and released in the UK in April 1949. Dickinson took over direction of the film at extremely short notice at the personal request of star Anton Walbrook, lest producer Anatole de Grunwald's film be cancelled altogether and all personnel at Welwyn Studios, at which this was the only active production, be thrown out of work. Anatole De Grunwald, a Russian *émigré* who moved to England with his family at the age of seven, was also a talented screenwriter, who worked uncredited with Dickinson to rewrite the script, based on Alexander Pushkin's short story, while the film was being shot. Made on an extremely low budget in difficult circumstances, *The Queen of Spades* looks absolutely sumptuous thanks to miracles being worked by the production team. Otto Heller's photography, all shadows and velvet blackness, and the almost entirely studio-bound production lends the whole film an air of gothic theatricality. The story concerns a lowly Russian army captain, embittered at his lack of money and status among an officer class made up of decadent, card-playing aristocrats, who kills an elderly countess in order to gain the mystical secret of winning at a fashionable card game. He eventually gains the secret, but it comes at a terrible cost.

A unique film in many ways, *The Queen of Spades* still has aspects in common with the Ealing and Powell and Pressburger films discussed above. Ian Christie, in his essay on the film, recognises that *The Queen of Spades*' elaborate theatricality (Anton Walbrook's performance was thought rather mannered by some) 'belongs to a particular moment in British cinema when the most creative and original filmmakers knew that they had to break with what had become conventionalised as "the documentary aesthetic"'.[4]

The latter part of the 1940s also saw an upturn in production of low-budget supernatural-themed productions, a genre that had died out in the war years after 1941's two comedies *The Ghost Train*—Arnold Ridley's 1923 play was on at least its sixth filmed version before it was reworked into a vehicle for popular radio comedian Arthur Askey and his sidekick Richard 'Stinker' Murdoch—and *Old Mother Riley's Ghosts*, in which Arthur Lucan's drag act Irish washerwoman character inherits what appears to be a haunted Scottish castle.

Horrors at the Bottom of the Bill

There was certainly enough business to go around in the latter half of the 1940s. The war years saw a boom in cinema attendances as audiences sought escape from the privations of the conflict, and in 1946, the film-going public was further swollen by the first rush of demobilised service personnel, making this the biggest ever year for cinema attendance in the UK. So fearsomely cold was the winter of 1946–1947 that people would visit the cinema simply to keep warm, either to save money or because a literally frozen transport system was unable to get coal to people to allow them to heat their houses.

Many of the most popular films of this era were, as ever, American, but this was an era in which even the smallest town in urban areas afforded moviegoers a choice of several independent cinemas plus one or more of the major chains. This meant that even the cheapest quota quickie shot in a week for a few thousand pounds was virtually guaranteed to pick up bookings from a buoyant film exhibition market hungry for new product.

Some of the results of the post-war trend for ghostly tales have not dated well and it is difficult to imagine them seeming very much better to contemporary audiences. Ivan Barnett's *The Fall of the House of Usher*

(1948) was an extremely cheaply produced version of Poe's tale, made with a largely amateur cast (with the exception of Gwen Watford, making her film debut). Without the budget to shoot his film with live sound, Barnett resorted to having the production's dialogue entirely recorded afterwards, his cast intoning their dialogue in a passionless monotone. Nevertheless, over a period of five years, the film found bookings at various British cinemas.

Director Dennis Kavanagh's haunted house story *The Night Comes Too Soon*, also from 1948, at least featured professional actors, led by the splendidly *basso profundo*-voiced Valentine Dyall, whose success in the BBC Radio horror series *Appointment with Fear* made him much in demand for such productions, and *Dead of Night*'s Anthony Baird. Other than in this respect, the film was in all honesty very little better than *The Fall of the House of Usher*, but it did sell to the American market, retitled *The Ghost of Rashmon Hall*. This appears to have been a miss-hearing of the name of the film's haunted house, which is clearly named at several points in the narrative as Ramersham Hall.

Even Tod Slaughter's film career spluttered back into a sort of life after wartime government restrictions curtailed his film career. The old ham's return in *The Curse of the Wraydons*, released in December 1946, was a very far cry indeed from the sharp and snappy horrors Slaughter was making with George King at the end of the 1930s. The story was based on *Spring-Heeled Jack*, one of the Victorian theatrical barnstormers with which Slaughter made his name at the Elephant and Castle Theatre and in London's West End. The poverty stricken production featured incidental music chosen, seemingly at random, from one of the music libraries servicing film and radio productions.

This put *The Curse of the Wraydons* at something of an advantage over Tod Slaughter's final star vehicle. *The Greed of William Hart*, produced in 1948, was the last film of B-movie specialist Oswald Mitchell, who died the following year. Even for the director of five productions in the mirthless Old Mother Riley comedy series, this bottom of the barrel effort hardly seems an appropriate send-off. Based on the true story of Edinburgh body snatchers and murderers Burke and Hare, *The Greed of William Hart* came complete with unconvincing backdrops, the cheapest sets imaginable, stick-on Victorian-style sideburns for the male cast members, and a very strange soundtrack indeed.

Once the film had been shot, horrified producer Gilbert Church was informed by the British Board of Film Classification that the film would not be passed in its current form. The story itself was acceptable, but the names of William Burke and William Hare could not be used, as even some 120 years after the real-life events that inspired the film, the subject was regarded as too sensitive. The solution was to redub the soundtrack with the new names Hart and Moore. This was done in the cheapest manner possible, with what appears to be a single actor dubbing just the names with an audible click on the soundtrack announcing the presence of the new dialogue. To make matters even worse, this used up all the money left in the film's budget for a musical score, so audiences had to make do with just the movie's overripe dialogue by future Hammer Films director John Gilling. Even a film as outrageously poor as this found an audience, and was even exported to America in 1953 under the title *Horror Maniacs*.

Some worthwhile productions did emerge from the B-movie sector during the 1940s. Vernon Sewell's 1945 film *The Latin Quarter*, the resolution of which revolves around a séance, had decent production values, despite the narrative moving at a snail's pace. This was one of four versions of the play *L'Angoisse* by Pierre Mills and C. Vylars Sewell directed at roughly ten-year intervals from 1934 onwards, his first being *The Medium* in 1934 and the last *House of Mystery* in 1961.

Butchers Film Services, that most venerable of B-movie distributors and producers that managed to stay operating through the ups and downs of the British film industry from the time of the Boer War to the Falklands War, made an entertaining hour-long canter through W. W. Jacobs' 1902 short story *The Monkey's Paw* in 1948. This story concerns the eponymous paw, on which the holder can make three wishes, which will come true, but with horrifying consequences. This starred sixty-seven-year-old Milton Rosmer with thirty-one-year-old Megs Jenkins incredibly convincingly playing his same-age wife, and it manages to work up to a fine pitch of tension, despite heavily rewriting the original source. This was first released on 1 November 1948, some nine months after Rosmer appeared in *Who Killed Van Loon?*. This was a forty-eight-minute crime second feature, which was one of the first productions by a small but enterprising film company that had recently reactivated after a short burst of activity in 1935 and 1936. The name of the company was Hammer Films, and during the 1950s, it would at first grow rapidly, then surprise everyone by becoming world famous.

4
Hammer Films 1946–56: Before the Horrors

When Hammer Films reactivated in 1946, it was just one of many small production companies that sprang up in the post-war reconstruction of the British Film Industry. The priorities of total war meant that much of the country's studio space had been used for purposes such as storage of government supplies, aircraft production, and even as a temporary home for the Royal Mint—as many in the film business joked at the time, at last a method had been found for a film studio to make money.

With the making of A-features being an expensive proposition, British feature film production remained largely in the hands of J. Arthur Rank's empire and Associated British Picture Corporation. Companies such as Hammer stayed alive by making products for the supporting programme. In the pre-television days of the 1940s and 1950s, cinema audiences would be treated to a programme of items before the main feature, including a newsreel, cartoons, a short film, and a B-picture of around an hour's length. Production of short films and B-movies kept a subculture of tiny, largely unheralded production companies in business, taking advantage of the quota of British films that had to be screened in the country's cinemas ever since the introduction of the Cinematograph Films Act 1927.

As exhibitors did not wish to reduce the number of popular American films they showed, the terms of the act were complied with by the production of what were often unfairly termed 'Quota Quickies'. Mainly crime thrillers and comedies, these films allowed a generation of performers and film technicians to learn their trade, occasionally providing a more interesting and accurate portrait of Britain to emerge than did the glossier products of Elstree and Pinewood.

Production companies making such films came and went, even the most successful of them—such as Mancunian Films who made a highly successful series of films starring northern English comedians such as Frank Randle and Norman Evans, whose regional appeal meant they did not show up on the radar of London-based studios—becoming little more than a footnote in film history. So how did the Hammer name become world famous and synonymous with gothic horror?

The circuitous route by which Hammer Films achieved immortality began not on the big screen, but with a BBC radio serial. Children across Britain thrilled to the serialised radio adventures of *Dick Barton—Special Agent* from the show's introduction on 7 October 1946 until its curtailment on 30 March 1951, when it was replaced by the rather less thrilling serial *The Archers*, which continues to this day. With Dick Barton's adventures reaching up to 15 million listeners, Hammer hit upon the idea of buying the rights to produce films based on the character. This was not an entirely original notion as Butcher's Film Services had begun to release B-pictures films based on the BBC's *Paul Temple* detective series in 1946.

Displaying the company's ruthlessly commercial streak even at this early stage, *Dick Barton—Special Agent* was designed to be a risk-free enterprise. Costing less than £20,000 to produce, Hammer was guaranteed £25,000 in booking fees. The frugal budget certainly shows on screen in a very odd film that is careful to include elements of the radio version of Barton audiences were familiar with—the show's iconic and stirring theme tune, 'The Devil's Gallop' by Charles Williams, was present and correct, along with the regular cast of Dick, Snowy, and Jock (albeit played by different actors). Even the basic plot, in which Nazi plans to poison London's water supply, could have come straight from the radio serial. Unfortunately, for large parts of the film, the story is ignored in favour of endless juvenile comic relief.

The film was a success, however, and Hammer quickly made two sequels, *Dick Barton Strikes Back* and *Dick Barton at Bay*, both of which paid a little more attention to their own plots and looked like more money had been spent on them. More films in the series were planned, with John Gilling's script *Dick Barton in Africa* being ready to shoot when star Don Stannard was killed in a car accident on the way home from the wrap party for *Dick Barton at Bay*. Despite not being the original Barton from the radio series, Stannard was a popular figure and nobody at Hammer had the heart to continue the series with a new star.

Despite this setback, Hammer had hit upon a successful formula by adapting popular radio properties, including versions of Ernest Dudley's outrageously rude psychologist/criminologist *Doctor Morelle* and *The Adventures of PC49*, popular on BBC radio from 1947 to 1953. Morelle had been played for Hammer by the cavernously voiced Valantine Dyall, who achieved fame as The Man in Black and introduced each episode of the radio horror series *Appointment with Fear*. The BBC retitled the 1949 series of *Appointment with Fear* as *The Man in Black* in an attempt to capitalise on Dyall's menacing image, and this was the title Hammer chose for their adaptation of the series, released in January 1950. Dyall introduced the story, which featured Sidney James giving an excellent performance as a rich man obsessed with yoga.

An effective enough creepy mystery story, *The Man in Black* is an effective illustration of just how far Hammer had come from the still recent days of *Dick Barton—Special Agent*. *The Man in Black* managed to achieve a positively sumptuous feel by being filmed extensively in the rooms and grounds of Oakley Court. This was a derelict Victorian-era Gothic Revival mansion adjoining Down Place in Bray, Berkshire, one of the many derelict country houses available for purchase in the 1950s that Hammer made its base of operations *in lieu* of available space in traditional film studios. Making a virtue out of necessity, Hammer used the rooms of these two houses to give their films a more authentic look than could have been achieved had they built sets in a studio on the budgets they were working with. Eventually, Hammer, having filmed in virtually every inch of every room in Down Place, outgrew the house, so they erected sound stages in the grounds and developed a true studio complex, Bray Studios.

Even at this stage, Hammer's solidly produced, modestly budgeted B-features were a class above those being made by other companies. The entry of American producer Robert L. Lippert was to take Hammer and its films to a different level. Lippert was the owner of a large chain of cinemas in California and its neighbouring state of Oregon, who entered the film production business after coming to the conclusion that his fellow film exhibitors were being overcharged for the quality of support features they were being offered. From 1945, Lippert began producing and distributing films, initially under the Screen Guild name, his drive to provide something different to attract audiences causing his to make his first film, *Wildfire: The Story of a Horse* starring B-movie cowboy star Bob Steele, in colour.

Screen Guild, which soon changed its name to Lippert Pictures, had a fast and busy production schedule including a great number of Westerns, but the company was happy to produce films in any genre that was currently popular. Therefore, Lippert film could be a musical, a jungle adventure, a science fiction thriller, or even a crime thriller of the type that would be dubbed by French critics as Film Noir. Frugal and commercially minded but not unadventurous, Lippert found a natural production partner in Hammer Films.

Hammer's skilled and efficient English production facilities could make a high-quality product for a fraction of the cost a similar film could be made for in Hollywood. Besides contributing a percentage of the production budget, Lippert also arranged for each of the films made under the arrangement to feature one of the many second-string Hollywood stars who were finding employment harder to come by as the studio system began to decline in the 1950s. This could be due to age, temperament, or bad luck, or in some cases, just the desire to have a paid visit to England. This Anglo-American partnership was also advantageous for Exclusive (at this point, the name used for most of Hammer's productions and for their distribution arm), which gained the rights to screen Lippert productions in the UK. These included such highly exploitable titles as the science fiction thriller *Rocketship XM*.

The first film made under the Lippert/Hammer deal was *Cloudburst* in 1951, starring Robert Preston, whose long and distinguished career was undergoing a temporary lull at the time. Now that Hammer's films were guaranteed distribution in the United States, they were competing in a bigger league. Along with the extra production funds provided by Lippert, this saw the quality of their films improve once again. Over a period of five years, a series of solidly entertaining noir-tinged thrillers emerged with an American star and, in some cases, showcasing startlingly good performances by actors who were given meatier roles than they were normally allowed. Therefore, Sidney James, who had already impressed in Hammer's *The Man in Black*, is excellent in the similar role of the wealthy, lonely, doomed Beveley Forrest in 1954's *The House Across the Lake*. Similarly, William Sylvester, star of many a British B-picture, might not have been the star of *The Stranger Came Home* (Paulette Goddard was imported for the occasion), but his intense performance represents probably the best work of his career.

By 1956, however, the deal between Hammer and Lippert had reached its end. Lippert's British and American pictures had attracted the attention of 20th Century Fox, who signed a deal with him to finance and distribute his films as supporting features to their feature films. His production unit ended up being more profitable than Fox's A-picture activities, and the deal only ended in the 1960s when Fox were no longer making enough films to need support features.

With the British film market contracting as television became the dominant entertainment medium, Hammer could have been in serious trouble as the Lippert deal ended, but one of the last films they made together pointed the way to the future.

Here Be Monsters: *The Quatermass Xperiment*

The American film market was going through convulsions of an epic nature in the 1950s. The major film studios had been legally ordered to divest themselves of their cinema chains, while the rise of television as a popular medium not only reduced the size of the audience, but radically changed its make-up. Trips to the cinema became less of a family affair and more an excuse for teenagers to get away from their parents; while Mum and Dad stayed in front of the television, the kids went to the movies, and film production began gearing to this younger audience.

Films began to look and sound different in an attempt to provide big screen spectacle that television could not compete with. Colour became more common, cheaper single-strip systems taking over from the bulky and expensive three-strip Technicolor, partially thanks to German technology taken by the Allies in the aftermath of the Second World War. While 3-D turned out to be a flash-in-the-pan gimmick (one that would return with depressing regularity over the following decades), widescreen systems proved a more fruitful way forward. Cinerama, which produced a huge image by running three projectors side-by-side, was hampered by its technical complexities, while larger film formats, such as VistaVision, were not practical for smaller cinemas. Anamorphic photography, led by 20th Century Fox's CinemaScope, was the greatest success; a wider image was produced by a special lens on the camera that squeezed the image onto regular 35-mm film, and another on the projector that unsqueezed it.

More germane to a discussion of horror films was one other method by which film producers tried to provide something that television could not: introducing previously taboo content. This was made possible by the slow death of the Hays Code—that censorious and strictly observed moral rulebook that American filmmakers had been forced to abide by since the mid-1930s. By the mid-1950s, the code was looking more than somewhat moth-eaten and anachronistic, and big-city audiences were increasingly able to see films from European and Scandinavian directors that made the products of the Hollywood studios look decidedly tame.

Horror films were increasingly popular once again, especially among the prized audience of American teenagers. On the small screen, the sale of the Universal horror pictures of the 1930s and '40s to television introduced classic horror characters such as *Dracula*, *Frankenstein*, and *The Mummy* to an enthusiastic, new, young audience. On the big screen, however, SF-horror was in vogue, the much-heralded opportunities and terrifying realities of the nuclear age bringing in a teen-friendly era of monster movies. *The Day the Earth Stood Still* was released in September 1951, a serious SF picture examining the morality of mankind possessing the atom bomb. What audiences remembered most was that visiting alien Klaatu (played by Michael Rennie, born in the Bradford suburb of Idle) who was in possession of a whacking great robot with death rays coming out of its eyes.

By the middle of the decade, audiences were thrilling to a series of monster films, especially after the success of Warner Bros giant ant film *Them!* in 1954. Giant creature films became a sensation for the next few years. Japanese studio Toho got in on the act with *Godzilla* (1954), which was released the US in 1956 in re-edited form with inserted scenes featuring Raymond Burr as *Godzilla, King of the Monsters*. This was so successful that it was reimported back into Japan the following year.

Amid the slew of irradiated giant wildlife threatening humanity, the Universal horror tradition was breathing its last, twenty-five years after the release of its *Dracula* in 1930. *Abbott and Costello Meet the Mummy* saw the comedy duo finally running out of classic monsters to 'meet', after which Universal dropped the increasingly cheap and shoddy film series. The main series of Universal horror pictures had really ended with *Abbott and Costello Meet Frankenstein* (1948), which signalled clearly that the studio's classic monsters were no longer regarded as frightening.

While the Universal horror series was expiring in ignominy, across the Atlantic, the horror genre was being reborn thanks to a television serial that had left the relatively small number of viewers of the fledgling BBC television service transfixed to their sets. There is a sense of the passing of the gothic torch about the fact that *Abbott and Costello Meet the Mummy* was released on 23 June 1955, while Hammer's *The Quatermass Xperiment* began its UK circuit run on 28 September.

The original BBC serial had been written by Nigel Kneale, then a BBC staff writer, and as such, he had no rights over the use of his work and the purchase of the film rights. Hammer, of course, had been making film versions of BBC serials since the company's return to film production in the mid-1940s and *Dick Barton—Special Agent*. Val Guest was hired to direct the film, which he also co-wrote with Richard Landau. Guest's background had been in comedy, where he found success as a writer in the 1930s with films for Will Hay and The Crazy Gang. He felt typecast in comedy and was grateful for the opportunities Hammer gave him in drama with films such as *The Men of Sherwood Forest* (1954) and *Break in the Circle* (1955).

Despite the huge reputation of Nigel Kneale's first *Quatermass* serial, television watching was still a minority pursuit in 1955 and Val Guest claimed never to have seen the television version. He read the scripts, however, and was immediately hooked. Guest's excitement for and commitment to the project are palpable on the screen. Richard Landau boiled down the original six half-hour scripts to a form that would eventually run a compact eighty-two minutes. Robert Lippert secured the services of Brian Donlevy, a star who was aging and over-the-hill even by the standards of the actors the producer had been persuading to cross the Atlantic to star in Hammer movies. Guest tailored the script to Donlevy's rat-a-tat delivery, redolent of 1930s gangster movies and a world away from the academic style of Reginald Tate, who had played the *Quatermass* role on television.

Hammer had worked with SF material before: *Spaceways* (1953) had really been more of a murder mystery and imported stars, Howard Duff and Eva Bartok, were thoroughly outshone by an excellent Alan Wheatley as a wily military intelligence investigator. This had been solidly directed by Terence Fisher, as had the bizarre *Four-Sided Triangle*, released the same year. This starred Stephen Murray and John Van Eyssen as childhood friends who become physicists when they grew up, sharing a passion for matter duplication experiments and for Barbara Payton. Payton loves Van Eyssen, but Murray convinces Payton to have a duplicate made of herself so Murray can have a copy of her, too. In a development that all concerned should have anticipated, Payton Mk 2 also loves Van Eyssen (goodness knows why—in this film, he displays all the sexual allure of processed cheese).

Ultimately, these were just two more cheap quickies made to make up the numbers of the Lipper co-production deal. With that deal rapidly coming to an end, Hammer had to make sure that *Quatermass* got noticed so they could find partners for future productions. The horror aspects of the story were pushed to the limits of acceptability in a film that was to be the most explicitly violent yet produced by a British film studio. Hammer exploited this fact for maximum publicity, and the fact that the film was designed to attract the 'X' certificate, which had only been introduced in 1951, by renaming Kneale's story *The Quatermass Xperiment*.

The story concerned the crash-landing in southern England of a space rocket launched by Quatermass's British Rocket Group. One member of the crew, Victor Carew, is found unconscious, but all that remains of the rest of the crew are empty space suits. Carew (played superbly by the gaunt, haunted-eyed Richard Wordsworth), it transpires, has been taken over by an alien organism and his mutating body contains the consciousness of the rest of the crew. Killing and taking on the memories and skills of others, plus that of plant life, Carew transforms into a shapeless monster that attempts to spread its spores to infect London from the top of Westminster Abbey.

The Quatermass Xperiment remains superb entertainment to this day, driven along by Guest's fast-moving direction and Donlevy's terrific lead performance. He is not remotely believable as a physicist, but his kinetic performance is the engine that pushes the film along at a breakneck pace. The film was an immediate success in Britain, but initially proved a tough sell in the US market. Robert Lippert offered the film to his usual American outlet, 20th Century Fox, under the title *Shock*, its British title being a non-starter in the US. Fox was pushing its CinemaScope format and only offering widescreen films to exhibitors, so it rejected the standard ratio Hammer film.

Eventually, United Artists picked up the US rights to the film, which had by now been retitled *The Creeping Unknown*, as it needed a film to run on a double bill with director Reginald LeBorg's *The Black Sleep*. This is notable for being the final movie featuring Bela Lugosi to be released during his lifetime, the posthumously released *Plan 9 from Outer Space* having yet to be conceived by the fetid imagination of Edward D. Wood Jr. In another example of the gothic film tradition passing on to Hammer, the difference between the two films is stark. *The Black Sleep* features ageing stars of the

Universal horrors in an era when the solidly carpentered B-movie production values of studios such as Universal and RKO were but a memory. Basil Rathbone seems to have lost the energy with which he threw himself into the Sherlock Holmes films, Lon Chaney Jr is sadly reduced by years of hard drinking from the strong, burly figure he cut in his star-making turn as *The Wolf Man* in 1941, while Bela Lugosi, who is not even given any dialogue, is a sad, shambling wreck. Brian Donlevy might have been a Hollywood has-been, but at this point, he was still able to inject a great deal of vim and vigour into his performance.

A more appropriate pairing cannot be imagined to demonstrate the qualities of *The Quatermass Xperiment* and the excellent work of the Hammer team: a fast-thrilling, location-shot production opposite a slow, dated, studio-bound film trying vainly to recreate the glories of a previous age. Another comparison between the two films was not lost on the studio executives at United Artists: Hammer brought in *The Quatermass Xperiment* for an estimated cost of under $116,500, for which they made a far more expensive-looking film than the $225,000 *The Black Sleep*. With tax and other financial incentives, such as the Eady scheme, Britain was suddenly looking like a very attractive filming location for low-budget genre film productions.

Harold Wilson and the Eady Levy

A key role in laying the financial groundwork for the British horror movie boom from the 1950s was played by none other than future Prime Minister Harold Wilson. To explain the background to this we need to go back to Clement Atlee's post-war Labour Party Government, elected by a landslide in July 1945. The costs of fighting the war had been financially crippling and Britain found itself short of dollar reserves, a situation not helped by the massive popularity with British audiences of American films, the profits from which went straight to Hollywood.

Chancellor of the Exchequer Hugh Dalton's attempt to address this situation in the summer of 1947 by placing a 75 per cent levy on American film imports proved disastrously counter-productive. The Hollywood studios simply refused to send new product to Britain, to the horror of film exhibitors. Instead of screening British films, the profits from which would stay in the UK, distributors exhumed from their vaults older American films. As Harold Wilson put it: 'We were actually paying out not 17 but 50 million dollars for the privilege of seeing *Hellzapoppin'* for the third time and *Ben Hur* for the twenty-third'.[1]

It fell to Wilson to sort out this mess when he was appointed President of the Board of Trade, an office today known as Minister for Trade and Industry, on 29 September 1947, becoming the youngest member of a British cabinet in the twentieth century at the age of thirty-one. Negotiations saw the levy lifted by March 1948 and American film imports resumed, but Wilson still wanted to solve the issue of the economy losing dollars via films while also boosting the prospects of the British film industry.

His next idea was to return to an idea the British Government had tried before—the quota. A quota of films of British origin to be screened in UK cinemas had been enshrined in law since the Cinematograph Films Act of 1927. By the 1940s, the level was set at 30 per cent, which Wilson then raised to 45 per cent. This approach failed as the British film production sector had not the resources to take up this new opportunity. The largest British film studio, Rank, was already overextended and ran into financial trouble, abandoning any attempt to become a bulk film producer. Its fearsome chief executive John Davis began a round of cutbacks while Rank concentrated on larger scale productions with export potential instead of smaller films made simply to fulfil the quota.

Wilson's next set of proposals met with long-term success, staying in place for the next thirty-five years. The Eady Levy, named after Sir Wilfred Eady, the treasury official who would put Wilson's ideas into practice, was a voluntary tax on cinema tickets, which was made statutory in 1957. The money raised went to the British Film Fund Agency, which distributed the money among British film makers, the National Film Finance Corporation (another Wilson creation that helped to finance British film production), the Children's Film Foundation, the British Film Institute, and to the training of film makers.

American film producers, both large and small, were attracted to the UK, some jumping through all manner of hoops in order to demonstrate that their films qualified as British enough to qualify for what became known as Eady Money. The results were undoubtedly positive for British filmmaking. Hammer, in the late 1940s just one of many small production companies making cheap B-pictures, signed a co-production deal with Robert L. Lippert. Together they made a long series of films for which Hammer provided the studio space, technicians, and a largely British cast of supporting actors—a largely British cast was one of the stipulations of receiving Eady funds—while Lippert provided a percentage of the budget and a second (or even third), rank American star, which helped make the films more attractive in both the American and home markets. Lippert was thought by some to be a front-man for 20th Century Fox, which was not averse to its bottom line being boosted by Eady money.

While Lippert remained based in the US, some American producers relocated to Britain to take advantage of the new financial arrangements. Albert R. Broccoli and Irving Allen formed Warwick Films, working on a similar basis to Hammer and Lippert, but on a much larger scale. Columbia

Pictures provided 50 per cent of the budget while the former talent agent Broccoli attracted a genuine A-list star in the form of Alan Ladd, who was able to take advantage to favourable US tax laws for Americans working overseas.[2] The company's first production in 1953 was a great success and led to Warwick making twenty-three films in Britain over the next eight years. Broccoli then went on to form Eon Productions to make the James Bond films along with a Canadian theatre and film producer who had also been attracted to work in Britain in the mid-1950s. His Woodfall Film Productions, formed with director Tony Richardson and writer John Osborne, had great success with social realist films such as *Look Back in Anger* (1959) and won four Academy Awards for *Tom Jones* (1963).

In the horror field, American producers such as Richard Gordon, the Amicus Films' pairing of Max Rosenberg and Milton Subotsky, and Herman Cohen moved to the UK, attracted in the same way as the examples above by Eady money, lower production costs, and a very high standard of technicians. These exploitation film producers should be given their proper due for the contribution they made to the British movie industry. Unlike some major studio productions that qualified for Eady funds despite hardly shooting a foot of film in the UK, they made pictures, which might have been smaller in scale, but which employed British actors and technicians in British studios. With the enormous success of Hammer Films' *The Curse of Frankenstein* (1957) and *Dracula* (1958) another, less tangible factor in the attraction of horror film producers emerged: Britishness was such a key component in the very makeup of the gothic horror genre that making them in the UK made sense on a very basic storytelling level.

Even the British weather worked better for horror productions: it is instructive to compare *Blood of Dracula*, an American-made film produced by Herman Cohen, which was first released in November 1957, with Hammer's *Dracula*, released in the US only seven months later. The bright Californian sun lent *Blood of Dracula*'s monochromatic photography a flat lighting scheme that worked against the development of even a shred of a gothic atmosphere. One can imagine the enormous impact the screaming reds of Hammer's Eastmancolor photography and the stylish gloom of the location scenes had on audiences who had grown used to such visual murk.

Post-*Quatermass*: Low-Budget SF Horrors

The *Quatermass Xperiment* had been a most unusual phenomenon: not only was it a genuine popular hit from an independent British studio, it operated within a genre that had previously been the sole purview of American cinema. As a result, there was a mini-gold rush of cheap SF offerings from small British studios.

A couple of British cheapies had pre-dated the release of *The Quatermass Xperiment*, and help to illustrate the quantum leap in the quality Hammer's film represented in term of home-grown genre production. *Devil Girl from Mars* was released in May 1954, a very stagy production (indeed it was based on a stage play) from low-budget producers The Danzigers starring Patricia Laffan as a villainous Martian woman with a robot that looked like it was made from cardboard boxes. Today the film is remembered for two things: Laffan's patent leather dominatrix outfit and the presence in the credits of future *Thunderbirds* producer Gerry Anderson in the credits, in his days as a freelance sound editor. *Stranger from Venus* was an Anglo-American production released in the US in August of 1954 and in the UK two months later. This featured Patricia Neil, who had previously starred in *The Day the Earth Stood Still*, and was retitled in some markets *Immediate Disaster* in order to forestall the possibility of legal action by 20th Century Fox, as the plotting of the two films was suspiciously similar.

Hammer quickly realised that audiences were reacting to the horror elements of *The Quatermass Xperiment*, a point not lost on rival producers. The British SF movies that followed considerably upped the gore element in ways that would have been unthinkable for American productions of the era. Thus, *The Strange World of Planet X* (1958) featured not only a *The Day the Earth Stood Still* plot device of a benevolent alien visitor, plus a bevy of marauding giant insects (a popular trope of American 1950s SF) but also the memorable sight of a soldier having his face eaten by a giant bug.

The Trollenberg Terror (1958) was made by future *Saint* television producers Robert S. Baker and Monty Berman, based on a *Quatermass*-influenced serial screened by the BBC's commercial rivals ITV. The film featured some crude low-budget chills, kicking off proceedings with the beheading of a mountaineer. Like *The Strange World of Planet X*, this also featured some laughably poor special effects, in both cases thanks to scripts that bit off rather more than their production budgets could chew.

Rather more striking was *Fiend Without a Face* (1958), a remarkably scary and bloodthirsty film by late-1950s standards that featured excellent stop-motion effects for the film's creature sequences. The creatures, produced by atomic radiation (naturally), were rather more imaginatively designed than the usual macro-photographed insects or men in rubber suits, being made up of an ambulatory brain and spinal column. In an economical movie, the creatures are invisible in the film's earlier sequences, becoming visible in a remarkably full-on climax in which cast members are killed while creatures are dispatched with shotguns.

5
Hammer Films 1957–70: The Rise of the Gothic

The Curse of Frankenstein

Sometimes a miracle happens and everything works perfectly on a film when it really should not have. *The Curse of Frankenstein* is a wonderful example of this. The project was first brought to Hammer by American writer/producer Milton Subotsky, who would return to the British horror movie scene in the 1960s. Subotsky had prepared a script that was quite close to the 1931 Universal adaptation. Hammer realised that not only was the script less than ideal (and could easily have breached some of Universal's jealously guarded copyrights), but also that since Mary Wollstonecraft Shelley's original was published in 1818, it was comfortably out of copyright. Having had unaccustomed mainstream success with *The Quatermass Xperiment* in 1955, Hammer was attempting to capitalise on this with a slate of horror films, and was preparing both *X The Unknown* and *Quatermass 2*. The idea of a gothic horror film therefore had some appeal, especially as *Frankenstein* was as much a period science fiction subject as a horror story, and it became clear audiences were reacting to the horror aspects of the *Quatermass* film.

The idea was given to Jimmy Sangster, Hammer's production manager and assistant director who was turned into a screenwriter with Joseph Losey's twenty-nine-minute short film *A Man on the Beach*—one of Hammer's sidelines to keep the company in profit was to make short subjects to fulfil the needs of distributors for supporting features in the newly fashionable colour and CinemaScope. This led to Sangster pitching the idea for a *Quatermass* sequel, which was reworked into *X The Unknown* when Kneale wrote his own sequel. Sangster still regarded himself as a production manager at this point (he filled this role on *X The Unknown* as well as writing the script), but *The Curse of Frankenstein* was to change his life.

The Curse of Frankenstein was sold brilliantly by Hammer, the trailer and poster promising a fast paced, colourful horror experience while keeping the film's biggest shocks under wraps. The original UK release trailer completely downplays the monster, never showing its face, and fails to mention Christopher Lee at all. Lee was no box office draw at this stage of his career, while Peter Cushing was a rising star thanks to his appearance as Winston Smith in BBC TV's legendary 1954 adaptation of George Orwell's *Nineteen Eighty-Four*. The poster does mention Lee, and shows us a tantalising glimpse of The Creature (as Frankenstein's creation was named here in order to differentiate it from the Monster of the potentially litigious Universal's version), its face half obscured by its huge, claw-like hand.

What this meant was that when Terence Fisher had the camera perform an under-cranked shock zoom as the creature's face is first seen, tearing the bandages from its face, the full shock value of the scene was achieved. The sequence is masterfully well done by Fisher and fully the equal of James Whale's introduction of Karloff in the 1931 version.

The use of Eastmancolor is also very skilful by Fisher and his cinematographer Jack Asher. Right from the opening titles, it is clear that colour is going to be a vital weapon in the film's arsenal, with the text in white on a red background with hellish smoke billowing in the background. Frankenstein rarely wears black, generally being seen in a green frock coat or a grey lab jacket. The jacket becomes steadily filthier as the film progresses, representing both a nice piece of continuity and a visual reflection of Frankenstein's descent from zealous explorer of the farthest reaches of science to coldly monomaniacal psychopath.

If all that *The Curse of Frankenstein* had to offer was shock value then it would not be half the film it was and would soon have been forgotten. What really lifted the film into something very special indeed was that it featured two superb performances by Peter Cushing, a known quantity, and Christopher Lee, heretofore regarded as little more than an unusually tall supporting player, usually in low-budget filler material. Cushing is the backbone of the film, giving a performance of subtlety and range as Victor Frankenstein moves from cold-hearted, cocksure young man—played in earlier scenes by an excellent Melvyn Hayes—to inspired, brilliant scientist, enraptured in his work and its possibilities, to obsession, unable to see past his goal to the chaos engulfing him.

If *The Curse of Frankenstein* was a showcase for Cushing's abilities, there were certainly hints in his earlier work of what he was capable of. Lee, on the other hand, came as a complete surprise, having had very little previous opportunity to exhibit his talents to their full. Encased in Phil Leakey's make-up, he was still able to give an absolutely masterful demonstration of silent pathos, uncomprehending sadness and rage. With Cushing as Hammer's Frankenstein, the sequels that would follow traced the story of the Baron, but to a large extent, they stood or fell by the quality of the creature he created.

Here, Hammer's Creature was fully the equal of what director James Whale and star Boris Karloff had created for that studio in 1931.

Although by major studio standards *The Curse of Frankenstein* was not an expensive film, Hammer no longer had the backing of the American studio contacts of Robert Lippert. Its production represented a considerable investment for the studio and its success was vital to Hammer's continued future. Nobody realised that its success would be so huge that it would alter the whole course of Hammer Films.

1957: From Blood Island to Castle Dracula

Hammer's releases in 1957 have the air about them of being made by a studio brimming with confidence. Warner Brothers were ecstatic when *The Curse of Frankenstein* was screened for them and arranged a major American release for the film, while it broke box office records in Britain on its release in May 1957. By this point, their next film was almost ready for release, an adaptation by Nigel Kneale of his own BBC television play *The Creature* entitled *The Abominable Snowman*. This once again featured Cushing, this time opposite American actor Forrest Tucker, in the lead role of the story played on television by Stanley Baker. While this was basically sold as a horror movie, Kneale's somewhat talky drama, shot by director Val Guest mainly on sets at Pinewood, with location shooting in the French Pyrenees, was really more of a straight drama with a mystical edge.

Other Hammer productions in the 1957–1958 period included another Val Guest picture, *The Camp on Blood Island*, a blood-curdling prisoner of war drama dealing with Japanese atrocities in Malaya, as well as *The Snorkel*, a rather clever murder mystery set in the south of France, and *Up the Creek*, a naval comedy, which gave Peter Sellers his first starring role.

It was clear from this slate of productions that Hammer's days as B-movie producers were behind them. Even the smallest of these films had a size and professional sheen about them that Hammer could only have dreamed about achieving five years earlier. There was one more film in the studio's schedule for the year, though. The overwhelming and unexpected success of *The Curse of Frankenstein* made a follow-up a given. Looking back at Universal's 1930s template (albeit in reverse), it was clear what this should be. Jimmy Sangster was set to work on scripting *Dracula*.

The film rights to Bram Stoker's most famous novel still lay with Universal, who fortunately, and presumably with an eye to the huge profits *The Curse of Frankenstein* had made for Warner Brothers, were willing to allow Hammer to make *Dracula* in return for the US distribution rights. The result was a film that was nothing short of revolutionary in the context of British film production. *The Curse of Frankenstein* production team was reassembled for what was Hammer's first colour production since that film. Naturally, this meant reteaming Peter Cushing and Christopher Lee, and as before Cushing, who was by this point Hammer's resident star, received far more screen time, while Lee made the visual impact—only this time even more so. Lee's performance as *Dracula* updated the template for the role set by Bela Lugosi in 1930 in interesting and intelligent ways.

The casting of the imposingly tall, young (aged thirty-four at the time of filming), and handsome Lee saw Hammer foregrounding the sexual potency of the vampire figure in ways that had not been seen for many years. Somewhat lost in the mists of time is the fact that Bela Lugosi, now often remembered as the elderly drug addict he was to become, was a very sexually attractive figure in 1930. This aspect of the vampiric myth was retained by the aloof, magnetic Gloria Holden in the underrated 1936 production *Dracula's Daughter*, but was subsequently de-emphasised in the wake of the censorious hand of the Hays Office's Motion Picture Production code's reshaping of America's cinematic output.

There is a reason why the later portrayals of *Dracula* in Universal's 1940s horror pictures are little remembered save as a niche interest among genre fans. Lon Chaney Jr was cast in the role of the Count for the confusingly titled *Son of Dracula* in 1942. His sad-eyed, bovine presence had proved effective in *The Wolf Man*, but in other roles he carried about him more the air of a furniture removal man than a horror star. John Carradine was cast in *House of Frankenstein* and *House of Dracula*. Aged thirty-eight when he took the role on, but looking at least ten years older, his emaciated visage suited the role of the ancient, undead character in many ways, but was hardly calculated to lend his Dracula sex appeal.

The casting of Christopher Lee in the role by Hammer, along with the loosening of censorship restrictions that had begun by the mid-1950s, allowed for a far more sensual reading of the story. This extends far beyond the physicality of Lee in the title role. Melissa Stribling, in the role of Mina, undergoes a startling transformation thanks to her encounter with Dracula from repressed Victorian wife to a woman who has clearly had her sexual horizons widened in a very big way. This aspect of the film was seized upon for its poster advertising campaign, which featured an image of Lee looming over a compliant-looking Stribling beneath the slogan 'The terrifying lover who died—yet lived'.

Lee's playing is something of a revelation. He was superb in *The Curse of Frankenstein*, but in some previous roles that required dialogue, he could appear stiff and dull. This could be another way of saying that he was not afraid of playing stiff, dull characters precisely how they were written, which is a selfless and brave move for an actor. Here he is natural, graceful, and animalistic—an absolutely magnetic figure who dominates the film.

The acting in the film is an interesting mixture, in which at times it looks like we are seeing modern screen acting being invented before our eyes. Cushing and Lee adopt a naturalistic style, which at times clashes with the cut-glass accents of the other cast members—the playing of the dialogue by the two leads makes John Van Eyssen (in the role of Jonathan Harker) sound like minor royalty in comparison.

Jimmy Sangster's screenplay is a masterpiece of compression, employing both his skills as a writer and his experience as a production manager to boil down Stoker's sprawling, continent-spanning novel to a pacey eighty-two minutes. This also allowed Hammer to bring in a handsome-looking film on the hardly extravagant budget of £81,000.

To this end, some liberties are taken with Stoker's plotting. Instead of moving from Transylvania to the northern English coastal town of Whitby, the film remained firmly set in central Europe. With the Count no longer looking to move house, Jonathan Harker's visit to Castle Dracula is no longer as an estate agent, but now as a librarian hired to work at the castle. In reality, Harker has been sent by Van Helsing to kill Dracula, an idea that also saves time in introducing Van Helsing. Much of the rest of the story remains fairly close to Stoker, retaining the key theme of an ancient peril being combatted by a foe armed not only with the latest in modern communications technologies, but with ancient, arcane knowledge.

Thus, Van Helsing represents the key gothic theme of the tension between ancient beliefs and rationalistic modernity. Sangster codifies the rules surrounding vampirism, which helps move the narrative along in an easily understandable way. Van Helsing explains the basics of vampire habits and how to kill them into an early Dictaphone, turning myth and superstition into scientific study. While the ageless vampire Dracula comes from the ancient world to threaten both the territory and physical bodies of the (late Victorian) present, Van Helsing is inverting the process to threaten Dracula with modern science.

Keeping the action within a relatively small geographic area helps give the film terrific pace, and this is an absolute gift to director Terence Fisher. Fisher was never a showy director, and here he further develops his style of keeping his powder dry for as long as possible, saving the visual flourishes for key points in the narrative for maximum impact. The best example of this is Dracula's first appearance, which manages to both establish him as a figure of great power and confound audience expectations. Dramatically lit, Lee sweeps down the staircase, his cape billowing behind him, in a single shot gliding in from the rear of the frame to a huge close-up only to unexpectedly reveal himself as a gracious and convivial host.

Dracula is a film that announces its intensions from the very first shot, as the camera pans in to a cold, grey tomb, which reveals the single world

'Dracula'. Bright, screamingly red blood falls onto the tomb, the sight searing itself into the retinas of an audience that had grown used to a British cinema, which was, literally and figuratively, bloodless. The response to *Dracula* was overwhelming, both in the home market and in the United States where Universal, still keen to differentiate the film from their own 1930 classic, retitled the film *Horror of Dracula*. Hammer had achieved the impossible: having caught lightning in a bottle once with *The Curse of Frankenstein*, they had not only repeated their success, but surpassed it. Hollywood studios, desperate to attract audiences as television ate away at their audience, fell over themselves to have Hammer remake their classic horror films. The era of Hammer horror had truly begun.

This represented a huge and unique opportunity for Hammer and for British producers in general who wished to work in the horror genre. As good as the *Quatermass* movies that brought Hammer to the attention of the American major studios were, they operated in a genre that American producers had already made their own and in which a British setting was something of an abstract detail. By switching to period gothic horror, Hammer discovered a way of delivering scares to audiences worldwide within a format of period drama in which British producers had traditionally operated. It is no coincidence that Terence Fisher learned his craft at Gainsborough Studios, the home of the 1940s gothic melodrama.

The Revenge of Frankenstein

The first order of business was to produce a sequel to *The Curse of Frankenstein*. What emerged was *The Revenge of Frankenstein*, principal photography on which began on 6 January 1958, reusing the same sets a mere three days after *Dracula* wrapped. Instead of Warner Brothers, a deal was now done with Columbia Pictures, with whom Hammer would work regularly, though not exclusively, for the next eight years.

The film carries on directly from the events of *The Curse of Frankenstein*, even giving us a date, 1860, for when the drama is set, instead of *Curse*'s vague 'more than a hundred years ago'. We last saw Baron Frankenstein on his way to the scaffold and here we return to see him saved from this fate. From here, the tone of the film alternates from the horror of the first film to a strain of black comedy expanded considerably from the first film, which perhaps indicates that writer Jimmy Sangster was already tiring of the gothic horror genre.

Sangster, with two huge international hits under his belt, was now a hot property as a screenwriter and wrote *The Revenge of Frankenstein* under a very tight deadline in between work for other studios. This meant that rewrites to *The Revenge of Frankenstein* script were by other hands, George Baxt providing a scene of broad comedy between two drunken grave robbers attempting to steal Frankenstein's body, one of whom drops dead when the Baron himself turns up to supervise their work.

A tone of rather more subtle black comedy is retained for the film's main plot, as the Baron relocates to Carlsbruck, setting himself up in a medical practice under the name of Dr Stein. Within three years, he is the most popular doctor in town, providing care to a well-heeled clientele, most of whom have nothing whatsoever wrong with them. He also provides free care at the local Poor Hospital, where the patients are desperately ill, but also provide a ready supply of parts for his new attempt to create life. There is a great deal of fun had in scenes of Frankenstein treating the complacent hack medics of the Medical Council who had previously rejected him with utter disdain.

Frankenstein is helped by Dr Hans Kleve (Francis Matthews), a member of the local medical council, whose other members have opposed 'Dr Stein's' arrival in their midst. This time, Frankenstein has built a perfect body, into which he transplants the brain of Karl, his crippled assistant, who saved Frankenstein from the gallows to do this. The operation seems to be a complete success, with Karl transformed into the tall, handsome, and strong Michael Gwynn. Things start to go wrong when Karl refuses to allow himself to be examined by the world's doctors, as Frankenstein plans to display his triumph of medicine to the world, arguing, 'All my life I've been stared at.'

Karl escapes from Frankenstein's house and soon there is a bigger problem: the new body starts to reject its transplants and Karl begins to lose control of his limbs. The once handsome face becomes twisted and sub-human as he physically degenerates and, worse still, Karl develops some very worrying cannibalistic tendencies. With his creation reduced to a rampaging monster, Frankenstein's true identity is exposed. He and Kleve put a drastic escape plan into action.

The ending of *The Revenge of Frankenstein* strikes, like much of the rest of the film, a tone a black comedy and is strangely low key. It is honestly hard to regard the film as more than a partial success compared to *The Curse of Frankenstein* and *Dracula*. It has too many changes of tone and Terence Fisher's direction strikes a note of discreet efficiency rather than the groundbreaking work of his previous two horror films. To be fair, asking him to make two films back-to-back of equal quality was probably a bit much.

The Hound and *The Mummy*: Hammer Hits the Big Time

After the heady triumphs of *The Curse of Frankenstein* and *Dracula*, and the profitable, if somewhat less ground-breaking *The Revenge of Frankenstein*, much had changed at Hammer. Not only had the studio managed, against the odds, to produce two massive worldwide hits, but Hammer had become a brand name. Although they continued to make films in other genres, to the public, Hammer meant horror. Major Hollywood studios had quickly come to the same conclusion, and many were throwing their vaults open to Hammer in the hope of having them remake items from their back catalogue. Not everything Hammer touched turned to box office gold, though, as evidenced by the fate of their next two productions, both of which attempted to add horror elements to stories from outside the genre.

The Hound of the Baskervillles was shot in September and October 1958 and released in the UK in late March 1959. Terence Fisher, who was directing all of Hammer's 'prestige' pictures at this point, returned, but the film was written not by Jimmy Sangster but instead by Peter Bryan. Although the end result was granted an 'A' certificate by the BBFC, the film was sold just much as a horror picture as it was a Sherlock Holmes movie. Peter Cushing was cast as Sir Arthur Conan Doyle's consulting detective and clearly relishes the opportunity to give a big, flamboyant performance. His Holmes changes moods often, at times suggesting the cold, calculating man of obsessive logic, which echoes his Baron Frankenstein, but just as often displaying an amused skittishness, as well as genuine warmth in his relationship with Dr Watson.

Watson is here played by André Morell, and in this piece of casting, Hammer's *The Hound of the Baskervillles* was revolutionary, eschewing the bumbling, hapless reading of Watson created for the Universal Pictures series of Holmes films starring Basil Rathbone and Nigel Bruce from 1939 to 1946. Both actors cast a long shadow over any other attempts to film Holmes for many years to come, and the role of Watson came with inherent difficulties. In the original stories, Watson is the narrator and we see the narratives through his eyes, which has a tendency to make him a somewhat passive figure. Many previous screen versions of Holmes side-lined the character, on occasion leaving him out completely, while the Universal series used him basically as comic relief. Morell's Watson is a competent man of action, far more suggestive of the former military doctor of Conan Doyle's stories.

Cushing and Morell work splendidly together, swapping amused glances in their reactions to the other characters. The other two major roles in the film were also cast with strong actors, with Francis de Wolff as Dr Mortimer and Christopher Lee as Sir Henry Baskerville. This was particularly important as this most famous of Sherlock Holmes stories removes the detective entirely for the central section of the narrative. Morell, de Wolff, and Lee are such powerful performers that the film remains gripping for the twenty minutes when Cushing is absent.

It should be said also that *The Hound of the Baskervillles* is an absolutely beautiful-looking film, and cinematographer Jack Asher, who had shot

Hammer's three previous horror pictures, reaches perhaps the peak of his collaboration with Terence Fisher here. Asher's working methods involved meticulous lighting set-ups including the creative use of coloured filters, which gave the films he worked on a strikingly rich colour scheme. This all took time, however, and no matter how glorious the results were on screen, it went against Hammer's fast and efficient working ethos. After 1960s *The Two Faces of Dr Jekyll*, the studio broke up the Fisher/Asher team and the cinematographer only worked on two more features for the studio: *The Scarlet Blade* (1963) and *The Secret of Blood Island* (1965). The look of Hammer's horror films was altered considerably by this change, with only the films directed by Freddie Francis having anything like the visual depth of the eight horror films Jack Asher worked on.

This was Peter Bryan's first script for Hammer, though, interestingly, he had been a camera operator for the studio earlier in the 1950s on such films as *Cloudburst* (1951) and *Stolen Face* (1952), after which he became a novelist. For *The Hound of the Baskervillles*, not surprisingly, Bryan played up the horrific aspects of the story, adding such details as a huge tarantula crawling up the arm of Sir Henry Baskerville, a long opening flashback sequence featuring the terrible crimes and terrifying death of Sir Hugo Baskerville, and a sacrificial altar on the moors on which it is planned that Sir Henry meets his doom. Unfortunately, like all screen versions of *The Hound of the Baskervilles*, Hammer's version has a basic problem—the hound itself is just a big dog in a mask and is nothing like as terrifying as Conan Doyle's description. In effect, despite the film's many other qualities, it is a monster film without a monster.

Sadly, this was reflected in the box office takings for the film. These were considerably smaller than Hammer's horror offerings, the lukewarm public reception for *The Hound of the Baskervilles* resulting in plans for a regular series of Cushing/Morell Sherlock Holmes films being shelved. Hammer had a crowded production schedule, though, which continued with *The Man Who Could Cheat Death*.

This time, Hammer was acting as a gun for hire for Paramount, a studio that did not have a rich heritage of horror movies to remake for a new generation. From the vaults, they disinterred *The Man in Half Moon Street*, a Barré Lyndon play the studio retained the rights to. Paramount had originally filmed the play in 1943, their version not being released until 1945. This was a common practice among major Hollywood studios when America entered the Second World War as an insurance policy against anticipated shortages of materials and star actors being called up to fight.[1]

Swedish actor Nils Asther had played the lead role in 1943, and for Hammer's reimagining of the material, retitled *The Man Who Could Cheat Death*, the studio chose Anton Diffring once Peter Cushing proved unavailable. This forty-two-year-old German actor had left his native country in the 1930s to escape persecution due to his being both half-Jewish and homosexual. With the fashion in popular British filmmaking in the 1950s being to make large numbers of war films, Diffring suddenly found himself in demand, ironically, like many German émigré actors, playing the very Nazis who forced him out of him homeland. Hammer clearly saw possibilities in Diffring beyond his normal range of parts, casting him both in *The Man Who Could Cheat Death* and in their abortive *Tales of Frankenstein* television series in 1958.

While Nils Asther played Dr Julian Karell with an amused manner and a roguish gleam in his eye, Diffring lacked the on-screen charisma to play the role (renamed for this version Georges Bonnet) in this way and his overplaying kills the film stone dead—one cannot help but wonder why director Terence Fisher did not reign him in. His cold, charmless air cuts against Jimmy Sangster's script, which positions Bonnet as an absolute woman-magnet, though he does bring a sadness to key scenes which is pitch-perfect.

The plot certainly had possibilities: Diffring plays Georges Bonnet, an apparently thirty-something artist who carries a terrible secret. He is actually 104 years old, kept young by a glandular operation every ten years. The surgeon who has been performing this operation is now elderly and dying, and a replacement must be found urgently or Bonnet will die. Christopher Lee—whom one could well imagine doing a much better job in the lead role—has an extended cameo as a surgeon who is asked to take on the job, and is the best thing about the film.

Even at eighty-three minutes (almost ten minutes shorter than the original), the film seems overlong and has the same faults as the original—although screenwriter Jimmy Sangster adds detail to the story, it still lacks action. The narrative only sparks into life during the film's too infrequent horror sequences (not helped by some very flat directing by Terence Fisher, whose use of long takes makes the whole thing look very stagey), and even then, the film's climax is fumbled unforgivably. While Ralph Murphy's original staged Nils Asther's sudden ageing in a very clever and convincing manner, which made it appear that he ages seventy years in a few seconds, Anton Diffring merely looks like he has dried mud all over his face.

Clearly Paramount had little confidence in the film Hammer delivered, as *The Man Who Could Cheat Death* stayed on the shelf for almost a year after filming completed in December 1958. This meant that the next Hammer horror film to enter production was released two months before its predecessor. This saw Hammer on more familiar ground, remaking another classic Universal monster of the '30s—1959 was the year of *The Mummy*.

The Mummy was on the floor at Bray Studios from late February 1959 to mid-April, and reunited the Hammer horror 'dream team' of director Terence Fisher and his cinematographer Jack Asher, writer Jimmy Sangster and the star acting duo of Peter Cushing and Christopher Lee. This time they were working for Universal Pictures again, the Hollywood major having made so much money from its American distribution of *Dracula* (or *Horror of Dracula* as it was retitled for American audiences) that it now let Hammer take their pick of any of their properties to remake.

This changed considerably how Jimmy Sangster set about constructing his script. Where his *Curse of Frankenstein* and *Dracula* scripts had avoided direct comparisons to the Universal films in order to keep Hollywood lawyers at bay, Sangster was now deliberately writing in as many references to them as possible. Thus John L. Balderston's script for Universal's 1932 version of *The Mummy* serves as a jumping-off point for the story, but large parts of the story and various character names are taken from the film's 1940 B-movie semi-remake *The Mummy's Hand* and its own sequels *The Mummy's Tomb* (1942), *The Mummy's Ghost* (1944), and *The Mummy's Curse* (1945).

Producer Michael Carreras tried, within Hammer's budget constraints—though it should be noted that *The Mummy* was made for something like double the budget of *Dracula*—to make a film with a bigger, more 'Hollywood' feel than the previous *Dracula* and *Frankenstein* films. To this end, an elaborate score was commissioned for the film from composer Franz Reizenstein, featuring not only a full orchestra, but also a choir. Carreras also had Jimmy Sangster add to his script a lengthy flashback sequence in ancient Egypt to explain the story of how Kharis came to be entombed alive and mummified. Although Carreras had in mind adding some razzmatazz and Hollywood production values to the film (though to be honest the results are hardly *Cleopatra*), the sequence does also serve a couple of other purposes.

The main plot of the film is about the discovery of the tomb of Princess Ananka by father and son Egyptologists Stephen and John Banning (Felix Aylmer and Peter Cushing), their accidental revival of the mummy guarding the tomb, and the mummy's vengeance on those who desecrated it. After the opening sequence, this does involve an awful lot of scenes taking place in Victorian drawing rooms and the flashback scenes, though studio-bound in themselves, do help to open out the narrative somewhat. The scenes also serve to expand Christopher Lee's role considerably. The importance of this cannot be underestimated as the rest of Lee's part involved the actor being entombed in physically very uncomfortable make-up designed by Roy Ashton, who was by now chief make-up artist after the departure the previous year of Phil Leakey.

Lee was being somewhat underutilised by Hammer—it should have been clear by now that Christopher Lee was a star actor, yet he had been overlooked for leading roles in films such as *The Man Who Could Cheat Death* and *The Two Faces of Dr Jekyll*, having to make do with smaller roles in which he outshone the stars of each film. One wonders if Lee would have accepted the role had it merely consisted of his playing a mute monster. Still, his performance as *The Mummy* was magnificent, representing the definitive performance of the character. The actors who donned the bandages in the 1940s (Tom Tyler and Lon Chaney Jr—Boris Karloff never actually played an ambulatory mummy in the 1932 film) played a shambling, slow moving, and not very frightening monster. Lee, on the other hand, was both a physically dominating presence and able to generate an astonishing amount of sympathy with only his eyes uncovered.

Production on *The Mummy* took place at Hammer's home studio of Bray, but also at Shepperton, partially for the swamp scenes, for which the jungle set erected on the Shepperton studio tank (a facility Bray lacked) for Hammer's war film *Yesterday's Enemy* was reused. With typical Hammer economy, the Bray Studios set used for Anton Diffring's home in *The Man Who Could Cheat Death* was redressed to serve as the nursing home to which Felix Aylmer is sent.

Released in the UK on 25 September 1959, the film was praised by critics, *The Times*' reviewer especially finding favour with Christopher Lee's performance as '…a figure of imperishable sadness whose expressive, sorrowful eyes his reanimated mummy retains'. While *The Mummy* performed well in the home market, Universal were ecstatic at the box office returns the film generated on its American release in December of the same year. These even outstripped those of *Dracula*, just over a year and a half earlier, and Hammer were back on top as the most successful movie producers in British cinema.

The Attractiveness of Evil: *The Two Faces of Dr Jekyll* and *The Brides of Dracula*

Just over two months after *The Mummy*'s UK release, on 23 November 1959, Hammer's next horror picture went in front of the cameras at Bray. Such was the sprawling nature of *The Two Faces of Dr Jekyll*'s production that the final two weeks of production in January 1960 took place at Elstree Studios in Borehamwood. This was another in Michael Carreras' efforts to have Hammer produce bigger productions, but while The *Mummy* succeeded in adding a touch of Hollywood-style gloss to the studio's gothic formula, this attempt to update Robert Louis Stevenson hit difficulties almost from the start.

Wishing to make a film with a touch more psychological complexity than the horror pictures Hammer had produced to date, Carreras hired playwright Wolf Mankowitz for a somewhat larger fee than Jimmy Sangster or Anthony Hinds attracted. Mankowitz proceeded to swap the physicality of Jekyll and Hyde by having the doctor as bearded, old, and gruff, while Hyde is an attractive young man. Neither man has an attractive personality, though.

Jekyll is obsessed with his work and neglectful to his wife, who he regards as his intellectual inferior. Hyde, on the other hand, is physically attractive but an abusive psychopath who cares about nothing beyond his own pleasure.

The film had two major factors working against it. Firstly, the central dual role was written specifically with actor Laurence Harvey in mind. Harvey was a somewhat limited actor, but extremely handsome and in the right role highly effective. When Hammer were unable to attract Harvey to appear in the film, for some reason they failed to opt for Christopher Lee, who would have been perfect in the part(s) and indeed is magnificent in the secondary role of Jekyll's duplicitous friend Paul Allen. Instead, the up-and-coming young Canadian actor Paul Massie was hired. One can understand Hammer's management not wanting to hire the same leading actors for all their horror films, but (like the late replacement Anton Diffring in *The Man Who Could Cheat Death*) Massie had nothing like the range the twin roles required. His attempts to portray the evil and depravity of Hyde with a fixed grin and a glassy stare constantly threaten to sink the film.

The second problem was that director Terence Fisher simply did not like Mankowitz's script, in which every character is in various ways unpleasant, flawed, or just plain evil. The audience has nobody to root for in a story, which is about the attractiveness of evil—Fisher could see no reason for us to like these characters, and was unable to make the audience care. Even the film's visual pleasures were reduced by the film being shot in the Megascope process, which demonstrated that widescreen photography did not suit Terence Fisher's visual style.

Once production was completed, behind schedule and at great expense by Hammer's standards, the film hit even more trouble. By modern standards, the debauchery contained in the narrative of *The Two Faces of Dr Jekyll* is very mild stuff indeed. It was too much though for Columbia Pictures, whom Hammer had made the film for, which passed the film on to one of its subsidiary companies. Eventually, the movie was sold on to American International, where it was released as *House of Fright*, after a period in which it laboured under the title *Jekyll's Inferno*. Under any title, the film did poor business and Hammer were in the unusual position, at the height of their success, of making a gothic horror film that lost them money.

If almost everything possible went wrong with *The Two Faces of Dr. Jekyll*, Hammer's next horror production worked triumphantly well despite a somewhat tortuous path to the screen. Hammer's main Hollywood studio customers at this point were Columbia and Universal, and the latter were extremely keen to have a sequel to *Dracula*. Jimmy Sangster was set to work on the project, the resulting script, entitled *Disciple of Dracula*, featuring both the disciple of the title and the Count himself. Interestingly, it would appear that Dracula's appearance in the story was relatively brief, perhaps recognising that the Count was a powerful but dramatically limiting character. It could also be read as a symptom of Hammer's curious reluctance to fully utilise Christopher Lee as a leading man.

Disciple of Dracula took a different turn when Hammer began planning a separate Christopher Lee vampire picture, *Dracula the Damned*. Peter Bryan was called in to remove all but a few mentions of Dracula from the *Disciple of Dracula* script, but then *Dracula the Damned* failed to proceed, leaving the original film, still referred to within Hammer as *Dracula II*, as a solo adventure for Van Helsing, provided that Peter Cushing could be convinced to return.

The studio eventually agreed on the title *The Brides of Dracula*, allowing them to use the magnetic box office appeal of the Dracula name despite, as events transpired, them having no actual Dracula film on their release schedule for 1960. The familiar production team was reunited for the occasion, with Terence Fisher directing alongside cinematographer Jack Asher, with Bernard Robinson outdoing his previous achievements to produce magnificent, spacious-appearing sets on the compact soundstages of Bray Studios. Peter Cushing, however, raised objections to the Sangster/Bryan draft of the script presented to him, particularly the ending in which Van Helsing uses black magic to conjure a swarm of bats to kill the nest of vampires. The idea was dropped but was too good to waste and was used instead for Hammers next vampire film, *The Kiss of the Vampire*.

With Cushing's services secured, an actor was needed to play the film's villain, the vampire Baron Meinster. David Peel was hired, a forty-year-old actor who, somewhat appropriately for a vampire, looked at least ten years younger and had never had a screen role anything like as big as this before. Peel, it would seem, knew which way the wind was blowing, appearing in only one other film (a tiny part in a French-produced remake of *The Hands of Orlac*, featuring Mel Ferrer and Christopher Lee) before retiring from acting.

A splendid supporting cast was assembled, with particular emphasis on the female roles. Jimmy Sangster had been criticised for not writing good roles for women in his scripts, and perhaps in response, *The Brides of Dracula* has probably the strongest female roles of any Hammer horror film.[2] Yvonne Monlaur plays heroine Marianne, a young school teacher and heroine of the film, a much larger and more satisfying role than that played by Yvonne Furneaux in *The Mummy*. Monlaur had appeared in the same year in Sidney Hayers' splendidly lurid *Circus of Horrors*. Theatrical *grande dame* Martita Hunt was cast as Baroness Meinster, mother of David Peel's Baron, their twisted relationship playing a key role in the film's opening half. Also playing a memorable role was Freda Jackson as the Meinster's servant Greta, creepy to the point of downright unhinged.

The end result of the production team's efforts was nothing short of superb, rivalling *Dracula* as the greatest vampire film Hammer ever made, and the film proved highly profitable for Universal. *The Brides of Dracula* operates for much of its length as a twisted adult fairy tale. The heroine Marianne is lured, in the old gothic manner, by Baroness Meinster to her huge chateau. There, she meets Baron Meinster, the Baroness's son, a handsome young prince complete with flowing blond locks, imprisoned and kept immobile by a golden shackle on his leg. Reversing the convention of traditional fairy tales, our very self-assured, active heroine—no passive screamer she—releases a beautiful male from captivity only to find that the charming prince is actually shockingly evil. The prince has turned into a frog. Although Marianne has unwittingly unleashed evil, in doing so, she saves her own life, as we learn that the Baroness has brought her to her home in order to feed her to her son.

The film also indulges in some comedy, though less so than *The Revenge of Frankenstein*. This is mainly in the form of Hammer regular Miles Malleson's cheerfully mercenary quack doctor, who acts as a sort of uncomprehending Watson to Van Helsing's Holmes (an interestingly similar relationship to that of Cushing's Baron Frankenstein and Thorley Walters' Doctor Hertz in 1967's *Frankenstein Created Woman*). Some fun is also had at the expense of Herr Lang (Henry Oscar), the self-important head of the girls' school where Marianne is employed, who cringes before any figure of authority—his servile reaction to Dr Van Helsing is precisely the same as his towards Baron Meinster.

The Times' anonymous film reviewer proved rather sniffy about the qualities of *The Brides of Frankenstein* in their review of 7 July 1960. 'There are some handsome sets … and the cast is too good for its material', was the verdict. The cast was so good that Peter Cushing did not even rate a mention in the article, as if his ubiquity in Hammer's horror pictures made him so taken for granted that he had become invisible.

The Werewolf and the Cat

There were still monsters in Universal's closet for Hammer to raid, and the studio's next gothic horror was, as it transpired, their only attempt at a werewolf movie. This was not to be a remake of either of Universal's main werewolf movies, *Werewolf of London* (1935) or *The Wolf Man* (1941), but instead an adaptation of another novel on the same theme that the studio owned the rights to: Guy Endore's 1933 story *The Werewolf of Paris*.

Hammer's original plan had been to first make another movie for Columbia, entitled *The Inquisitor*. This was to have been set during the Spanish Inquisition, but ran into trouble when it became clear to the Hollywood studio that a film on this theme would never be cleared by the Catholic Legion of Decency. Even in the early 1960s, the Legion of Decency was so powerful that that a 'C' for Condemned rating could spell doom for a film's American box-office prospects. Earlier in 1960, Warwick Films big-budget feature *The Trials of Oscar Wilde* was a major financial failure after its subject matter attracted a 'C' rating.

Perhaps not surprisingly, Columbia backed out of the project, but Hammer's customary production efficiency meant that large Spanish-style sets were already in an advanced stage of preparation on the Bray Studios backlot. Not about to see these expensive sets wasted, Hammer brought forward their plans for *The Werewolf of Paris,* producer Anthony Hinds (who also wrote the film under his traditional *nom de plume* of John Elder) changing the setting from France to Spain to accommodate *The Inquisitor*'s sets.

Terence Fisher, still entrusted with Hammer's prestige horror pictures, returned to direct, but now worked with a different cinematographer. Arthur Grant took over these duties, the meticulous working methods of Jack Asher proving too time-consuming for the ever-cost-conscious Hammer management. Grant's style was far more realistic than Asher's and the studio's horror pictures took on a different look in this period of its history. The films still looked more expensive than their budgets might suggest, but a certain expressive sheen had been lost.

The Curse of the Werewolf also saw some new names in front of the camera, with top-billing going to Clifford Evans, a powerful forty-eight-year-old Welsh actor who had worked steadily and with distinction but, at this time, mainly on television rather than film. The part of the poor lad stricken with the werewolf curse went to Oliver Reed, a very promising young actor Hammer had placed under contract. Reed previously stood out in two uncredited roles for the studio: as a club bouncer in *The Two Faces of Dr Jekyll* and as Lord Melton in *The Sword of Sherwood Forest.* With his dark, brooding looks and stocky frame, Reed was physically perfect for the role and he was already a fine actor.

John Elder's script in effect splits the story into two sections. The first part of the film is framed rather like a fairy tale, narrated at key points by Clifford Evans. This tells the story of a beggar (the angular, expressive face of Richard Wordsworth once again proving ideal) who appears at the door of a cruel nobleman (Anthony Dawson) on the day of his wedding. After making fun of the beggar, the nobleman has him thrown into jail, where he remains for many years, forgotten by all but the jailer and his mute daughter. The daughter grows up into the strikingly beautiful Yvonne Romain, who is herself thrown into the same jail by the now hideously aged nobleman. The beggar rapes the young woman, then dies, and when the nobleman tries to force himself on her again the following day she kills him.

Fleeing the castle, she is discovered in the forest by Don Alfredo (Clifford Evans), who is kindly, cultured, and educated. It transpires that the woman is pregnant, and gives birth on Christmas Day (an ill-omen), dying in childbirth.

Don Alfredo and his housekeeper raise the boy, whom they name Leon, as if they were his parents, though we discover that he has a taste for blood and the local goats keep disappearing. This takes up almost half of the film's ninety-one-minute running time, with the rest of the film's length being taken up by the story of the adult Leon, a fine, strong lad (by now played by Reed) who goes to work at the local vineyard. There he meets and falls in love with the owner's daughter Christina (Catherine Feller), the couple's budding romance being doomed both by their difference in social status and by Leon's taste for blood finally developing into him turning into a werewolf.

The result was a film that, with its twin themes of gothic horror and doomed romance, could have been written expressly for Terence Fisher's directorial strengths. The levels of violence in the film (which were not especially greater than those in previous Hammer films) and Leon being the product of rape proved to be especially controversial when *The Curse of the Werewolf* was sent to be assessed by the BBFC. Part of the problem was not due to the content of the film itself, but due to the political situation surrounding the issue of film censorship at the time. While the situation was nothing like as bad as during the notorious moral crackdown in Britain during the mid-1950s, a huge furore had been stirred up by the release of Michael Powell's *Peeping Tom* in May 1960.[3]

That film was the subject of thunderous condemnation, not only in the popular press, but also from elsewhere. On 20 April 1960, the National Union of Teachers announced at its annual conference in Blackpool that it was launching a campaign against horror films.[4] The climate in Britain was hardly conducive to the kind of full-blooded gothic horror represented by *The Curse of the Werewolf*, which was released with around five minutes of censor cuts to a chorus of press hostility.

In contrast, Universal were more than happy with the film Hammer delivered to them, which was released to positive reviews as part of a double bill with one of the studios most unusual and little-known horror films. This was *Shadow of the Cat*, a film that Hammer did not even take a credit for. Instead, despite the film being made by Hammer's regular crew of technicians, it was officially made by BHP Productions.

Shadow of the Cat followed *The Curse of the Werewolf* onto the studio floor at Bray on 14 November 1960, just twelve days after Terence Fisher's film completed its principal photography. Unusually for a Hammer horror picture in this period, this low-budget film was from a producer other than Michael Carreras or Anthony Hinds, in this case Jon Penington. The director chosen for the assignment was John Gilling, who had written several films for Hammer during the 1950s 'Exclusive Films' period. He had experience directing horror pictures of wildly different types though, being responsible for the 1952 Bela Lugosi/Arthur Lucan comedy *Mother Riley Meets the Vampire* and the rather more recent Burke and Hare drama *The Flesh and the Fiends*, which had been released in London in February 1960. Gilling went on to become one of the directors most associated with Hammer Films during the 1960s, directing swashbucklers such as *The Scarlet Blade* and *The Brigand of Kandahar* plus horror pictures including *The Plague of the Zombies* and *The Reptile*.

Gilling and returning cinematographer Arthur Grant certainly ladled on the gothic atmosphere for *The Shadow of the Cat*, the opening sequence of the murder of Ella Venable (Catherine Lacey, who would have somewhat more memorable horror appearances in *The Mummy's Shroud* and *The Sorcerers*) taking place in an old dark house on a stormy night directly after the old lady reads a passage from Edgar Allan Poe's *The Raven*. The murder was committed by Andrew the butler, in cahoots with the victim's husband Walter (André Morell), who wants her money. The film takes a bizarre turn when the murderers realise that Ella's cat Tabitha has witnessed the murder, and become manically obsessed with killing a perfectly ordinary, well-fed housecat.

The film boasts a great cast of stalwart British B-picture actors and a few names familiar from previous Hammer productions. Freda Jackson returns from *The Brides of Dracula*, once again playing a creepy servant, while Barbara Shelley makes a welcome return as Ella's niece, who tends to the bedridden Morell. She also acts as the film's much-needed voice of reason, informing the cast at regular intervals of the absurdity of fully grown adults being terrified of a cat. Morell calls in his grasping relatives, including the cheerfully criminal William Lucas, his wife, Vanda Godsell, and Lucas's father, Richard Warner, offering them a share of the loot if they can both find Ella's will and kill the cat. Everyone who tries to kill Tabitha is killed in various fairly absurd ways, while a suspicious newspaperman (Conrad Phillips) and Police Inspector (Alan Wheatley) investigate Ella's disappearance.

Perhaps to compensate for the badly handled central premise of the film—the original idea of George Baxt's script had been to have the cat represented by hints and shadows, rather than an actual tabby cat—*The Shadow of the Cat* is acted at a pitch of hysteria, which fails to make the film any more convincing. While this experiment by Hammer in producing its own horror B-pictures can be, at best, regarded as being only a partial success, it was a notion they would return to later in the decade with rather happier results.

The Phantom Strikes!

Hammer's next gothic horror was a much higher-budgeted affair, and another in their series of reworkings of Universal horror movies. Universal had been planning a new version of *The Phantom of the Opera* for some time, having had great success with the property in 1925, starring Lon Chaney, and 1943, starring Claude Rains as The Phantom (the latter being the only one of the 1930–40s cycle of Universal horror films to be shot in Technicolor). With Hammer becoming the preeminent maker of gothic horror films during the late 1950s, Universal abandoned plans to make the film in-house and handed over the project to the English studio.

The subject matter of Gaston Leroux's story, with large scale opera scenes integral to the plot, demanded a somewhat higher budget than was normal for Hammer, which began production at Bray Studios on 21 November 1961. The opera scenes for the film were shot on location at London's Wimbledon Theatre, which was hired for three weeks for the production. Anthony Hinds wrote the screenplay, once again using his *nom de plume* John Elder, and Terence Fisher directed, as he had all of Hammer's prestige horror pictures.

Herbert Lom, the Prague-born actor who had been a leading character player in British films since his breakthrough role in *The Seventh Veil* (1945), brought a commanding presence to the role of The Phantom. Although Lom was new to horror films, he had previously appeared in one Hammer/Exclusive production, *Whispering Smith Hits London* (1952). Heather Sears, at this point seen as a potential star actress after roles in *Room at the Top* (1959) and *Sons and Lovers* (1960), played Christine, the opera singing object of The Phantom's attentions, while Edward de Souza played the romantic male lead. The latter tends to be a somewhat thankless role in versions of this story, though in the 1943 version, it was actually top-billed thanks to the casting of singing star Nelson Eddy in the part. Rather more effective was Michael Gough, playing as the manor-born, sneering, villainous Lord Ambrose d'Arcy, who passes The Phantom's music off as his own.

The resulting film is certainly handsomely mounted, counting as one of Hammer's best-looking pictures of this period, and is well played by Lom and de Souza, though Heather Sears is a trifle colourless in the female lead. Lom's impact is somewhat lessened by his lack of screen time—he does not show up until some fifty minutes into the film—and the decision to give his character a full-face mask, drastically reducing his ability to express emotion.

The script, not surprisingly, increases the horror quotient somewhat from previous versions, though The Phantom's status as a tragic, wronged hero is protected by a killer dwarf (Ian Wilson) committing most of the murders. How much The Phantom knows of the dwarf's activity is left unclear. The shocks are rationed, but very good when they arrive, and The Phantom's lair in the sewers of Paris is very well-realised by production designer Bernard Robinson. The results were good but not ground-breaking in any real sense, yet one's reaction to the film depends somewhat on how much opera the viewer has patience for. Structurally, this is a problem for the film, as staging large sections of an opera about Joan of Arc at a crucial stage of the narrative kills the pace of the film stone dead.

Hammer's *The Phantom of the Opera* was well-received in America, but was not a success in the UK market thanks to a bizarre decision by the film's British distributor Rank to ask at a late stage for the film to be suitable for an 'A' certificate. A film that had been designed for an 'X' rating and had been carefully paced was ruined by this decision. Also affected was Terence Fisher's career with Hammer: it is notable that the studio began giving horror assignments to directors other than Fisher from this point on and it would be two years before he would start work on another for them.

A veil shall mercifully be drawn over Hammer's disastrously poor gothic horror comedy remake of *The Old Dark House*, a collaboration with American horror director/producer William Castle that demonstrates just how good *Carry On Screaming* (1966) really is. Universal, meanwhile, wanted another Dracula sequel from Hammer. *The Kiss of the Vampire* was the studio's attempt to make *Dracula III*—like *The Brides of Dracula*, the Count himself was once again absent.

Shooting began at Bray on 7 September 1962, with Anthony Hinds' script (as ever using his John Elder pseudonym) reworking material originally developed, but not used for *The Brides of Dracula*. Most notably, the original ending of that film rejected by Peter Cushing was utilised, in which black magic is used to call a swarm of bats that attack the nest of vampires. This ending could now be used because of some changes that were wrung for *The Kiss of the Vampire*. Peter Cushing was not cast, despite the script containing an extremely Van Helsing-like character. Instead, the role of Professor Zimmer went to Welsh actor Clifford Evans, who had previously impressed as Don Alfredo in *The Curse of the Werewolf*.

Changes were also apparent behind the camera: Terence Fisher was not called to direct one of Hammer's A-picture horrors for the first time. Tasmanian director Don Sharp was chosen instead, a figure new to both Hammer and horror pictures who was to spend the next few years heavily involved in the genre, as well as associated films such as Hammer's own *Rasputin the Mad Monk* (1966) and Harry Alan Towers' *The Brides of Fu Manchu* (1966). Sharp brought with him a cinematographer new to Hammer, regular *Carry On* director of photography Alan Hume.

The pair certainly began the film with style with a memorable sequence of a vampire being staked through a coffin lid with a spade, the camera seeming to travel through the wood of the coffin to see the results. The way this scene is played by Clifford Evans is interesting, as although it is shot for maximum effect, Professor Zimmer is subdued and close to tears. Zimmer is a much rougher character than Van Helsing, haunted by the evils he has witnessed and driven to drink—when he tries to warn English honeymooning couple Gerald and Marianne against visiting the superficially charming Dr Ravner, he is too drunk to be taken seriously. As already discussed, Zimmer's methods are also very different to those of Van Helsing—Peter Cushing's vampire hunter uses the symbols of Christianity, in contrast to Zimmer's use of black magic.

Dr Ravna (Noel Willman) is also quite different to Hammer's previous vampires. Although he is the head of a vampire cult, he lacks personal magnetism and seems to be of a slightly lower order of bloodsucker—what one might describe as an upper-middle-class vampire, as opposed to the aristocracy of Baron Meinster and Count Dracula. Although the film is effective, there is a sense of the creative treading of water: if Hammer were to continue making vampire pictures, they needed to inject something different into the mix.

Although it is not especially more violent than previous Hammer horror films, *The Kiss of the Vampire* suffered from the same censorship difficulties that *The Curse of the Werewolf* had, the BBFC being in an especially censorious mood during this period. While an edit of the film was eventually assembled that was acceptable for the Board's examiners, the film encountered a different set of problems in America. While Universal were more than happy with the film Hammer delivered, the bat-attack ending they were finally able to use proved too similar to that of Alfred Hitchcock's *The Birds*, which was due for release in March 1963. Thus, *The Kiss of the Vampire* was held back until September 1963 for US audiences, while Britain had to wait until January 1964.

An even worse fate awaited the film when it was eventually sold to American television, which was so squeamish about horror content that the title of the film was changed to *Kiss of Evil* to avoid mention of vampires. As with other Hammer films of this period sold to US television, so much footage was cut that an especially filmed subplot was created by other hands so that the film could make its required length.

Monsters Old and New: *The Evil of Frankenstein*, *The Gorgon*, and *Curse of the Mummy's Tomb*

While Hammer's ongoing vampire series was still attracting audiences, particularly in America, the studio's next move was to reactivate its *Frankenstein* movie sequence with *The Evil of Frankenstein*. This went onto the studio floor at Bray in October and November 1963, just over a year after *The Kiss of the Vampire* wrapped. This was originally offered to Columbia as part of Hammer's ongoing contract with them, but eventually wound up at Universal. This meant that some elements of that studio's 1930s and 1940s *Frankenstein* cycle of films found its way into Anthony Hinds' script and the general look of the film. The most notable story element was the discovery of Frankenstein's monster preserved in ice, which featured in Curt Siodmak's 1943 script for *Frankenstein Meets the Wolf Man*.

The general look of the film also owed a little to Universal, with the Baron's castle being equipped with a laboratory, a touch more like those of the Karloff-era films than anything in Hammer's first two *Frankenstein* movies. The most striking similarity, however, was the monster, a blue-grey faced creation that adopted the distinctive square-headed look created by Jack Pierce for Boris Karloff. This was a decidedly mixed blessing as this make-up, though iconic, had ceased to be frightening by the mid-1960s—within a year of *The Evil of Frankenstein*'s filming, *The Munsters* premiered in the US on the CBS network featuring Fred Gwynne as a comic Frankenstein monster.

Worse still, Hammer had not learned the lessons of Universal's sometimes unwise casting of the Frankenstein monster after Karloff retired from the role. Boris Karloff, Christopher Lee, and even Michael Gwynn succeeded in the role because they were not only physically suitable, but also excellent actors able to project a performance through the make-up. For *The Evil of Frankenstein*, Hammer chose Kiwi Kingston, a 6-foot 5-inch wrestler with no known previous acting experience. The previous two Hammer Frankenstein films featured the monster as an actual character, both the result of and the victim of Baron Frankenstein's obsessive experiments and, in some strange way, the moral centre of the stories. Now, the monster was just a stumbling, hulking menace used as a guided missile.

Nevertheless, there is much to enjoy in what amounts to a reboot of Hammer's *Frankenstein* sequence of films. Crucially, unlike with the *Dracula* sequels, the studio were able to cast their original leading man, and Peter Cushing was as excellent as ever in what was to become his signature role. He looks older and more careworn than in the previous films, travelling Europe to continue his work and being chased away by the reactionary, anti-scientific forces of the church before he can make a breakthrough. Out of both money and options, the Baron and his assistant Hans (Sandor Elès) return to his home town, only to find his castle has been ransacked.

The Evil of Frankenstein has quite an episodic plot, with a large chunk of the film being devoted to a long flashback sequence that retells the story of the Baron's first attempt at creating life and its apparent destruction. Back in the present day, Frankenstein and Hans discover the monster frozen in ice and set to work reviving it while also plotting revenge on the Burgomaster and Chief of Police who have stolen his possessions. A further plot strand is introduced when Frankenstein recruits a carnival mesmerist (Peter Woodthorpe) to control the actions of the monster.

The whole thing works surprisingly well, which makes it especially sad that so much good work and a decent, pacey job of direction by Freddie Francis have been so overshadowed in the memories of many who saw the film by the movie's disastrously poor monster. An especial point of interest is that *The Evil of Frankenstein* ignores the timeline established by *The Curse of Frankenstein* and *The Revenge of Frankenstein*, thus restarting the Hammer

Frankenstein sequence from scratch. The films in the series that follow are sequels to *Evil* rather than the first two in the series.

Hammer continued to make efforts to break away from producing cycles of gothic horrors based exclusively on Universal's 1930s and 1940s film characters. One such attempt was *The Gorgon*, an idea brought to the studio by the writer John Llewellyn Devine, which had the interesting notion of transplanting the title character of Greek myth to Hammer's traditional location of early twentieth-century central European. The story was turned into a script by John Gilling—whose work was subsequently rewritten by Anthony Hinds, much to Gilling's disapproval—and went before the cameras at Bray from early December 1963 to mid-January 1964.

This saw Hammer's 'A-team' of director Terence Fisher and stars Christopher Lee, Peter Cushing, and Barbara Shelley reunited, with curiously muted results. Interestingly, Lee this time was given top billing for a role that is somewhat smaller than Cushing's (he does not properly enter the narrative until some fifty minutes into the film). This is perhaps an indication of how important Lee was to Hammer and how much more valuable his time was now that he was an international leading man, by now living in Switzerland and appearing in films across Europe.

There are things to enjoy about *The Gorgon*. Terence Fisher conjures a nicely gloomy air of gothic decay, aided enormously by some lovely sets by Bernard Robinson. After a lively beginning featuring a hanging and characters being turned to stone, the film becomes somewhat talky and studio-bound. Fisher's trademark deliberate pacing seems rather too slow as the film determines to hold back on showing its monster until the film's climax. The Gorgon herself proved to be one of Hammer's more spectacular misjudgements, an original idea of using a headdress containing live grass snakes being rejected in favour of pneumatically powered rubber snakes. With fast cutting, this might just have passed muster, but in unsparing close-ups, the results were both unconvincing and unfrightening.

Released by Columbia in the US in February 1965, British audiences had seen the film the previous October on a double-bill with the considerably livelier *Curse of the Mummy's Tomb*. This had been shot from 24 February to 27 March 1964 at Elstree and saw a return to Hammer by Michael Carreras. Sir James Carreras and his only son Michael always had a difficult relationship, which had prompted Michael to leave Hammer to strike out on his own. Occasionally, he would return to the family business as an independent producer, and here he was writer, producer, and director. Union rules meant that one person was not allowed to be both producer and writer, the same reason Anthony Hinds wrote under the pseudonym John Elder. For his *nom de plume*, Carreras made reference to his friend Hinds' choice, choosing Henry (his own middle name) Younger.

Curse of the Mummy's Tomb was in many ways a remake of Hammer's 1959

The Mummy, set in 1900 with a rampaging mummy killing members of the expedition that opened its tomb. The film's stars were two of the stalwarts of the British B-movie scene: Terence Morgan and Ronald Howard. They were joined by Fred Clark as the American showman who plans to exhibit the mummy, leading lady Jeanne Roland, and George Pastell, the latter playing exactly the same role as he had done in *The Mummy*. The film definitely has a hand-me-down, B-movie feel to it, but it is well made, lively, and good fun—some much-needed light to contrast the gloom of the top half of the double-bill it was part of in the UK.

Hammer, Beyond the Horrors: War Movies

It would be useful at this point to pause our narrative of Hammer Films' gothic horror output to look at the wider range of productions the studio released from the mid-1950s onwards. The massive success of *The Curse of Frankenstein* and *Dracula* saved Hammer's finances at a time when, with its cycle of Anglo-American thrillers having ended with the completion of its co-production deal with Robert L. Lippert, the continued future of the company was in very real doubt.

Hammer did not, however, turn its entire production effort towards the making of horror films, continuing throughout the 1950s and most of the 1960s to make movies in a wide variety of genres. It should be remembered that nobody knew how long the vogue for gothic horror would last and Hammer were caught in an unusual situation: they existed largely on co-production deals with major American studios, but increasingly those studios wanted more horror pictures, which tended to make more money than Hammer's other films. If Hammer were painted into a corner of only producing horror films, they would be left high and dry if fashions changed and commissions for these films stopped coming in.

Much of the British film industry busied itself in the 1950s making endless war movies, replaying the Second World War as the national wartime narrative hardened into a set of cinematic clichés. *The Steel Bayonet* (1957) was Hammer's first effort in this field, a drama set in the North African theatre of conflict in 1943. This being Hammer, the film sets out to be distinctive and presents an ahead-of-its-time picture of a near-exhausted group of men struggling to survive against the odds with their own high command being as much a threat to their lives as the German Army. Starring Leo Genn and Kieron Moore, the toughness of the film was reflected in a no-nonsense poster campaign with the slogan 'It Stabs to the Guts of War!'

The Steel Bayonet did well enough for Hammer to look at continued war movies with a different angle and they hit the box office jackpot with their next effort, *The Camp on Blood Island* (1958). This is probably the Hammer war movie that has developed a reputation similar to the company's horror movies and was sold in the UK with an image of a topless, sword-wielding Milton Reid as a Japanese executioner and the screaming ad-line 'Jap War Crimes Exposed!' The film itself remains a really thrilling and engaging piece of work, despite the unlikely casting of the likes of Ronald Radd and the ubiquitous Michael Ripper as Japanese officers.

David Lean's *The Bridge on the River Kwai*, which had been released in the UK in October 1957, was a major studio hit and proved that audiences were interested in the experiences of British soldiers fighting in the Far East. Those soldiers who had suffered at the hands of the Japanese Army disliked the film though and *The Camp on Blood Island*, which was released six months later, was somewhat closer to their real experiences. Director Val Guest even went to the trouble of hiring naturally very thin actors (including *The Quatermass Xperiment*'s Richard Wordsworth) whose physiques more closely resembled victims of the Japanese Army than the suspiciously healthy looking prisoners of David Lean's film.

The Camp on Blood Island is set in a Malayan POW camp run by brutal Japanese Commander Yamamitsu (the aforementioned Ronald Radd). The British prisoners, led by Colonel Lambert (André Morell), must keep the news from the Japanese that they have actually lost the war or Yamamitsu will order them all killed. Amazingly, the script, by Val Guest and John Manchip White, was based on a real incident. This was another big success for Hammer for Val Guest, who had recently directed the first two *Quatermass* films and *The Abominable Snowman*.

Guest also directed Hammer's next war movie, *Yesterday's Enemy* (1959), which was also set in the Far East, this time Burma after the Japanese invasion. British audiences were promised 'The Most Outspoken Film of Our Time!', while America posters yelled 'War is Hell!' The film, based on a BBC Television production and reportedly based on true events, took the highly unusual step of portraying British war crimes. Stanley Baker, the forceful Welsh actor who was quickly becoming the pre-eminent British screen star of the day, played the leader of a group of British soldiers making their way through the Burmese jungle. In attempting to keep his men alive, Baker makes tough and morally dubious decisions, including the killing of civilians. The film is somewhat studio-bound, but remains extremely powerful and one of the hidden gems of the Hammer archives.

Hammer only made one more war movie, *The Secret of Blood Island* (1964), which this time was directed by Quentin Lawrence from a John Gilling script. Shot in Eastmancolor, the film was released in April 1965 in the US by Universal Pictures, who saved money by ordering prints in black and white. This speaks volumes about the company's opinion of the box-office potential of a film with a frankly silly plot about a female British secret agent (Barbara

Shelley, who played a different character in *The Camp on Blood Island*) being hidden by the men of a Malayan POW camp.

The company did co-produce one other film that deserves mention at this point: *Ten Seconds to Hell* (1959), one of the earliest productions by Seven Arts Pictures, who would collaborate with Hammer on many productions over the next decade before acquiring Warner Brothers from Jack Warner in 1967. Set in a ravaged post-war Berlin, major American stars Jack Palance and Jeff Chandler feature as former German soldiers who are now members of a bomb disposal team. The production was based at Berlin's famous UFA studios and proved an especially difficult shoot with American director Robert Aldrich clashing both with the Anglo-German crew and star Palance. Seven Arts were less than happy with the results and recut the picture without Aldrich's knowledge, which is possibly the reason for the film's clunking voice-over narration.

Psychological Horrors

Running alongside Hammer's ongoing series of gothic horrors were horror-tinged psychological thrillers inspired by the huge success of Alfred Hitchcock's *Psycho*, which was released in the US in June 1960 and in the UK in August of the same year. This was a much lower-budgeted production than Hitchcock's normal glossy suspense thrillers, which allowed the director to go much further in the direction of horror than he had been allowed to previously by American movie studios. The results changed the face of American horror and made an enormous amount of money. The combination of low-budget horror and high profits attracted the attention of Hammer, who began working on their own variations of the idea.

This was more than fine by Hammer's most celebrated screenwriter, Jimmy Sangster, who had grown tired of writing gothic horrors and was inspired not only by *Psycho*, but also by *Les Diaboliques*, Henri-Georges Clouzot's 1955 French classic of murder and suspense. Sangster's first attempt in this area was Hammer's neat little murder mystery *The Snorkel* (1958), which bears some similarities with *Taste of Fear*, Hammer's first full-blooded psychological thriller. First screened in London in April 1961, this starred Susan Strasberg as Penny Appleby, a young woman crippled after a riding accident, who travels to the south of France to stay with her father and his new wife (Ann Todd), who she has never met. Her father has gone away on business, but Penny keeps seeing visions of his dead body. Is she going mad? She enlists the help of the household's friendly chauffer (Ronald Lewis) and is suspicious of the attentions of the family's sinister doctor (Christopher Lee).

Taste of Fear (known in the US as *Scream of Fear*) was the first Hammer production to be directed by Seth Holt, one of the great lost talents of British cinema. A renowned film editor, Holt became a superb director whose career was hampered by a serious drink problem, which at times affected his health so much he was unable to work. For *Taste of Fear*, Holt adopted a deliberate pace, which makes the shock sequences dotted at intervals throughout the film even more effective. He gives the film a sophisticated and literate feel quite different to Hammer's other films and teases excellent performances from the cast. Particularly notable is Ronald Lewis, a Hammer contract player, who here gives possibly the best screen performance of his career. Lewis was a talented actor who did not get the breaks required to become a major star and whose career declined after his Hammer contract expired in 1965.

Jimmy Sangster's script does not bear a moment's scrutiny once the film has finished, but it really keeps the audience on its toes and generates a great deal of suspense. The film was not a great financial success in the UK and US, but was very successful in the European market, making enough money for Hammer to initiate a series of similar films written by Sangster. The next in the series was *Paranoiac*, which was released in the UK in May 1963. Sangster's script was based on Josephine Tey's classic 1949 crime novel *Brat Farrar*, which had been on Hammer's schedule for some time. The version of the story that eventually appeared expanded the horror elements in Tey's story of the return of the long-lost heir to a family fortune. The major change was the character of Simon Ashby, the heir whose position is threatened by the arrival of Tony (Alexander Davion), who claims to be his older brother. Simon, it transpires, is not only an abusive drunk but also an unhinged murderer—as played by Oliver Reed, he is really unhinged, the actor giving a performance so over the top that it is quite memorable. Janette Scott is top billed, but truth be told, her role is secondary and somewhat thankless; however, the film is terrific fun, packed with incident and very stylishly shot by Freddie Francis and his cinematographer Arthur Grant.

Paranoiac—in which none of the characters are identifiably paranoid—was released in the US on 15 May 1963, some time before the film was seen by British audiences. On 29 May, however, UK moviegoers were treated to the next Jimmy Sangster thriller, *Maniac*. This had originally been announced for production in 1960, at which point it would have starred Peter Cushing and George Sanders. While this version failed to come to pass, three years later, Columbia contract artist Kerwin Mathews became the rather lower-profile star of a film, which is perhaps the least interesting of this strand of Hammer's productions.

Mathews plays an American painter in the Camargue in the south of France who begins an affair with his landlady (Nadia Gray) whose husband is locked up in an insane asylum after killing with an acetylene torch a man who raped their daughter. Mathews helps to hatch a scheme to help him escape with the idea that the husband would be perfectly happy for their affair to continue. Perhaps not surprisingly, things do not go as planned as the escapee (Donald Huston) turns out to be a homicidal maniac.

Maniac is a considerable disappointment, the pace of the narrative grinding to an agonisingly slow pace after an inventively shot and gruesome opening murder scene. Part of the problem is the structure of the story, which is both highly unlikely and does not really start until some forty minutes into the film. Michael Carreras directs and does a fair job with a couple of set-piece sequences, but generally demonstrates that his real talent was as a producer.

Nightmare has some of the same faults as *Maniac*, starting with a real bang as schoolgirl Jennie Linden suffers a vivid nightmare about being locked in an asylum with her insane mother. Linden is a (rather overage) pupil at Hatcher's School for Young Ladies who has been traumatised by seeing her mother murder her father when she was a young girl. This becomes the subject of a campaign by her guardian and the nurse hired to look after her (David Knight and Moira Redmond) to drive her murderously insane. *Nightmare* at least looks stylish and unusual, in part due to being shot during the freezing winter of 1963, but mainly thanks to Freddie Francis' well-staged direction. Ultimately, the film was sunk by key plot developments that are too silly for words.

By this time, the standard Sangster plot device of someone trying to drive a woman insane was wearing a little thin from repetition. At least *Hysteria* attempted to alter the formula by having the story concern an amnesiac man who may or may not be going insane and turning into a killer. It helps also that the character is played by Robert Webber, a busy American character actor giving a typically solid performance—Webber never played likeable types, and although he does not really sell the vulnerability of his character, he does make for a convincing potential killer. As with virtually all of these films, the plot is not the most believable, but the action keeps moving (save for a misjudged flashback sequence in which we discover the events that led up to Webber's amnesia) and Freddie Francis, returning once again as director, keeps the action moving so we do not notice the holes in the plotting. Webber was not asked back for future Hammer films; however, his on-set behaviour made the *Hysteria* shoot an uncomfortable experience.[5]

The main body of Hammer's psychological thrillers ended here. *Fanatic*—shot for the most part at Elstree Studios in the autumn of 1964 and released in the spring of the following year—was very much sold as a shocker in the same vein ('Sledge Hammer Suspense to Shock You from Your Seat' screamed the posters). Director Silvio Narizzano's film, in which religious fanatic Tallulah Bankhead keeps Stephanie Powers hostage in her creepy old house, is far more a jet-black comedy that wore its American release title, *Die! Die! My Darling!*, exceedingly well.

It was somewhat against the currents of Hammer's release schedule at the end of the 1960s, when they returned to the psychological thriller form with *Crescendo*, which was shot during 1969 at Elstree Studios with location work in the south of France. This was a project that had been doing the rounds for some time and had originally been written by Alfred Shaughnessy with Michael Reeves attached as director. When Hammer managed to secure funding for the film, Alan Gibson directed in a style that indicated just how much tastes had changed in the intervening four years. He kept his camera constantly mobile, shooting through cars and railings, employing wide-angle lenses and focus-pulls in a style that was of its time, but made what was actually quite a studio-bound film consistently visually interesting.

The content of the film had also moved on quite a bit since the mid-1960s, with scenes of nudity and drug-taking that pushed the edges of acceptability for mainstream cinema at the time. Stephanie Powers returned to Hammer to play an American music student visiting the French home of a deceased composer she is studying. There, she becomes caught in a psychodrama involving the composer's crippled failed pianist son (James Olson), his mother, the maid who keeps him supplied with sex and drugs, and Joss Ackland as an oddly menacing manservant.

Crescendo was not a notable financial success for either Hammer or Columbia—in the UK, it was the supporting feature to *Taste the Blood of Dracula*—but it remains a fascinating entertainment with a unique, brooding atmosphere.

Comedies

Interestingly, several of Hammer's comedies made in this period also had a military setting, which perhaps should not be surprising as military service represented a powerful shared experience among a large section of the movie-going audience. *Up the Creek* was released in May 1958 and featured Peter Sellers in one of his first featured roles outside of spin-offs from his legendary radio series *The Goon Show*, which was to finish its nine-year run on the BBC Home Service on 28 January 1960. Here, he played a sort of Irish variation on Phil Silvers' Sgt Bilko, a naval chief petty officer running several businesses on the side along with the crew of a Royal Naval destroyer. His schemes are little changed by the arrival of an inexperienced, accident-prone new captain (David Tomlinson) who is soon drawn into the various scams.

Up the Creek proved unexpectedly successful and was exported to America where *The New York Times* reviewer described the film as 'diverting and spasmodically amusing, if not precisely uproarious', which is a fair enough description. A sequel was rushed into production, which was a fine idea, save for the fact that Peter Sellers was unavailable, having been booked to appear in Jack Arnold's *The Mouse that Roared* (1959). This set Sellers on the road to international stardom, while *Further Up the Creek* would appear a mere six months after *Up the Creek* with comedian Frankie Howerd cast in an equivalent role to that of Sellers. Howerd's performance was quite different to that of Sellers; the chameleon-like Sellers would have been able to play the role in almost any accent, while Howerd brought his established gangly, semi-camp persona to the part.

The two *Up the Creek* films had been directed and co-written by Val Guest who had previously directed Howerd in his 1954 comedy film debut *The Runaway Bus*. Guest had by this point been given his big break as a director of dramatic features by Hammer, having helmed *The Quatermass Xperiment* (1955), *Quatermass 2* (1957), *The Abominable Snowman* (1957), and *The Camp on Blood Island* (1958) among others for the company.

I Only Arsked! (1958) was unusual for Hammer in that it was based on a television property not from the BBC, but by Manchester-based commercial television contractor Granada Television, which provided ITV's programming to the north of England. Continuing the military theme of the company's comedies, this was the film version of Granada's very successful sitcom *The Army Game*, which ran from 1957 to 1961 over 154 episodes—a huge run for a British comedy. Directed by B-movie veteran Montgomery Tully, the film starred several cast members of the original series, including Bernard Bresslaw, Alfie Bass, and Charles Hawtrey. Interestingly, there was a second, unofficial *Army Game* film that featured several actors from the show who had left after a major shake-up of the series cast after its second season. Thus, actors associated with *The Army Game* such as William Hartnell, Charles Hawtrey, and Norman Rossington were seen by cinema audiences from 1 August 1958 in *Carry On Sergeant*, which was to launch the long-running *Carry On* film series.

The Ugly Duckling, which was released on 10 August 1959, saw Hammer attempt to make a comedy star of the hulking Bernard Bresslaw, an accomplished actor who had achieved national popularity as Private 'Popeye' Popplewell in *The Army Game*. Here, though, Bresslaw was cast as Henry Jekyll, a shy, awkward young man whose life is changed when he discovers a medical formula that changed his persona to the sophisticated and confident Teddy Hyde. Yes, you are reading this correctly: Hammer's first version of the classic Jekyll and Hyde story was a comedy vehicle for Bernard Bresslaw. *The Ugly Duckling* proved less than popular with audiences and Bresslaw never became a comedic leading man, though he remained a popular performer for the rest of his life, particularly after he joined the *Carry On* film team with *Carry On Cowboy* (1965).

Don't Panic Chaps was released to UK cinemas in November 1959 and was directed by George Pollock who would become most famous for directing

MGMs four *Miss Marple* films starring Margaret Rutherford. A return to military comedy, this saw British and German soldiers, led by German Dennis Price and English George Cole, left forgotten on an Adriatic island during the Second World War and living together in peace until the beautiful Nadja Regin is cast adrift on the island. This was a co-production with ACT Films, the filmmaking arm of filmmaking union Association of Cinematograph Technicians, which got into film production in an attempt to find work for technicians who were struggling during slumps in British film production. The company stayed in the business of producing commercial films from 1951 until 1962, after which the name was revived occasionally for documentaries on Trades Union and political themes.

Watch it, Sailor! (1961) was another naval-themed comedy, this time featuring Dennis Price, a comedy star who made an enormous impression in his breakthrough role of the vengeful Louis, killing his way through the D'Ascoyne family in *Kind Hearts and Coronets* (1949), but whose career subsequently declined due to alcoholism. He remained a popular figure, however, and appeared in Hammer's *The Horror of Frankenstein* (1970) and *Twins of Evil* (1971), and the Amicus production *The Haunted House of Horror* (1969) among many other horror appearances during the last days of Price's career before his death in 1973, aged fifty-eight but looking many years older.

Hammer's final comedy in this period was *A Weekend with Lulu* (1961). Probably the most *Carry On*-style of the company's productions, this was directed by John Paddy Carstairs, the professional name of John Keys, the brother of Hammer producer Anthony Nelson Keys. Bob Monkhouse was top billed, best known as a stand-up comedian who maintained an acting career in the 1950–60s as a sort of British version of his comedic hero Bob Hope as a result of his role in *Carry on Sergeant*. Alongside him as the other half of a hapless pair trying to organise a caravan holiday to France (*Lulu* is the name of the caravan) was *Carry On* star Leslie Phillips, while *Carry On* regulars Sidney James, Kenneth Connor and Shirley Eaton were also seen.

By this point, though, it had become clear that Hammer's future lay with its horror and drama productions, which tended to be easier to export and were attracting major co-production deals from American studios. Therefore, Hammer did not make another comedy film for ten years, until the success of *On the Buses* saved Hammer's finances at a point in time when its gothic horror films were beginning to decline in popularity.

Historical Dramas

The Curse of Frankenstein and *Dracula* gave Hammer an opening to the world of American major studio film production. The company worked with virtually every major studio in Hollywood, though not exclusively. Columbia Pictures signed a long-term deal with the company, which was eventually to last until 1965 and encompassed many of the studio's non-horror dramas. The year 1959 saw Hammer begin a series of costume dramas, which span off into two very different directions.

The Stranglers of Bombay steered closer to their horror films, but is an interesting historical adventure set in 1830s colonial India about the murderous Thuggee cult. Guy Rolfe (a strapping 6 feet 4 inches and a well-preserved forty-nine years old at the time) is excellent as the hero Harry Lewis, a captain in the East India Company, the trading company-*cum*-private army that ran Britain's Indian colonies. Lewis is pitted against both his uncaring employers and the fanatic Thuggees—led by the Cypriot George Pastell, who played almost every nationality on earth during his acting career, often for Hammer—in a fairly brutal story. Terence Fisher's film was advertised as being in Strangloscope, a widescreen process that was in reality exactly the same as Hammerscope, which was in turn another name for Megascope. The budget, however, did not stretch to colour photography for cinematographer Arthur Grant.

The Sword of Sherwood Forest (1960) on the other hand was aimed at a much younger audience and Terence Fisher worked with director of photography Ken Hodges to present a colourful adventure. This was yet another television spin-off from Hammer, this time from ITC's highly popular series *The Adventures of Robin Hood*, which ran from 1955 to 1959 over 143 episodes. This was British commercial television's first American success, launching Lew Grade as an international television impresario. The show's star, Richard Greene, formed a production company with the show's producer Sidney Cole, bought the series rights and took the project to Hammer, who immediately saw the export possibilities and readily agreed to make the film. The film looked fabulous (shot, unusually for Hammer, at Ireland's Ardmore Studios), and director Fisher was certainly familiar with the subject matter, having directed several episodes of the television series in that pre-*The Curse of Frankenstein* period when it looked like his late-blooming career was winding down.

It was perhaps unwise for the producers to replace much of the regular cast of the television series. Besides Greene, none of the other television cast members who had become familiar and loved were hired for the film. Alan Wheatley, a familiar Hammer face of old, was replaced in the key role of the Sherriff of Nottingham by none other than Peter Cushing, who never disappointed an audience in his life, but was not the person audiences were used to.

Therefore, there began a series of juvenile historical mini-epics made for the bank holiday audience. *Captain Clegg* (1962) featured Peter Cushing in the central role of Doctor Blyss, a parson who leads a double existence as the titular Captain Clegg, leader of a band of smugglers. Peter Graham Scott directed this tale, based on Russell Thorndike's novel *Doctor Syn*, which had previously been filmed in 1937 by Gaumont British under this title, starring George Arliss. The rights to Thorndike's novel were claimed by Walt Disney, which resulted in Hammer changing the names of the characters and the title of the film to avoid the attentions of Disney's lawyers. The stock company, which had developed for Hammer's historical pictures, was reassembled, including Yvonne Romain, Oliver Reed, Milton Reed, and the ubiquitous Michael Ripper, this time joined by Patrick Allen as the Royal Naval captain sent to catch Clegg.

Hammer beat Disney to the punch by some distance, releasing *Captain Clegg* to UK cinemas on 25 June 1962, twelve days after its American release. Disney's version, *Dr. Syn, Alias the Scarecrow*, did not reach UK screens until 22 December 1963. The title of Hammer's version changed again for the film's American release via Universal—the studio had been due to make a version of Richard Matheson's post-apocalyptic vampire novel *I Am Legend* under the title *Night Creatures*. The BBFC, having read the proposed script, informed Hammer that a film based upon this script would not be passed for UK release. The project was abandoned, but Hammer owed Universal a film entitled *Night Creatures*, so this became the American release title of *Captain Clegg*, the film thus being sold as rather more horrific than was the original swashbuckling intention.

The Pirates of Blood River saw Christopher Lee return not only to Hammer, but also to British filmmaking after a period working in Italy—Lee worked extensively in Europe during the 1960s, partial due to his setting-up home in Switzerland in the summer of 1962. The idea was for Hammer to produce something a bit more light-hearted than the gothic fare they had become famous for, but the shoot, under the auspices of notoriously bad-tempered director John Gilling, was very tough on the actors. Lee looks to have had a whale of a time as the eye-patched villain Captain LaRoche, while Oliver Reed returned as Brocaire, one of his band of pirates. Distributors Columbia provided two of their own contract players to act as the main heroes of the tale, Kerwin Matthews, best known for playing Sinbad in the Ray Harryhausen adventure *The 7th Voyage of Sinbad* in 1958, and Glenn Corbett, who spent most of his career in American television.

Columbia double-billed *The Pirates of Blood River* with another Harryharusen picture, *Mysterious Island*, on its release on the ABC circuit in August 1962, reaping huge profits for what became the post popular double-bill of the year. The market for such things having been thoroughly established, Hammer assigned John Gilling to direct another swashbuckler for 1963 release, *The Scarlet Blade* (retitled *The Crimson Blade* by Columbia for its March 1964 US release). This was, unusually, a swashbuckler set during the English Civil War with Jack Hedley cast in the title role as a swordsman attempting to free King Charles I, played by Robert Rietti, more usually employed as a voice artist, from the clutches of Lionel Jeffries, tyrannical Roundhead Colonel Judd. Oliver Reed appears once again, this time as the duplicitous Captain Sylvester who moves from Cavalier to Roundhead camps as his own interests dictate.

If *The Scarlet Blade* featured something of a second eleven cast, *The Devil Ship Pirates* saw Hammer's star name Christopher Lee return to action (as did some of *The Scarlet Blade*'s sets), this time under Australian director Don Sharp. Lee looked both dashing and menacing as the bearded Captain Robles, leader of a band of pirates separated from the main Spanish Armada after its defeat by the Royal Navy. In a period rewrite of film noir *The Desperate Hours*, writer Jimmy Sangster has the damaged ship put into a remote English coastal village for repairs, the crafty Robles convincing the locals that the Spanish have won the battle and they are all prisoners. Looking far more expensive than Hammer's budget should have allowed, Bernard Robinson's sets and Michael Reed's Hammerscope widescreen photography give *The Devil Ship Pirates* an epic feel.

The film was released in May 1964 in the US and in August of the same year, catching the school holidays again in the UK, this time double-billed with an Italian peplum entitled *The Secret Seven/Gli invincibili sette* (1963) by Alberto De Martino. Absolutely nothing to do with Enid Blyton, this was a late entry into the sword and sandal genre made popular by the *Hercules* series of films, which would soon be swept away by the huge success of the spaghetti westerns. Despite this hardly being so enticing a prospect for its intended young audience as *The Pirates of Blood River* double-bill, *The Devil Ship Pirates* still managed to be one of the top earning British films of 1964.

Unfortunately, Hammer was unable to produce another hit costume adventure film, their next attempt being possibly the worst. *The Brigand of Kandahar* was Hammer's final film under the studio's long-running production partnership with Columbia Pictures, and it has the deadly air of a contractual obligation. Even the major cast members were at the end of their contracts with Hammer; Ronald Lewis in the title role was appearing in his final substantial movie appearance of any description while Oliver Reed was destined for much bigger things and Yvonne Romain was soon to try her luck in Hollywood. This is one of those films that is based entirely on other films rather than real life as Anglo-Indian army officer Case (Lewis) is thrown out of the army after his commanding officer (a miscast Duncan Lamont) trumps up charges of cowardice against him. Case is promptly sprung from jail by Eli Kahn (Reed), leader of a tribe fighting the British. Case throws in his lot with Kahn in order to gain revenge against the British.

Director John Gilling salvaged stock footage from Terence Young's 1957 film *Zarak* on which Gilling was associate producer for the film's more spectacular scenes. The rest of the film is frankly awful, Lewis stiff and incredibly unconvincing as an Indian, while a scenery chewing Reed never for a moment seems anything other than English. *The Brigand of Kandahar* proved too juvenile for adults and too serious and violent for children, and managed to appeal to neither. The fact that Hammer bothered to make such an old-fashioned film at all was a worrying sign. Yes, it was a cheap, throwaway film, but Hammer had grown to prominence making low-budget films to the best possible quality. The sharp little 1950s Brit Noirs of the Robert Lippert era or even Val Guest's gritty, crime-on-the-streets drama *Hell is a City* (1960) suddenly seemed like they were from another era and beyond Hammer's capabilities.

The company's final two costume dramas were released in 1967, *A Challenge for Robin Hood* being released in July and at least having the advantage of being in no doubt whatever as to the audience it was aimed at. While schoolboys with the price of a movie ticket were no doubt pleased to see the film, this did show more signs of flagging inspiration. This was Hammer's third Robin Hood movie, the first being *The Men of Sherwood Forest* back in 1953, displaying a lack of imagination either on Hammer's part or on that of film distributors (Warner-Pathé in the UK and 20th Century Fox in the US). Secondly, Barrie Ingham as Robin Hood gave a perfectly adequate performance, but severely lacked the roguish charm of Errol Flynn or the fatherly appeal of Richard Greene.

Most bizarrely of all came *The Viking Queen*, which was released to no acclaim whatsoever on 25 March 1967 in the UK. Director Don Chaffey's film, shot in Ireland, was an attempt to construct an epic film with the background of the Roman occupation of Britain. Uncomfortably cast American import Don Murray plays kindly Roman Justinian (as we all know, ancient Romans should always be played by actors with impeccable Received Pronunciation accents) who rules Icena alongside Queen Salina, played by the previously unknown Carita. This displeases people on both sides, especially the brutal Octavian, played by Hammer fan-favourite Andrew Keir. The results were odd in the extreme, larded with brutal tortures, including burnings and whippings while at the same time seeming incredibly out of place in the movie landscape of 1967.

This was to be the last of Hammer's non-horror period dramas, and it proved to be an expensive misstep. The film ran over badly schedule and budget, and completely failed to attract an audience, thus incurring the displeasure of the film's US distributor 20th Century Fox. By the time the dust had settled on the debacle of *The Viking Queen*, it was 1968 and the warning signs were plain to see for James Carreras and his Hammer team. The studio was running out of major Hollywood studios still willing to deal with them, and as a production company, it was being backed into a corner. With the studio's comedies being a thing of the past and its straight dramas having hit the buffers, despite Hammer's best efforts, increasingly they were being forced into becoming a studio that only made gothic horror pictures. If these went out of fashion, Hammer might not have a long-term future.

Double Your Money: *Dracula: Prince of Darkness* and *Rasputin the Mad Monk*

Sir James Carreras and the Hammer management always had an eye on the balance sheet. Double-bills were still popular in the mid-1960s as hard-pressed cinema chains sought new ways to entice customers from in front of their televisions and into movie houses. Hammer had found some success with producing its own double-bills such as with 1964's *The Gorgon* and *The Curse of the Mummy's Tomb*. These two films were, however, entirely separate productions, made by different crews and were even shot in different production facilities—Bray and Elstree. It would, Hammer calculated, be far cheaper to produce two films in tandem with shared casts, crews, and the same sets, redressed for the occasion.

The disadvantage of this approach was that if the two films were shown together audience members would quickly work out what had happened and might (perhaps unfairly) feel cheated. Instead, a plan was formed in which four films would be made in pairs, which could then be shown either individually or as two double-bills, the top half of each bill swapping its sibling with the other. Thus, Christopher Lee was tempted to star in *Dracula: Prince of Darkness* and went straight on to appear in the title role of *Rasputin: The Mad Monk*, a historical drama with some horror trimmings added for Hammer's core audience. A large castle set was constructed on the Bray backlot, which served both as Castle Dracula and as a rather tatty-looking Russian royal palace.

Meanwhile, Hammer's resident production designer Bernard Robinson also supervised the construction of a large village set that served as the main outdoor filming location of two films directed by John Gilling, *The Plague of the Zombies* and *The Reptile*. Between 26 April and 22 October 1965, Bray Studios was a hive of activity as four full-length films were shot, one of the most remarkable achievements in British filmmaking history.

The two Christopher Lee features were definitely the A-pictures of the exercise, *Dracula: Prince of Darkness* reuniting most of the key personnel of *Dracula* from 1958. Anthony Hinds' story idea was passed on to Jimmy Sangster to adapt into a full script. Although Sangster had written for Hammer regularly, he had little interest in the gothic horror genre and this was his first script of this type since 1960s *The Brides of Dracula*. For the occasion, he dusted off his occasional penname of John Samsom.

The other three films in the package were ideas that had been floated previously but had fallen by the wayside for various reasons. A production of the Rasputin story was first proposed and provisionally scheduled for production in 1961 but dropped, possibly due to the danger of legal action from Prince Yousoupov, one of the killers of Rasputin, who was very much alive at the time of filming and who had sued previous studios that had made versions of the story.

Rasputin: The Mad Monk was written by Anthony Hinds/John Elder, who also wrote *The Reptile*, a project that had been turned down by Universal the previous year under the title *The Curse of the Reptiles*. *The Plague of the Zombies* was written by Peter Bryan and was a toned-down version of another project previously offered to Universal, known previously as *The Zombie* or *Horror of the Zombie*.

While production on the films went smoothly, the films themselves are worthy of closer examination, both for their content and for a snapshot of where Hammer were in a creative sense by 1966. *Dracula: Prince of Darkness* remains one of the most famous films the studio ever produced, and even fifty years after its production, it retains the power to shock and disturb. The film reuses many of the tropes established in Hammer's previous three vampire films, but the presence of Lee as Dracula invigorates the entire production. Effective as *The Brides of Dracula* and *The Kiss of the Vampire* were, we are here in the presence of the lord of the undead.

The film is intelligently structured, holding back the big reveal of Dracula until the halfway stage. Ten years after the events of the first Dracula film, a group of four English travellers (Barbara Shelley, Francis Matthews, Suzan Farmer, and Charles Tingwell) are in an inn on the way to Karlsbad. A monk, Father Sandor, advises them not to go, but they ignore him. The coach driver taking them ejects them in the forest before they can arrive at Karlsbad, too frightened to travel any further at night. They are then met by a driverless carriage, which takes them to a mysterious castle, where meals and warm beds await them, provided by the manservant Klove (a splendidly lugubrious Philip Latham) on behalf of his long-dead master, Count Dracula.

Everything that happens for the first half of *Dracula: Prince of Darkness* is a build-up to the revival of Dracula, which is spectacularly well-achieved. Alan Kent (Charles Tingwell) is stabbed to death by Klove, who hangs his body upside down and cuts his body, the mixing of his blood with Dracula's ashes reviving the Count. This sequence remains powerful even today and it is somewhat surprising that it was passed almost uncut by the BBFC in 1965, though the Board did object to the original idea of Alan being decapitated. This is the centrepiece of the film, Terence Fisher's deliberate pacing creating a mounting sense of dread and horror as we realise what Klove is about to do.

In this first half of the film, the most impressive acting comes from Barbara Shelley. She is simply wonderful as Helen Kent; prudish, nervous, and frightened, she is the only person in the group who seems to realise what danger they are all in. After the revival of Dracula, Helen is the first to be vampirised by Dracula, and her demeanour is transformed in a similar manner to that of Melissa Stribling in the 1958 *Dracula*. Christopher Lee's performance is somewhat different to that which he gave in the first film: stripped of dialogue (both Lee and Sangster claimed responsibility for this), Lee abandons the front of affable civility he began the first film with. Instead, we are treated a full-throttle performance of animalistic intensity.

The main opposition to Dracula here is Andrew Keir's Father Sandor, a big, bustling outdoors type who serves to replace the character of Van Helsing here—it is interesting to note that, in a further development of Lee's billing above Cushing in *The Gorgon*, here he is the sole star name. Hammer's curious reticence towards giving Lee major roles (as seen in the supporting roles he was cast in for *The Man Who Could Cheat Death* and *The Two Faces of Dr Jekyll*) had finally dissipated. Andrew Keir's Father Shandor is a very well-drawn character, designed to be as different as possible to Van Helsing and he drives the action of the film in its second half.

Other highlights include the staking of Helen by Father Shandor and his monks, a strongly horrific scene, and the scene in which Dracula attempts to turn Diana (Suzan Farmer) into his slave by having her lick blood from his chest. Although they are interrupted by the sound of Charles' (Francis Matthews) voice, the scene remains wildly sexual. Filled with well-staged horror set-pieces, *Dracula: Prince of Darkness* is ultimately let down by a rushed and unconvincing ending. One wonders if there was an imperative, driven by the desire to show the film as the top-half of a double-bill, to restrict the film's running time to ninety minutes. Had the filmmakers been given an extra fifteen minutes in the film's second half, one cannot help but think that a better paced and staged denouement could have been arranged.

Terence Fisher's *Dracula: Prince of Darkness* crew wrapped filming on Friday 4 June 1965, and the following Monday, largely the same personnel, headed by *Kiss of the Vampire*'s Don Sharp, started work on *Rasputin: The Mad Monk*. Four of the same cast members also stayed on for the new film (Lee, Shelley, Matthews, and Farmer), joined by Richard Pasco, returning from *The Gorgon*, and Dinsdale Landen. The film told a rather fictionalised account of the rise of Rasputin from a drunken penniless monk to the Russian royal court during the last days of the Romanov dynasty, his magnetic personality and talent for healing allowing him to use and abuse women along the way.

Remarkably, the entire story of his rise and eventual murder is told with absolutely no mention of the approaching revolution that would shortly sweep the Romanovs from power. It is a real pleasure, though, to see Christopher Lee give a big, loud performance and have him carry a film in a way that he never had for Hammer before, even in the Dracula movies. Although Anthony Hinds added a few nasty moments to help fulfil the expectations of Hammer audiences (Dinsdale Landen, for instance, gets his face burned with acid), *Rasputin: The Mad Monk* was basically a historical melodrama, and no worse for that fact.

As different sets were being used, most notably Bernard Robinson's outdoor village, a whole eight days went by between Don Sharp completing principal photography on *Rasputin: The Mad Monk* and John Gilling's crew starting work on *The Plague of the Zombies*. Oddly enough, the industrious Gilling would direct both this and its sister film *The Reptile*, keeping the same director of photography, Arthur Grant, and camera operator Moray Grant. Several crew members worked on all four films, including Hammer's regular make-up artist Roy Ashton, hair stylist Freda Steiger, and sound editor Roy Baker.

The Plague of the Zombies saw Hammer taking on about the only horror film monster of the 1930s and 1940s, which they had yet to adapt for modern audiences. Universal had steered clear of the zombies during their horror cycle, but other producers had managed some success with the theme. Independent producers Edward and Victor Halperin produced the strikingly atmospheric 1932 film *White Zombie*, starring Bela Lugosi, along with its lesser sequel, *Revolt of the Zombies* (1936). Boris Karloff appeared in an odd crime/zombie hybrid for Warner's *The Walking Dead* (1936), but the only other major success of the period was producer Val Lewton's *I Walked with a Zombie*, a 1943 B-picture made for RKO, which borrows the narrative structure of *Jane Eyre* and moves it to Haiti.

The Plague of the Zombies took the opposite approach and transplanted the voodoo-influenced plot to a Cornish village, where the locals are dying off from a mysterious sickness. Local doctor Brook Williams is baffled and calls on his old professor, André Morell, to help him work out what is going on. Morell discovers that zombies are afoot, and mixed up somewhere in this development is the local squire John Carson. The casting of the film is spot on, with Morell providing a commanding presence as the moral centre of the film and Carson bringing his trademarked smooth manner and smoky James Mason-esque voice to the hissable squire. Particularly memorable is Jacqueline Pearce as the unfortunate Alice, who gives a natural unaffected performance as the doctor's ailing wife, only to return as one of the screen's most memorable zombies.

Although *The Plague of the Zombies* did not make a huge impact on its release in January 1966, the film was somewhat revolutionary in its portrayal of the living dead. Unlike previous incarnations of the monsters, here they are terrifying, green-faced creations who we see instinctively attacking people (albeit, in one memorable sequence, this happens during a dream). This was to prove highly influential on the next generation of horror filmmakers, notably George A. Romero, who borrowed much of the visual representation of the monsters for his genre-changing 1968 film *Night of the Living Dead*.

It is interesting to note that Romero solved a major problem of the zombie genre that eluded Peter Bryan's *The Plague of the Zombies* script—that of a convincing motive for them to be brought into existence. In *The Plague of the Zombies*, they are basically free labour for the squire's tin mine, which is too dangerous for live humans to work in. This leads to an amusingly silly scene in which zombies are whipped to make them work harder, which one might imagine would have a limited effect on the dead. Romero's masterstrokes were to remove not only the link with voodoo, but also any question of an outside motive for their appearance. There is some mention in *Night of the Living Dead* of the zombie outbreak being caused by spores from a returning spacecraft, but human motive for the creation of zombies is irrelevant to the Romero cycle of films.

Gilling and his crew wrapped filming on *The Plague of the Zombies* on 8 September 1965, beginning *The Reptile*'s shoot on the following Monday. Jacqueline Pearce returned as the title character, joined by Hammer regular Michael Ripper who had played the village policeman in *The Plague of the Zombies*. For *The Reptile*, Ripper got probably his biggest role in a Hammer film as Tom Bailey, an old seaman turned village publican who befriends newcomer Harry Spalding (Ray Barrett) and helps him investigate the death of his brother. His death was caused by the bite of a human-sized reptile living in the house of the decidedly odd Dr Franklyn (*The Kiss of the Vampire*'s Noel Willman returning for his second major Hammer role), his oppressed daughter, and their sinister manservant (Jacqueline Pearce and Marne Maitland, respectively).

Although *The Reptile* proved nothing like as influential on the horror genre as *The Plague of the Zombies*, it certainly has its pleasures. Gilling directs quite snappily, the rough-hewn Australian Barrett offers something quite different to the standard Hammer leading man, and John Laurie is great fun, overacting like crazy as Mad Peter. The effects of *The Reptile*'s bites are effectively horrible, giving the film some regular gruesome highlights. The whole thing falls away quite badly in its final third, in which the script makes the mistake of having Dr Franklyn verbalise the absurd plot. This is followed by yet another burning house climax, which was becoming a rather too regular method employed by Hammer scriptwriters to quickly wrap up their plots.

Dinosaurs and Cave Girls

Michael Carreras was drafted back in for the studio's next attempt at something big and splashy outside of the horror genre, which resulted in Hammer racking up a major success with *One Million Years BC*. This took a huge amount of money at the box office on its American release in February 1967. A remake of producer Hal Roach's 1940 picture *One Million BC*, there really is no way that this ahistorical mixture of cavemen and dinosaurs should have worked. The mixture of Ray Harryhausen's stop-motion effects, which still look impressive fifty years later, and the iconic imagery of Raquel Welsh, complete with fur bikini and false eyelashes, proved irresistible to audiences. Thanks to extensive location shooting in the Canary Islands and expensive, time-consuming special effects, *One Million Years BC* was even costlier to produce than *She*, Hammer's biggest budget film to that time.

More in line with Hammer's usual budgets was *Slave Girls* (aka *Prehistoric Women*), a typical piece of Michael Carreras camp featuring *One Million Years BC* co-star Martine Beswick who was a hot property at the time after appearing in the 1965 James Bond movie *Thunderball*. The real follow-up to *One Million Years BC* was *When Dinosaurs Ruled the Earth*, which financial inflation saw costing considerably more than its predecessor. Although the film was profitable, Jim Danforth's ground-breaking Oscar-nominated special effects were so slow and expensive to produce that the film was not released until October 1970, some two years after the completion of principal photography.

This process was so far removed from Hammer's normal production philosophy that the last of Hammer's caveman epics, *Creatures the World Forgot*, filmed in Namibia and South Africa, dropped the dinosaurs altogether. The film was released in April 1971, only six months after *When Dinosaurs Ruled the Earth*. Michael Carreras was keen to produce more films along these lines, including more science fiction-themed ideas such as *When the Earth Cracked Open* and *Zeppelin Vs Pterodactyl*, but was unable to interest potential studio backers. This is a genuine pity as the basic idea was sound, which was proved when the British horror boom petered out in the mid-1970s and Hammer's rival Amicus found success with similar material.

Witches and Monsters

The bread and butter of Hammer's production schedule continued to be horror. *The Witches*, unusually, was brought to Hammer from an outside source. The film rights to Peter Curtis' novel *The Devil's Own* had been purchased by actress Joan Fontaine, who had become a major star in 1940 after being cast in the lead role of Alfred Hitchcock's first American film, *Rebecca*. By 1966, Fontaine was a well-preserved forty-nine years of age, but she had not made a theatrically released film in four years, so was keen to use this project to re-establish herself.

Hammer's regular production partners Seven Arts took on the project and production began at Bray Studios. Unfortunately, the story of a highly strung schoolteacher who returns to England from teaching in Africa to find a black magic coven operating near her new village school was not a success. *The Witches* (which retained the title *The Devil's Own* for its American release) was fatally compromised by director Cyril Frankel having a different vision for the film to its writer, *Quatermass* creator Nigel Kneale. Aside from his famous science fiction work, Kneale wrote satires for the BBC such as the 1968 production *The Year of the Sex Olympics* and he intended something rather more blackly comedic than the somewhat dull final result. Admittedly, the silly finale does raise a few unintentional smiles, but sadly, *The Witches* failed to revive Joan Fontaine's movie career and she spent the rest of her career working in television.

Frankenstein Created Woman

Michael Carreras, despite not being directly employed by Hammer, was in charge of major non-horror adventure movies such as *She* and *One Million Years BC*, which were big international hits for the company and kept their reputation high in Hollywood. These were expensive films to produce and Hammer's bread and butter output remained its gothic horror pictures. Shot in July and August 1966, *Frankenstein Created Woman* was evidence that the company was beginning to increasingly rely on its *Frankenstein* and *Dracula* franchises. While this did not bode well for the long-term health of Hammer, Anthony Hinds' script fizzes with fascinating ideas and is one of the very best of the series.

Peter Cushing returned as Baron Frankenstein, this time based in a small, unnamed central European town and working with local physician Dr Hertz (Thorley Walters, a favourite of director Terence Fisher). Frankenstein's hands—damaged, one presumes, in the fiery climax of *The Evil of Frankenstein*—can no longer perform surgery, so the boozy and befuddled Herz provides medical assistance to the Baron as well as food, lodgings, and the financing of his experiments. Those experiments have changed tack radically from his previous attempts at creating life and he has now developed a way of trapping the human soul after the death of its host body and transferring it into another.

Cushing and Walters work together tremendously well in a Holmes and Watson manner, with Walters kindly but uncomprehending Hertz acting as an effective foil to Cushing's brilliant but cold and acerbic Frankenstein. This is quite different to how Cushing played Sherlock Holmes in Hammer's *The Hound of the Baskervilles*, but bears interesting similarities to more recent interpretations of the role. While these two protagonists carry the story forwards entertainingly, the heart of the film and its most interesting themes lay elsewhere.

Susan Denberg and Robert Morris play Christina and Hans, star-crossed lovers who each carry deep traumas. Hans witnessed his father's execution at the guillotine when he was a child, while Christina was born with physical and facial disfigurements. The film examines themes of class arrogance (three posh-boy thugs stride into Christina's father's inn as if they owned the place and abuse Christina, knowing their social position means that they will get away with it) and sexism (Christina is victimised for being poor, weak, and female).

Despite his intellectual brilliance, Frankenstein is not infallible and fatally lacks insight into other people's needs and motives. Hans is executed unjustly for the murder of Christina's father, after which Christina drowns herself. Rescuing the bodies, Frankenstein captures Hans' soul and transplants it into Christina's body, with no thought of the potential for disaster or psychological damage if either personality should emerge. While the 'new' Christina, physically cured by Frankenstein and with new soul intact, at first seems to have no memory of her former life, eventually she becomes a beautiful, unhinged avenging angel wreaking vengeance on the three young dandies who murdered her father.

While the scripts and performances of *Frankenstein Created Woman* are generally excellent (though Susan Denberg as Christina is clearly dubbed—her appearance in the 1966 *Star Trek* episode 'Mudd's Women' reveals that she had a deep, throaty voice) the film still falls a little short of Hammer's top rank of films. The production looks rather cheap, limiting Terence Fisher and his cinematographer Arthur Grant's ability to give it much visual personality. The town in which the action takes place is noticeably underpopulated, and some of the costumes—particularly the suits and top hats of the dandy murderers—look stagy and unrealistic. *Frankenstein Created Woman* remains a fine film, appreciated rather more by modern audiences than it was during its release in the US during March 1967 and in the UK during June of the same year. It demonstrated, though, ways in which Hammer needed to modernise if the studio were to stay ahead of the game.

Further evidence for the need to freshen things up at Hammer came with *The Mummy's Shroud* (1967), writer-director John Gilling's last film for Hammer, which was also the last film the studio made at its long-term home of Bray Studios. From this point on, Hammer productions would be largely made at what was at this point known as ABPC Studios Elstree. Shot in September and October 1966, and released in both the US and UK on the bottom half of a double-bill with *Frankenstein Created Woman*, *The Mummy's Shroud* looks like it was made in very cramped conditions and in general has a very threadbare air about it. Worse yet, the film is a virtual remake of *The Curse of the Mummy's Tomb*, which was itself a retread of Hammer's original 1959 version of *The Mummy*. John Gilling and Anthony Hinds reportedly wrote the script in five days—and it shows. All concerned were too professional to produce anything slapdash, but *The Mummy's Shroud* comes perilously close at times.

This time around, André Morell and David Buck play the unlucky British explorers who rouse the ire of a living mummy, but the whole thing had been done too often before and some storylines that passed muster in 1964 suddenly appeared dated by 1967. The expedition is being financed by John Philips and Elizabeth Sellars has a nicely written role as his brittle, unhappy wife, rather enjoying her husband's discomfort as the danger from the mummy grows larger. Credit should also go to George Partleton for some decent mummy make-up, which crumbles to dust quite effectively—a better achieved effect than some of the vampire disintegrations in Hammer movies.

What Hammer needed was something new and different to take them out of their comfort zone of making period gothic horrors. Their next horror film provided just what was required, ironically by returning to Hammer's original horror movie hero, Professor Bernard Quatermass.

Devils in the Pit, Devils in the House

Quatermass and the Pit, the third of Nigel Kneale's massively popular television SF/horror serials, was first broadcast on BBC Television from 22 December 1958, running over six thirty-five-minute episodes until 26 January 1959. Despite his extreme reservations about the casting of Brian Donlevy in the role, Kneale collaborated with Hammer on a third script, but the vogue for science fiction monster films had waned and Hammer's then-new production partner Columbia passed on making *Quatermass and the Pit*. It was to be nine years before the film would finally enter production, by which time Hammer's films were being distributed by 20th Century Fox in the US, and Brian Donlevy's days as the lead in major studio productions were behind him.

In point of fact, British audiences were used to *Quatermass* being played by different actors, three different ones having played the role of the professor for Kneale's 1950s BBC Television serials. Reginald Tate, who played the part in *The Quatermass Experiement*, died shortly before *Quatermass II* was due to begin shooting. John Robinson stepped into the role at the last minute, but ironically, when the part was recast for the BBC's production of *Quatermass and the Pit*, Hammer regular André Morell was hired. One of Hammer's other second-string leading men, Andrew Keir (fresh from appearing in Hammer's disastrous Roman Britain epic *The Viking Queen*), was cast instead, becoming one of the actors most closely associated with the part.

A director new to Hammer was hired for the film, the vastly experienced Roy Ward Baker who was used to working on complicated, large scale films such as the famous 1958 recreation of the Titanic disaster *A Night to Remember*. Baker would work extensively for Hammer in the next few years as horror rose to become the dominant genre in British popular cinema. Roy Ward Baker was also employed by a studio which would become Hammer's greatest rival among horror film makers in Britain—Amicus, which we shall look at in the next chapter.

Nigel Kneale's script for *Quatermass and the Pit* does some very interesting things with the format of the films. Having written two stories in which the Earth (or south-eastern England, at least) was threatened by menaces from space, Kneale now devised a terrible threat from within, uncovered beneath London during excavation for a new underground railway station. Professor Quatermass, becoming involved almost by accident, discovers that the strange object that has been partially uncovered is not an unexploded bomb, as the military suspect, but instead an ancient alien spacecraft that may have affected the course of human life on earth.

How the character of Quatermass is portrayed changes across the course of the three Hammer films in fascinating ways: in *The Quatermass Xperiment*, Brian Donlevy's Quatermass is a human bulldozer, completely unburdened by doubt or any consideration of factors outside his own mission; in *Quatermass 2*, the character now does have doubts, and while he remains a man of action who drives the film's plot, he is tired and frequently terrified; and in this third film, Quatermass has softened, helped, obviously, by the change of actor. While he is in the thick of the action, his narrative purpose is to explain to the audience what is happening to the other characters, not to push the action along. Quatermass is swept along by events and does not even get to save the day in the end, an honour that goes to James Donald's Dr Roney.

Quatermass and the Pit is a film with the courage of its convictions, trusting the audience to understand what is quite a complex plot and containing dialogue that really matters to its understanding in scenes, which are never static or dull. Roy Ward Baker's direction is terrific in this regard—fast moving and mobile even during scenes, which must have been technically difficult to achieve. The reputation of *Quatermass and the Pit* has deservedly increased over the years and it stands as one of Hammer's very best films of the '60s.

Quatermass and the Pit was retitled *Five Million Years to Earth* for American audiences, Fox encountering the same problem that United Artists had in the '50s—the Quatermass name was meaningless to audiences outside the UK. A similar problem was encountered by Hammer's next horror picture, the Dennis Wheatley adaptation *The Devil Rides Out*. To British audiences, Wheatley's name was synonymous with horror and his titles famous, but 20th Century Fox executives thought the title sounded like a Western, renaming it *The Devil's Bride* for the film's eventual American release in December 1968.

Christopher Lee returned for another solo Hammer starring performance, this time as wealthy nobleman and expert on the occult the Duc de Richleau, who finds himself in opposition to the Satan-worshipping Mocata. In the latter role was Charles Gray, who gives a splendidly feline performance as the smiling face of evil. Mocata has gained influence over the Duc's young friend Simon (Patrick Mower) and he and his friends must withstand terrifying apparitions in order to escape.

In another unusual departure for Hammer, the story is set in the late 1920s, which makes for some attractive costumes and period motor vehicles. Unfortunately, the film was not a success in the vital American market and it must have looked quite dated by late 1968. Terence Fisher returned to direct, but here his style seems quite static and flat, despite the picture looking like quite an expensive production. Notoriously, *The Devil Rides Out* proved rather too expensive, with time and money running out before the complex optical effects could be completed. As already mentioned, Charles Gray is excellent, while Paul Eddington give the film a lift with his natural comedic instincts. Elsewhere, the playing is rather stiff: Leon Greene's performance as the *Duc*'s sidekick Rex was hampered by his being dubbed throughout by Patrick Allen—while this might possibly have passed muster for US audiences, in the UK, it was somewhat distracting as Allen had one of the most famous voices in Britain, heard daily in literally thousands of advertising and documentary voiceovers.

Uncharted Seas: Hammer in Trouble and the Return of Dracula

The Devil Rides Out gained very positive reviews in the UK and remained one of Christopher Lee's favourites of his own films, but failed to find an audience in the US. The fact was that Hammer had racked up a series of box office disappointments in a short space of time—as well as *The Devil Rides Out* failing, *The Lost Continent*, *Quatermass and the Pit*, and *The Viking Queen* had all underperformed in the US market, burning up much of the goodwill created by major hits such as *She* and *One Million Years BC*.

The Lost Continent was scripted and produced by Michael Carreras, based on Dennis Wheatley's novel *Uncharted Seas*, and was slated to be directed by Leslie Norman at Elstree at the end of 1967. Carreras dismissed Norman during production, taking over these duties himself on a production, which fell so far behind schedule and over budget that James Carreras came very close to closing the film down. *The Lost Continent* is a fascinating oddity in which survivors from the sinking of a tramp steamer encounter monsters and the descendants of peoples marooned centuries earlier. Fascinating or not, an expensive failure was the last thing Hammer needed at this point, which was the end result when the film was eventually completed and released in June 1968.

Crucially, this slate of films represented a concerted attempt by Hammer to build upon their two hit adventure films and break out of a gothic horror genre which has proved highly successful but could not last forever. This run of flops had major implications for the studio. Firstly, the pool of potential Hollywood major studio backers available to Hammer was getting smaller. Hammer's deals with Columbia and Universal had lapsed with little prospect of revival, while its relationship with Paramount had floundered at the first hurdle with the debacle of *The Man Who Could Cheat Death*. Now Fox was becoming disillusioned with Hammer and allowed their distribution deal to end with *The Vengeance of She*, an ill-starred sequel with little connection to the original that sank without trace on its release in April and May 1968.

Fortunately for Hammer, its long-term production partner Seven Arts, run by Kenneth Hyman who had produced several films for Hammer over the years, bought out Jack Warner's controlling interest in Warner Brothers in 1967. Kenneth Hyman was appointed head of production for the newly formed Warner Brothers-Seven Arts and Hammer once more had a favoured position with a Hollywood major. This would prove a temporary reprieve, however, as the new company only lasted for two years before it was bought out by the conglomerate Kinney National. Even with this new circumstance, the types of film Hammer could gain financing and distribution for were becoming more limited and more *Frankenstein* and *Dracula* pictures were soon on the production slate.

Dracula Has Risen from the Grave was the first fruit of Hammer's new deal with Warner Bros-Seven Arts, the agreement being made by Sir James Carreras on the understanding that Christopher Lee had signed on to return as Dracula. Unfortunately, in reality, no such agreement had been made with Lee who was, perhaps understandably, somewhat displeased at this turn of events. As well as there being some doubt as to the participation of the film's star, Hammer also found itself without a director when Terence Fisher was hit by a car and put out of action. Fortunately, Britain's other great specialist horror movie director of the era, Freddie Francis, was available and able to help smooth things over so filming could commence at Pinewood Studios on 22 April 1968.

In spite of Hammer's problems securing finance for future productions, the start of shooting on *Dracula Has Risen from the Grave* saw the studio's past performance as a generator of export funds being recognised by the award of the Queen's Award for Industry. This new production was to give Hammer a much-needed international hit, helping to set the direction Hammer was to take for the next five years.

This new *Dracula* film certainly looks very nice, Francis' instincts as a cinematographer prompting his director of photography Arthur Grant to be a little more creative than his normal rather plain style. Coloured filters are used for key scenes, recalling the methods of Hammer's former cinematographer Jack Asher. Most interestingly, a subtle yellow filter is used for scenes in which Dracula appears in order to give the impression that his appearance causes the very air around him to look sickly.

Anthony Hinds' plot also has some interesting new twists, having a recurring theme of religious faith. The Van Helsing substitute this time is a Monsignor (Rupert Davies) who finds a village in his area, which has abandoned the church due to their fear of Dracula. In his fight against Dracula, the Monsignor's supposed allies are the local priest (Ewan Hooper), a frightened man who has lost his faith, and an atheist student (Barry Andrews). This sets up the film's set piece—Dracula is staked through the heart but as the process is not carried out by a person with the enquired religious belief, it fails to destroy the Count. Dracula is motivated this time by revenge: on his revival, he discovers that he has been evicted from Castle Dracula thanks to an exorcism carried out by the Monsignor, so he targets his opponent's daughter (Veronica Carlson).

Not everything about the film works, unfortunately. Barry Andrews does not make a convincing academic and the revival of Dracula, via a trickle of blood from a head injury from the local priest, is both underwhelming and badly achieved. There is also a sense in *Dracula Has Risen from the Grave* that the title character is somewhat underutilised. Not only does Dracula not get enough screen time, but one feels that such a powerful screen presence should be trying to achieve more than chasing around after the Monsignor's daughter. On the positive side, Christopher Lee brings to his performance the same animalistic grace he displayed in *Dracula: Prince of Darkness*, but now with a subtle layer of sadness not seen in his other readings of the role.

In a reversal of the situation seen in Hammer's previous *Dracula* picture, which featured a show-stopping resurrection but a rushed and half-hearted ending, *Dracula Has Risen from the Grave* has possibly the most memorable vampire destruction in cinema history as the Count finds himself impaled on a giant cross, weeping tears of blood.

Changing Times: *Frankenstein*, Moon Flights, and Lesbian Vampires

It is symptomatic of the problems Hammer were having with obtaining finance for new productions that the company only had two releases during 1969, in sharp contrast to the six Hammer films released to cinemas during the previous year. *Frankenstein Must be Destroyed* began shooting during January 1969 at Elstree Studios, fifteen months after scripting for the film began—an eternity by Hammer's normal fleet-footed standards. Anthony Hinds, who had scripted most of the studio's gothic horrors at this point, was busy working on the Hammer-20th Century Fox television series *Journey to the Unknown*. Instead, Anthony Nelson Keys and assistant director Bert Batt came up with a fascinating idea, which first (and only) time writer Batt was allowed to work up into a screenplay.

This time Frankenstein acts like a cuckoo in the nest of his landlady Anna (Veronica Carlson) and her fiancé (Simon Ward), a doctor at the local insane asylum. Blackmailing them, he forces them to eject the other tenants and help him in his latest medical quest. This time, he attempts to repair the brain of his former scientific collaborator Dr Brandt, who is now an inmate of the asylum, by surgery. When Brandt has a fatal heart attack, he takes his plan a step further by transplanting the brain into the body of the asylum director Professor Richter. As in *Frankenstein Created Woman*, the Baron is undone by his own lack of human empathy. When Brandt wakes up mentally cured, he is horrified to find himself in a new body with huge operation scars on his head. When he tries to make contact with his wife, who is terrified by his new appearance, Brandt plans revenge on Frankenstein.

While Frankenstein remains a Holmesian 'desiccated calculating machine' (to quote Aneurin Bevan in a different context), he is now even more ruthless and manipulative than before. This represents an interesting development in the character who is now as irredeemably awful and self-centred as he was in *The Curse of Frankenstein*. The years of toil, disappointment, and public opprobrium have stripped the humanity from him. It becomes all too clear that Frankenstein is now the monster and his latest creation merely another victim.

Terence Fisher handles the film admirably, conjuring moments of macabre Hitchcockian tension, such as a burst water main revealing and animating a corpse. All concerned were dismayed by Sir James Carreras' insistence on a hideously out of character rape scene between Frankenstein and Anna. This does allow, though, for a sharp contrast between this and him telling Anna how he would like his eggs in the morning, which recalls *The Curse of Frankenstein*'s famous 'pass the marmalade' scene. It was a real shame that illness restricted Fisher to only direct one more film assignment after this one, as he was clearly still at something like the top of his game with *Frankenstein Must Be Destroyed*. Peter Cushing, at this point fifty-five years of age, was starting to look a little frail, and Hammer would recast the role, taking a radical new approach when they returned to the character the following year in *The Horror of Frankenstein*.

In many ways, *Frankenstein Must Be Destroyed* was the last of the traditional Hammer gothic horror productions, the films that followed having a different feel to them as Hammer attempted to adjust to an increasingly permissive censorship regime and changing audience tastes. One attempt to move with the times was Hammer's other 1969 release, the big-budget (by Hammer standards) 'Space Western' *Moon Zero Two*. This was another attempt by Michael Carreras—still not directly employed by Hammer—to broaden the range of Hammer's output. This was not necessarily a bad idea since public interest in space was at a high point in the lead up to the first manned landing on the moon.

Directed by Roy Ward Baker, writer-producer Michael Carreras based his script on a storyline for a Western, which should have delivered a thrilling result. Unfortunately, what was undoubtedly a good-looking film—the space suits were reused in British science fiction productions throughout the 1970s— was slow-paced and dull. *Moon Zero Two* lost money for Warner-Seven Arts and it is notable that Hammer only made one more film outside of the horror and comedy genres (the latter, as we shall see, making an unexpected comeback in 1971) over the next five years.

It was time to return to tried and tested formulas, and Hammer returned rather quickly to its most profitable franchise with *Taste the Blood of Dracula*. This was originally written à la *The Brides of Dracula* to be a *Dracula* sequel in name only, with a new disciple of the Count being created from a ceremony using Dracula's blood. Warner-Seven Arts were having none of this and a decidedly unwilling Christopher Lee was convinced to return for what looked suspiciously like the smallest appearance all concerned could get away with. With Lee on-board, Anthony Hinds reworked his story so that the Count's disciple, Lord Courtley (Ralph Bates), is killed during a black magic ceremony. Dracula, for reasons left unexplained, is revived after the ceremony and swears revenge on the three jaded, sensation-seeking middle-aged men (Geoffrey Keen, Peter Sallis, and John Carson) responsible for Courtley's death. He turns the men's children into his weapons of vengeance in probably the film's most interesting plot device, which brings the 1960s generation gap into the film's narrative, as well as an interesting strain of feminist revenge fantasy. The three men thoroughly deserve their fate, especially Geoffrey Keen's Hargood, whose drunken threats to beat his daughter Alice are charged with an atmosphere of sexual abuse. *Taste the Blood of Dracula's* lively direction was by Hungarian Peter Sasdy who had previously helmed two episodes of *Journey to the Unknown* and would direct two more films for Hammer in the following year.

Before this, Roy Ward Baker would return to direct Hammer's most sexually explicit film to date. With Hammer's long-established production team starting to break up, outside producers were starting to work for the company. Thus, Michael Style and Harry Fine (a partnership sometimes known as Fine Style) produced *The Vampire Lovers*, one of the key Hammer films of the '70s. This time, Sir James Carreras signed a co-production deal with American International Pictures who had maintained a strong UK production presence in the making of horror films. The partnership appears not to have been a happy one; despite the film being a financial success, AIP made no more films with Hammer, the studio preferring instead to work with Amicus or to produce them itself via its British subsidiary company.

The Vampire Lovers is based on the novella *Carmilla* by J. Sheridan Le Fanu; it features Ingrid Pitt as the title character, a female vampire who is left in the care of General von Spielsdorf (Peter Cushing)—Le Fanu's character was written as a teenage girl rather than the buxom thirty-something Pitt. After Von Spielsdorf's daughter dies of a mysterious malady, Marcilla (as Pitt's character is known at this point) is passed on to another family, where she becomes close to their young daughter (Madeline Smith) who soon becomes sick herself.

Peter Cushing's role here is something of an extended cameo and the part of the film's vampire hunter goes to Douglas Wilmer, looking ridiculous in an enormous wig in earlier scenes in which his character is meant to be some years younger. Despite the injection of co-production money and quite a starry cast of old stagers and up and coming actors (George Cole looks very out of place, while Kate O'Mara, Dawn Addams, and Jon Finch all appear to somewhat better effect), *The Vampire Lovers* was a cheap production and Hammer no longer had the ability to disguise the fact very well. The selling point of the film was sex and regular scenes of naked young women chatting in their rooms or engaging in lesbian and/or vampire activities.

The script this time was by Fine and Style along with Tudor Gates, and the film sorely misses Anthony Hinds' affinity with gothic themes. *The Vampire Lovers* comes across today as a jaded middle-aged man's idea of a sexy exploitation movie and is far less fun than one might expect. While Hammer found the subject matter saleable enough to make two sequels, popularly known as the Karnstein Trilogy, they did so without AIP's participation.

Into the Seventies

For the first time in many years, Hammer were reliant on British funding, thus Sir James Carreras began an agreement to make a series of films for EMI Films, the successor company to Associated British, beginning with a double-bill package of *Scars of Dracula* and *The Horror of Frankenstein*. There was a real sense of desperation in the air as Hammer were not only returning to their two most famous characters far too often, but also putting them together like this betrayed the fact that they were not the special events that they had been ten years previously. Potential audience members were also treated to some of the ugliest poster art in Hammer's history.

First onto the studio floor at Elstree was *The Horror of Frankenstein*, for which Jimmy Sangster was convinced to return to the franchise. Sangster was offered the proverbial carrot that he could both write and direct the picture, adapting an original storyline by actor/writer Jeremy Burnham. In modern parlance, *The Horror of Frankenstein* was a reboot of the series, in effect remaking *The Curse of Frankenstein* for a new era with a younger lead actor, the floppy-haired Ralph Bates, who had previously played Lord Courtley in *Taste the Blood of Dracula*. Never a particular fan of the gothic horror genre, Sangster chose to make the film as a black comedy. The resulting film was both cheap-looking and—to this writer at least—possibly the least funny British comedy film until Hammer's own *On the Buses* film arrived the following year.

Scars of Dracula also bore clear signs of a low budget with obvious backdrops in many scenes and Dracula even having to apologise for his castle's poor state of repair. It did have Christopher Lee once again and this time plenty of him, and even a few sequences that were based directly on Bram Stoker's writing. It was also the most explicitly violent *Dracula* film Hammer would make—Roy Ward Baker's film goes far heavier on the gore not only than previous *Dracula* movies, but also than future ones the studio would make. The film also has a fashionably permissive attitude towards sex while being oddly reticent about portraying nudity, somewhat in contrast to *The Vampire Lovers*.

Plot-wise, *The Scars of Dracula* is fairly basic: the Count is established in his castle terrorising the local villagers, having been resurrected after a passing rubber vampire bat pukes blood onto his lips. He is opposed by Simon (a callow and rather uncomfortably cast Dennis Waterman) who is searching for his missing brother Paul (Christopher Matthews). On top of this is added heaps of violence, not all of which makes sense; for example, Dracula stabs to death one of his vampire brides, a method of dispatching vampires previously unseen on film, while the Count and his servant Klove (interestingly, Anthony Hinds gave him the same name as Philip Latham's servant in *Dracula: Prince of Darkness*) have a relationship that is pretty clearly sadomasochistic.

Jimmy Sangster's directorial career at Hammer continued with *Lust for a Vampire*, a quickly mounted sequel to *The Vampire Lovers* (which had originally been assigned to Terence Fisher before the director fell ill) scripted by Tudor Gates and produced once again by Fine and Style. With AIP having turned down the opportunity to work with Hammer again, EMI stepped once more into the breech having been happy with the returns on *The Horror of*

Frankenstein/*Scars of Dracula* double-bill. Peter Cushing had been meant to appear in the secondary role of occult-obsessed teacher Giles Barton, but had to pull out due to the illness of his wife, Helen, to be replaced at short notice by Ralph Bates. Despite the lack of American funding, *Lust for a Vampire* is actually a better-looking film than its predecessor with the key role of Mircalla now played by Danish model and small-part actress Yutte Stensgaard. This was her biggest movie role by some distance and she brings a kind of supernaturally calm presence to the proceedings, which proves surprisingly effective. Mircalla is ensconced at a girls' boarding school at which she romances and drinks the blood of her fellow pupils. A new teacher, writer of gothic tales Richard Lestrange (Michael Johnson), arrives and promptly falls in love with Mircalla. This goes about as badly as can be expected, unlike the film itself, which is surprisingly enjoyable. The sight of Yutte Stensgaard's Mircalla, covered in blood and half-naked, became the most famous Hammer film image of the 1970s and neatly sums up the company's output in this era.

If *Lust for a Vampire* was more solidly carpentered than some recent Hammer productions, *Countess Dracula* looked positively opulent. Shot at Pinewood from 27 July to 4 September 1970, the reason Peter Sasdy's film had such finely detailed sets was that they were still standing at the studio from the 1969 filming of the historical drama *Anne of the Thousand Days*. This highly exploitable title *Countess Dracula* was attached to a Jeremy Paul script about the legendary Hungarian noblewoman Elizabeth Bathory. In this version of the tale, the ageing Countess discovers that bathing in the blood of virginal young women magically restores her lost youth. Abandoning her lover Captain Dobi (Nigel Green, excellent as always), she romances young Imre instead, but she needs to repeat the process to maintain her new looks and reverts to a hideous old crone in between times.

This was a very Hungarian tale indeed, with producer Alexander Paal hailing from Hungary (this was to be his last film, Paal dying two years later at the age of sixty-two) as did director Peter Sasdy and star Ingrid Pitt, in the title role, and co-star Sandor Elès (returning from *The Evil of Frankenstein*). One thing that was not genuinely Hungarian was Ingrid Pitt's voice; much to the actress's annoyance, the decision was made to overdub her with an unknown actress.

The flurry of activity at Hammer Films could not disguise the fact that the company was facing an increasingly difficult future. The Hollywood majors had pulled out of most their European production arrangements, leaving Hammer only a loose agreement with Warner Brothers, who only seemed interested in more *Dracula* movies. With much of Hammer's old guard of production staff breaking up, help was needed to help steady the ship in the increasingly troubled waters of the British film production sector. Michael Carreras, the prodigal son, was called on to help give Hammer a new direction for the new decade.

6

Amicus Productions: Milton Subotsky and Max Rosenberg

Rock! Rock! Rock!

Before we return to the story of Hammer films, we need to take our narrative back by some twenty-five years and change the scene from Hertfordshire to rural post-war Ohio. In 1945, a local phenomenon developed in that eastern state of the US in what is known as the Great Lakes region. A twenty-three-year-old former armed forces radio DJ called Alan Freed found that the mix of hot jazz and pop music recordings had become highly popular with a young audience, which was part of that newly minted post-war phenomenon: the teenager.

By 1951, Freed was based in Cleveland, one of the largest cities in the state, and had gained enormous popularity after having developed his radio show to feature a mixture of blues, country and western, and rhythm and blues, which crossed racial barriers. Many of the songs were notable for an unusual frankness in describing sex and relationships, which spoke like no other music to white teenagers. The existing terms for such music—country and western, blues, or even 'race music'—were all loaded with connotations of 'black' or 'white' music and were in any event inadequate to describe the development of a new musical form that was mixing ingredients from all of these sources. Alan Freed dreamed up a catchy new term that eventually caught on: rock 'n' roll.

This burgeoning scene was breaking nationally, especially in the Southern States in which a blues-influenced version of country and western was developing known as rockabilly. As Nik Cohn notes in his seminal history of rock and pop, *Awopbobaloobob Alopbamboom*, Freed had branched out to stage shows with roaring success: 'In 1951 ... Alan Freed launched a series of shows at the Cleveland Arena and immediately drew crows three times as big as the venue's capacity. These shows featured coloured acts but were aimed at predominantly white audiences'.[1]

Largely denied radio airplay from major stations, what rock 'n' roll needed to break into the mainstream was a singer with mass appeal. In other words, a white singer: one who could attract young fans in the same way as the young Frank Sinatra had in the 1940s and that Johnnie Ray had since breaking through to massive chart success with 'Cry' in late 1951. A well-built, darkly handsome former truck-driver from Tupelo, Mississippi, called Elvis Presley was causing a sensation with live shows and his early recordings on the small, Memphis-based Sun Records label. The huge RCA Victor record label bought his contract, releasing his first single for them, 'Heartbreak Hotel', in January 1956. The record became a number one hit throughout the world. Rock 'n' roll had leapt almost in a single bound from the status of a semi-underground regional phenomenon to a global musical movement.

The birth of rock 'n' roll also inadvertently launched the first serious and sustained competition for Hammer in the production of British horror films. In March 1955, Metro-Goldwyn-Mayer released director Richard Brooks' high school drama *The Blackboard Jungle*, its use of Bill Haley and the Comets' 'Rock Around the Clock' causing a sensation, earning the film huge profits and rocketing what had been a B-side to number one in the billboard charts for eight weeks. Film producers raced to capitalise on this trend, including a fledgling pair of producers called Max Rosenberg and Milton Subotsky.

The older of the pair by some seven years, Rosenberg gained his first experience in the film industry in 1943 when he made *The Good Old Days*, a nostalgic documentary made up from turn of the century newsreel footage Rosenberg bought for $10,000. The film turned a large profit and launched him into the movie business. Rosenberg then formed Motion Picture Ventures with the legendary film entrepreneur Joseph E. Levene, importing important European films into the US market such as *The Blue Angel*, which back in 1930 had made Marlene Dietrich into an international star, and Roberto Rossellini's ground-breaking *Rome, Open City* (1945).

He fell into the television business in the 1950s, making a children's educational series along with one Milton Subotsky. Subotsky was a writer who had served in America's Signal Corps during the Second World War where he made army training films. After the war, he wrote for television during what is now known in the US as the medium's first 'Golden Age', which lasted roughly between television's post-war re-establishment (around 1947) and 1960. The cheapness of production in an era when most dramas were recorded as if they were live productions, the relative wealth, and thus the assumed tastes of those who could afford a television set, together with the absence of established ground rules all worked to create a healthy spirit of experimentation. It could not last, and by the 1960s, American television had become a byword for formulaic production line entertainment. Before this, however, anthology series proliferated and Subotsky provided scripts and stories for series such as *The Lock*, which presented mystery and suspense stories, and *Lights Out*, which was more concerned with the horrific and supernatural.

Subotsky and Rosenberg saw this new market in youth music as their entry into film production and quickly gained funding for *Rock! Rock! Rock!* The producers had a special advantage in appealing to this market as Milton Subotsky was quite a successful composer of rock 'n' roll tunes. His work in this field included the rockabilly classic 'Lonesome Train (on a Lonesome Track)' recorded by Johnny Burnette and the Rock 'n' Roll Trio in 1956, and later 'Space Ship to Mars', a Gene Vincent B-side in 1962.

Rock! Rock! Rock! starred thirteen-year-old model Tuesday Weld in what was clearly a shoestring production (setting the pattern for future Subotsky and Rosenberg productions) set in a café in which, bizarrely, the rockin' teens applaud when a record finishes on the jukebox. The presence of Alan Freed in the cast and Subotsky's inside knowledge meant the production attracted some big musical names, including Frankie Lymon and the Teenagers and Connie Francis, who provided Tuesday Weld's singing voice. Freed was capitalising on his onscreen fame while the going was good, appearing in three films in 1956. *Rock! Rock! Rock!* first appeared on American screens on 7 December 1956, only a week before the next quickly shot production to hire Freed, *Don't Knock the Rock*.

The performance of *Rock! Rock! Rock!* was healthy enough for a follow-up, *Jamboree*, to be released a year later. Subotsky and Rosenburg, who were operating under the Vanguard Productions banner at this point, then made the tough prison drama *The Last Mile*, released in February 1959 and starring Mickey Rooney. This would be the Subotsky/Rosenberg partnership's final film in America, although Max Rosenberg did produce a couple on his own: *Girl of the Night* (1960) and *Lad: A Dog* (1962). The future of the partnership lay across the Atlantic, in England, where they relocated in 1960 to take advantage of the country's favourable tax laws designed to encourage film production, as well as the generally much lower cost of production compared to Hollywood.

This pair of New York-born producers made Shepperton Studios their base of operations, where they made their first British production, the remarkable horror film *City of the Dead* (1960). Directed by John Moxey (who moved to America at the end of the decade with considerable success, having changed his name to John Llewellyn Moxey on the advice of a numerologist), this remarkably creepy film featured Christopher Lee in a tale of Satanism in a small New England town. In an interesting and genuine case of parallel story development, *City of the Dead* featured a very similar plot structure to Alfred Hitchcock's *Psycho*, which was filming at almost exactly the same time at Universal Studios in Hollywood.

The duo had already had some dealings with British studios, as their projected follow-up to *Rock! Rock! Rock!* was none other than a colour remake of *Frankenstein*. The script was taken to Columbia pictures who liked the idea, but did not have confidence in the makers of a teen musical to pull it off. Instead, they put them in contact with James Carreras at Hammer Films who had recently made a big splash with their SF horror *The Quatermass Xperiment*. Hammer also liked the idea, but disliked the script, which Subotsky claimed hewed closely to Mary Shelley's original novel. Instead, they assigned Jimmy Sangster to write a new script, which resulted in 1957's epoch-making success *The Curse of Frankenstein*. The blow of having their script rejected was somewhat softened for Subsotsky and Rosenberg by their sharing in a percentage of the considerable profits.

After the success of *City of the Dead*, which John Moxey succeeded in making look far more expensive than its budget merited, the pair returned to the familiar ground of the teen musical, only this time with a British twist. At this point, a new name was introduced for the duo's British production company: Amicus. *It's Trad, Dad* (1962), one of director Richard Lester's first films, cost £50,000 to make—a tiny amount even by Subotsky and Rosenberg's standards—and made back £300,000 in the UK alone. The film was seen across Europe and even scored an American release, though the lack of a trad jazz revival in the US necessitated a title change to *Ring-A-Ding Rhythm*. *It's Trad, Dad* took its title from a British jazz revival of the period, but actually featured an impressive array of British and American pop talent including Helen Shapiro, Chubby Checker, Gary 'US' Bonds, and Del Shannon. A follow-up was a foregone conclusion and *Just for Fun* arrived in 1963, this time directed by Gordon Flemyng with photography by future cult director Nicolas Roeg. The line-up of stars was slightly less stellar than previously, with Bobby Vee top-billed above The Crickets (who retained some marquee value despite the 1959 death of their leader Buddy Holly) and Freddy Cannon.

Horror in Small Doses

By now, Amicus had a working methodology that allowed them to make films on a regular basis over an extended period, through various crises that afflicted the British film industry. An idea for a film would be formulated and an approximate budget calculated. When a proportion of these funds had been raised, a director (most often Freddie Francis) would be contracted and pre-production would begin. Funds would continue to be raised right up until shooting began, at which point the director would learn how much money he had to make the film for, often far less than the original sum agreed on.[2]

Subotsky would write the productions, partially as a money-saving device so an outside writer would not have to be paid, but mainly because the literate

New Yorker was not only a passionate movie lover, but also a well-read aficionado of horror literature; however, his efforts would often require heavy rewriting—his script for *The Skull* (1966), from a story by Robert Bloch, was less than half the required length.[3]

Subotsky was especially fond of Ealing Studios' classic 1945 portmanteau horror film *Dead of Night* and his attempt to duplicate this film was to give Amicus its own unique identity as a maker of horror films. The first film in the series, *Doctor Terror's House of Horrors* (1965), was a fairly solid collection of stories by Subotsky with an excellent cast (Christopher Lee, Peter Cushing, a young Donald Sutherland, and trumpeter/singer Roy Castle) and only one weak episode, which featured disc jockey Alan Freeman as a man whose house is attacked by sentient plant life. As with many Amicus productions, the film is made to look far more expensive and stylish than it really should thanks to Freddie Francis' expert use of the Techniscope widescreen format.

A wide format that did not use anamorphic lenses and saved considerably on filming costs, Techniscope offered the interesting side-effect that deep focus effects and extreme close-ups were possible, which could not be achieved with the more expensive CinemaScope and its later development Panavision. As this was a format generally used on lower budgeted action movies and horror films, the unique possibilities of Techniscope tended to remain untouched by directors working in these fields. The format, however, became a central part of the extreme visual style developed for *A Fistful of Dollars* and *For A Few Dollars More* by Sergio Leone and his cinematographer Massimo Dallamano. In his work for Amicus, Freddie Francis was one of the very few British directors to utilise Techniscope to its fullest.

If Hammer had the precise, unshowy Terence Fisher as its key director (though Fisher was capable of visual fireworks if a scene demanded it), Amicus had Freddie Francis as a sort of in-house director. Amicus had very few permanent staff—low overheads were key to Subotsky and Rosenberg's operation—and Francis has no problems with turning down an assignment from the company if he did not fancy it. Nevertheless, Amicus and Francis made no less than six films together in the two years between *Doctor Terror's House of Horrors* (1965) and *Torture Garden* (1967), with the director later returning for Amicus's most famous film, *Tales from the Crypt* (1972).

Francis had been a renowned cinematographer before making the jump to directing his own films, winning the Academy Award for Best Cinematography (Black and White) in 1960 for *Sons and Lovers*, which was directed by another famous former cinematographer, Jack Cardiff. In the following year Francis had photographed one of the most stylish, affecting gothic horror films ever produced; director Jack Clayton's masterpiece *The Innocents*. This was a film version of Henry James' 1898 novella *The Turn of the Screw*, featuring Deborah Kerr as the new governess in charge of two children who appear to be possessed by the spirits of their uncle's former valet Quint (Peter Wyngarde) and Miss Jessel (Clytie Jessop), who both died after conducting an abusive sexual relationship. The Innocents is masterfully photographed by Francis in a monochrome colour scheme featuring the inkiest of blacks, working with the innovative editing and sound to create a unique, chilling atmosphere. A sense of dread and bone-chilling horror is created quite subtly, while the audience sees almost nothing that might be described as conventionally horrific.

As a director, Freddie Francis became somewhat typecast as a maker of horror films, which was a genuine shame as he proved to be a superb visual stylist whenever circumstances and budgets allowed. Unlike some directors with a background in photography, Francis also proved to be an 'actor's director', his presence alone able to attract famous performers to a production. He deserved more recognition than he received and the chance to work with a wider range of material.

As producers, Rosenberg and Subotsky were generally willing to give Francis free rein and he would heavily rewrite Subotsky's scripts—often as a practical measure to ensure that the finished product would actually be of feature film length. Perhaps as a result, Francis' work for Amicus was generally more inventive and interesting than that which he did for Hammer, where he was more hemmed in by the more formulaic requirements of *Frankenstein* and *Dracula* sequels.

Robert Bloch, Spies, and Galactic Pepperpots

Milton Subotsky might not have been the most skilled of scriptwriters (at least in Freddie Francis' opinion as he makes clear in his memoirs), but he was genuinely enthusiastic and knowledgeable on the subject of horror cinema and literature. It is hardly surprising therefore that Amicus had the background knowledge to hire Robert Bloch, the renowned writer of science fiction and supernatural tales, for an extended run of films. The company's first contact with the writer came when they bought the film rights to his story *The Skull of the Marquis de Sade*, which they filmed to great effect in 1965 as *The Skull* (the famous Marquis' surviving descendants were somewhat litigious, so his name was dropped from the title). The script to the film was credited to Milton Subotsky, but was rather too short and needed considerable input from Freddie Francis and a flexibly creative atmosphere on set to make work.

For Amicus' next production—a stylishly macabre murder mystery with horrific overtones released the following year under the title *The Psychopath* (despite the presence of no actual psychopaths in the film's narrative)—Bloch began providing scripts for Subotsky and Rosenberg. Bloch had been writing since the 1930s, beginning as a teenage fan of legendary horror writer H. P.

Lovecraft, to whom he wrote a fan letter. Lovecraft offered any assistance he could to the would-be writer and a friendship began as Bloch plunged his considerable energies into creating horror fiction. Soon, Robert Bloch's work was appearing in the pages of *Weird Tales* magazine alongside his hero and inspiration.[4]

Following Lovecraft's death in March 1937, the nineteen-year-old Bloch, much of whose writing had at this point took place within Lovecraft's unique world, re-evaluated his own writing. As a result, he broadened his range considerably, branching out into science fiction and a wider range of horror writing. A particular speciality of Bloch's became the adaptation of legendary or real-life characters for fictional purposes, beginning with his 1943 story *Yours Truly, Jack the Ripper*. This strain of his writing was to bring Bloch lasting fame with his 1959 novel *Psycho*, which took the real-life case of mother-obsessed multiple murderer Ed Gein as its starting point. The Gein case was to inspire many future horror films, including *Deranged*, *The Texas Chain Saw Massacre* (both 1974), *The Silence of the Lambs* (2001), and *House of 1000 Corpses* (2003).

In 1959, however, it was Alfred Hitchcock who had the notion of bringing Bloch's version of the story to the screen. Hitchcock devoured Bloch's novel and used both the crew and the fast, cheap methods of his popular television series *Alfred Hitchcock Presents* (which enjoyed a ten-year run from 1955) to create probably the most extreme contemporary horror film made to that date. On its release in 1960, many film critics were repulsed, particularly *The Observer*'s C. A. Lejeune, who walked out of the press screening she attended and subsequently resigned from her post at the paper. Audiences proved rather more willing to see the film through to its end and the film quickly became a milestone in horror and suspense cinema. At a stroke, Hitchcock had reformed the entire genre and made Robert Bloch a famous writer, though Bloch received little by way of direct financial reward.

At about the same time, Bloch moved to Hollywood and became a busy writer of television and film scripts, among his work being no less than ten contributions to *Alfred Hitchcock Presents*. Bloch was to write five films for Amicus, his work generally contributing to an upgrading of the quality of the company's productions. One exception to this trend was *The Deadly Bees* (1967), a perfectly dreadful horror-mystery that is notable only for creating the entire killer bees film genre—possibly the only film genre in which every example is absolutely terrible. The Bloch touch can be seen working to rather better effect in the second Amicus portmanteau horror production: *The Torture Garden* (1967). As an experienced writer of short stories for pulp magazines, this form suited Bloch down to the ground. The first story, *Enoch*, sees greedy playboy Michael Bryant planning to murder his dying uncle (the always excellent Maurice Denham), but falling under the spell of an evil cat. The idea of an evil cat remains a standard horror movie trope and Bloch's classically macabre touch can also be seen in the story *The Man Who Collected Poe*, which indulged his love both of Edgar Allan Poe and of a cleverly punning title. *Terror Over Hollywood* revealed the secret behind how certain film stars appear forever young, reflecting Bloch's horrified fascination with the movie business in which he was now earning his living, while *Mr Steinway* is the story of a concert pianist whose piano becomes jealous of his girlfriend.

It was a sign of Amicus's rising fortunes that a pair of genuine Hollywood stars were recruited for the films, albeit in Burgess Meredith and Jack Palance, two actors who were considerably past their box-office peak. Meredith was a highly regarded character actor who had retreated to the stage in the 1940s and 1950s after falling foul of the Hollywood blacklist during the dark days of Joseph McCarthy's communist witch-hunt. By 1967, he had unexpectedly become an internationally famous screen star once again thanks to his performance as The Penguin in the spoof superhero television series *Batman*. His fees were still affordable on Amicus's low budgets and he gave a richly theatrical performance as Dr Diablo whose fairground sideshow provides the framing device for the film.

Among the customers paying Diablo extra for an especially frightening experience is Palance, who stars in *The Man Who Collected Poe*. Palance became a major Hollywood star in the 1950s, his broken nose and high cheekbones coming as a result of a previous career as a boxer and reconstructive surgery after baling out of a burning aircraft during the Second World War. His terrifying physiognomy and often overwrought acting style helped make Palance one of the greatest heavies in movies, especially after his 1953 breakthrough role in *Shane*. *Torture Garden* began a new phase in Palance's career, during which he worked extensively in Europe, bringing his unique presence to many spaghetti westerns (Sergio Corbucci's *The Mercenary/Il mercenario* (1968) is especially good). He also essayed some notable horror roles, including very creditable versions of *The Strange Case of Dr Jekyll and Mr Hyde* and *Dracula* for producer Dan Curtis.

After *Torture Garden*, Amicus withdrew from the horror genre for several years, instead dipping into forms such as the spy movie (*Danger Route*) and SF, the latter in the form of the cheap-looking *They Came from Beyond Space*, helmed by the studio's favourite director Freddie Francis, and the incredibly cheap and cheerful *The Terrornauts*, from veteran B-movie director Montgomery Tully. Under the flag of convenience, AARU Productions, Subotsky and Rosenberg also made two films based on the BBC's SF serial *Doctor Who*. This had become a national obsession soon after it first began broadcasting in November 1963 when Terry Nation's fascistic pepper pots, the Daleks, first appeared.

Doctor Who and the Daleks was released on 23 August 1965 in time for the August school holidays and was based on Terry Nation's first Dalek serial, adapted for the occasion by Subotsky. This was followed a year later by a sequel, rather clumsily entitled *Daleks—Invasion Earth 2150AD*, based on Terry Nation's epic six-episode TV story *The Dalek Invasion of Earth*. The films contained none of the cast members familiar to television viewers, which is hardly surprising as the series was being made virtually the whole year round at this point—cast members' holidays had to be written into the plot of whichever serial was being made at the time. Thus, instead of William Hartnell's spiky, wilful, often downright self-centred Doctor, film audiences instead got Peter Cushing attempting the role as a kindly, forgetful old duffer. Truth be told, this did not represent Cushing's best work and the film series ended, having failed to make a significant impression on the all-important American market.

By 1969, with the backing of Columbia Pictures, Amicus even made attempts to get into straight drama with *A Touch of Love*, written by novelist Margaret Drabble, and *The Mind of Mr Soames*, about a man who has been in a coma since birth being woken and introduced into the world. A big budget was raised and star names such as Terence Stamp and Robert Vaughn were recruited, but the film failed to make an impact with audiences.

Return to Horror: Amicus Drips Blood

Rosenberg and Subotsky made the decision to return to the horror genre and contracted Robert Bloch to put together another portmanteau horror script for them. Released in February 1971, *The House that Dripped Blood* was a very odd mixture of stories indeed. The contraction of the British film industry meant that the studio could hire very good actors, providing a decent payday for a few days' work. The linking story features the police investigation into the disappearance of horror film star Paul Henderson, during which the inspector on the case discovers the terrible fate that befell the previous tenants of Henderson's manor house.

Unfortunately, the stories are somewhat weaker than in previous Amicus films. In *Method for Murder*, Denholm Elliott plays a writer of horror stories who finds himself inspired to new heights of creativity when he moves into the house, but finds that his latest literary creation has manifested itself physically. Elliott was perfect for this kind of role, and as his former callow handsomeness began to degenerate thanks to alcohol and the effects of an interesting social life, his acting deepened. His trademark jittery desperation is seen to great effect here and in later films such as Hammer's *To the Devil... A Daughter*. It is a shame that the story he features in here has such a weak ending.

Right: 'Weird happenings in a house of mystery': This typical 1930s British understatement somewhat undersells Boris Karloff's 1933 British horror film *The Ghoul*.

Below: Bela Lugosi and blind assassin Wilfred Walter menace Norwegian cutie Greta Gynt in *Dark Eyes of London* (1939).

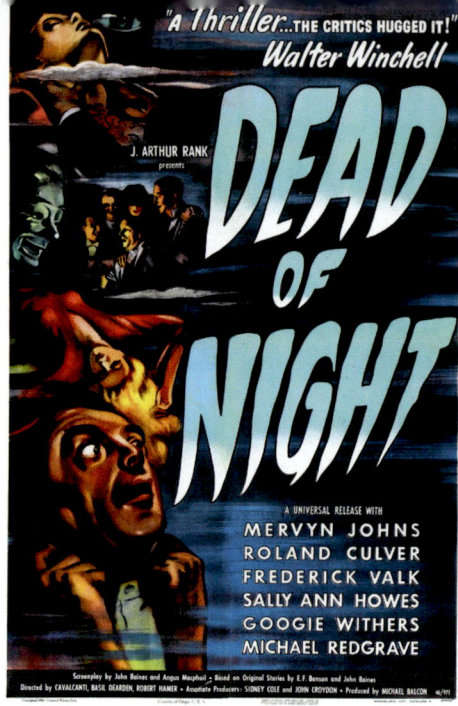

Above left: American poster art for *The Face at the Window*. Horror reached a new peak of popularity in 1939, and Tod Slaughter's Victorian horror melodramas found eager US distributors.

Above right: Universal's poster art for *Dead of Night* (1945) sold the film as a thriller, but what audiences got to see was probably the first acknowledged classic of British horror cinema.

Below: Original poster art and trailers for *The Curse of Frankenstein* (1957) cleverly denied audiences a view of Phil Leakey's make-up effects for Christopher Lee's creature.

Above and below: While the British release poster for *The Quatermass Xperiment* pushed the film's 'X' certificate for all it was worth, American audiences were promised a cute, three-armed smoke monster and a flying cat.

Above: *Blood of the Vampire* (1958) featured notorious theatrical ham Sir Donald Wolfit, Jimmy Sangster's script not even making him a vampire.

Below: Casting the tall, imposing Christopher Lee as Dracula gave Hammer's publicity department the chance to sell the Count as a sexually dangerous figure—the terrifying lover who died, yet lived.

Barricaded windows fail to halt the attack of invisible fiends.

M-G-M Presents "FIEND WITHOUT A FACE"

Above: The monsters in *Fiend Without a Face* (1958) were conveniently invisible for most of the film, but when they did show up, they did not disappoint.

Right: Yesterday's Enemy (1959) was one of a series of Hammer productions taking the bloody horror and adult content of their breakthrough horror pictures and applying them to the war genre.

Above: The Brides of Dracula (1960) saw Hammer producing a *Dracula* sequel without the Count. The result was a wonderfully twisted fairy tale for adults.

Below: The City of the Dead (1960) was a marvellously atmospheric gothic horror starring Christopher Lee that was the first horror production of Amicus pairing Milton Subotsky and Max Rosenberg.

Above: *The Curse of the Werewolf* (1961) saw Hammer giving Oliver Reed his first starring role in a Spanish-set reworking of the werewolf myth; however, the film ran into censorship difficulties.

Below: *Village of the Damned* (1960) saw the fictional residents of the real Berkshire village of Letchmore Heath fall into comas ahead of the birth of cinema's spookiest children.

Above: *Repulsion* (1966), Roman Polanski's first English-language feature after his escape from Poland, was for Compton Films, previously better known for horror and softcore sex pictures.

Left: *Dr Terror's House of Horrors* (1965) saw Amicus try to emulate the success of *Dead of Night*, which changed the course of the company's productions.

Above: Quatermass and the Pit (1967) was a cult success but not a big success in America. In Britain, the ABC cinema circuit double-billed it with the Anglo-German production *Circus of Fear*.

Right: Curse of the Crimson Altar (1967) featured a striking-looking Barbara Steele, but the film was not worthy of her talents, nor those of Boris Karloff and Christopher Lee.

FRANKENSTEIN MUST BE DESTROYED!

THE SCREEN'S MOST FANTASTIC FIEND ...AND HAMMER SAY SO!

ETER CUSHING · MON WARD · FREDDIE JONES · VERONICA CARLSON · THORLEY WALTERS · MAXINE AUD

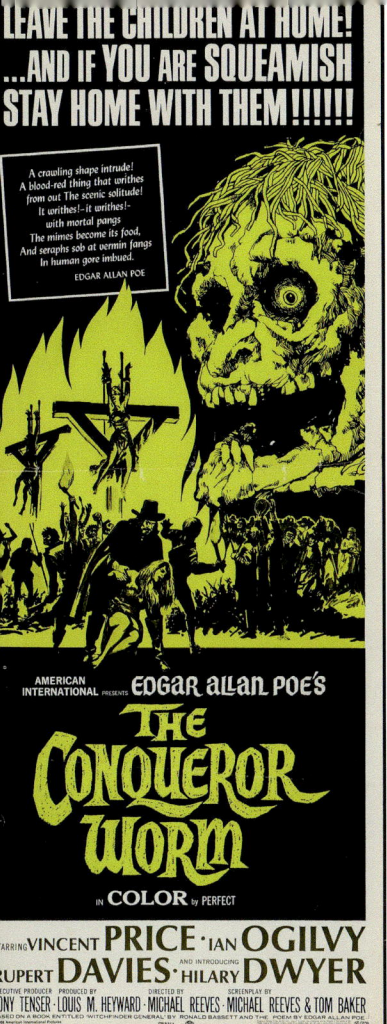

Opposite above: Frankenstein Must be Destroyed (1969) was something of the end of an era for Hammer, after which their long-established team began to fragment.

Opposite below: The cleverly designed UK poster art for Ken Russell's *The Devils* (1971) sees Oliver Reed's head surrounded by red-tinted naked nuns, visually suggesting both a crown of thorns and a splatter of blood as well as the film's notorious climactic orgy.

Above left: Witchfinder General (1968) so impressed backers American International Pictures that they retitled it as *The Conqueror Worm* and used it to relaunch their Edgar Allan Poe film series.

Above right: Blood on Satan's Claw (1970) was an interesting and well-made attempt by Tigon British to recreate the success of its *Witchfinder General*.

Above: *Mark of the Devil* (1970). British writer-director Michael Armstrong's film was turned into an ultra-violent Euro clone of *Witchfinder General*.

Below left: Japanese poster art for *Dracula AD 1972*, Hammer's attempt to relocate the Count to a London that was no longer swinging.

Below right: *The Satanic Rites of Dracula* (1973) saw Christopher Lee return one last time as Count Dracula, though by now, the law of diminishing returns had taken effects.

 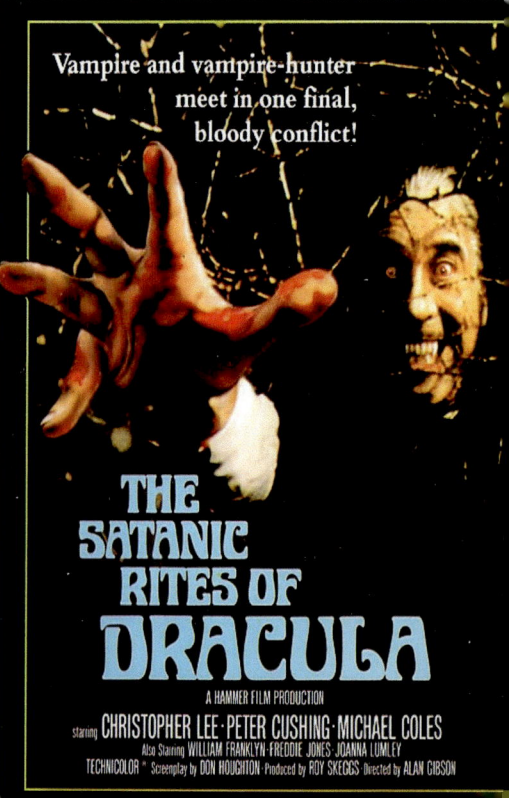

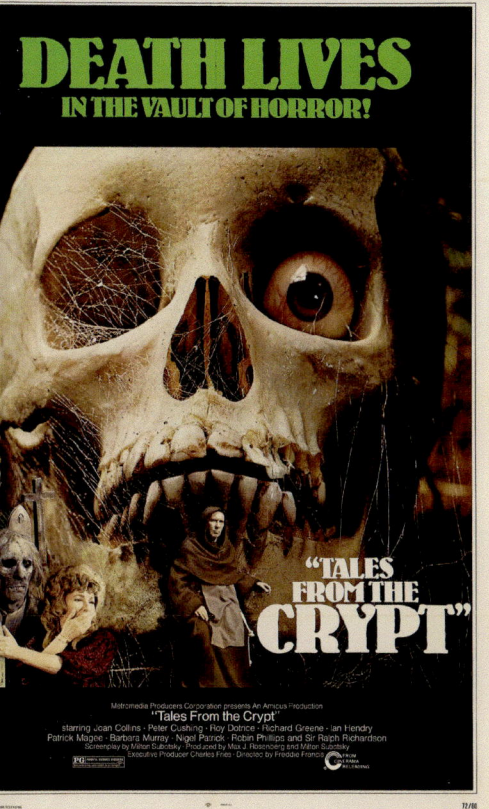

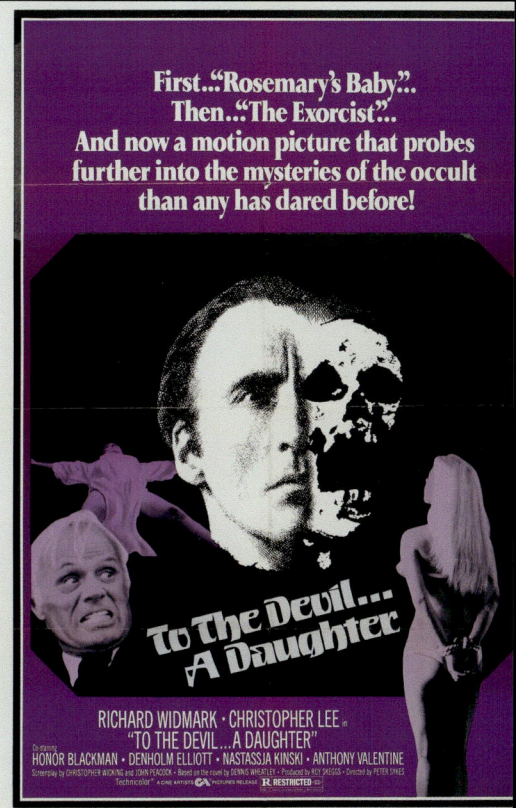

Above left: An all-star cast and mordantly amusing scripts saw Amicus achieve its biggest hit with the portmanteau film *Tales from the Crypt* (1972).

Above right: Hammer took on modern horrors, such as *The Exorcist*, with *To the Devil… A Daughter* (1976), scoring its last big hit in the process.

Right: Classic exploitation movie poster art from the American release of Pete Walker's *House of Whipcord* (1974). The film was rather grimmer in tone than this image might suggest.

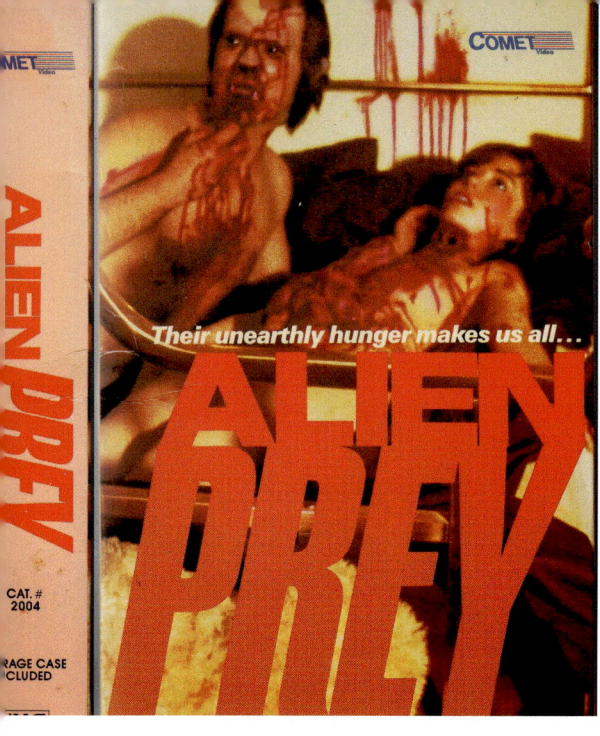 

Above left: By the time Norman J. Warren's *Prey* (aka *Alien Prey*) was released in 1977, low-budget horror pictures were starting to migrate to home video for their widest exposure.

Above right: Norman J. Warren's SF-horror *Inseminoid* (aka *Horror Planet*) was the largest-scale film the director was to make and brought his run of imaginative low-budget horrors to an end.

Below: *Xtro* (1982) was, at heart, a gory low-budget sibling to Steven Spielberg's hugely successful *E.T.*, and it did not care who knew it.

Above: Poster art for Ken Russell's hallucinatory *Gothic* (1986) explicitly referenced Henry Fuseli's 1781 painting *The Nightmare*.

Right: *Hellraiser* (1987) was the key British horror film of the 1980s, making writer-director Clive Barker a horror superstar, and it led to an absurdly long series of sequels by other hands.

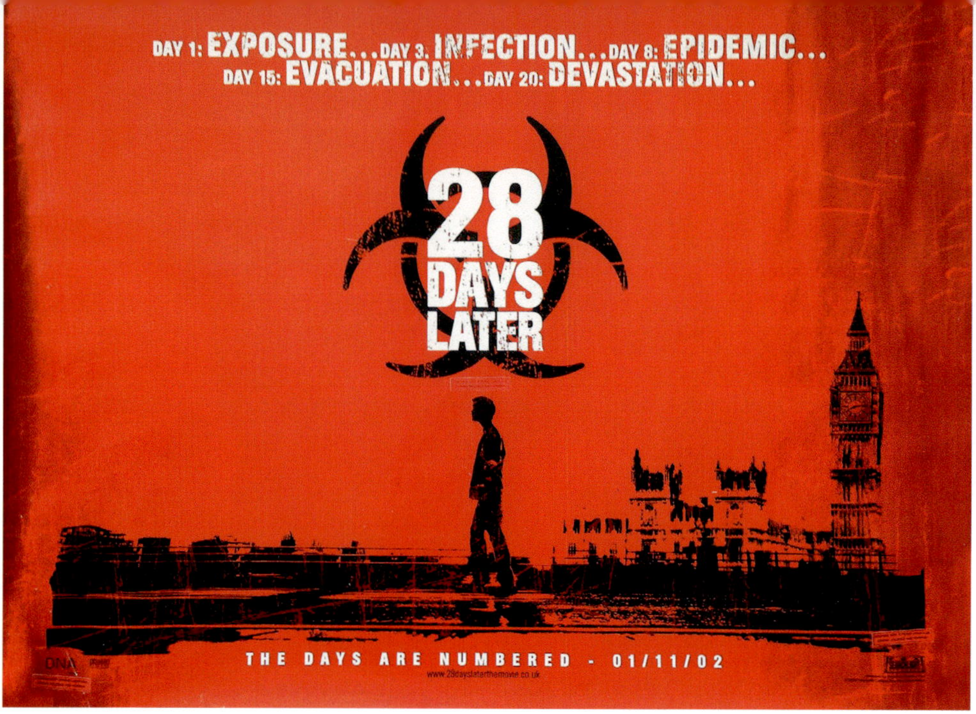

Above: Director Danny Boyle's *28 Days Later* (2002) was ground-breaking in its use of digital video cameras, completely reinventing the zombie movie in the process.

Below: The revived Hammer Films had a massive success with *The Woman in Black* (2012), and starred Daniel Radcliffe, who was superb as the bereaved, cursed young lawyer.

Waxworks is even less effective, which is a shame as Peter Cushing and Joss Ackland are a very effective pair of actors. They play two old friends who become obsessed with a female waxwork figure they see in a wax museum, but the very slight story really is not worthy of them. The highlight of the film is the next tale, *Sweets to the Sweet*, in which Nyree Dawn Porter is hired as a private tutor to a young girl and her cold, distant father. The father is played by Christopher Lee, giving one of his most subtly effective performances as it is slowly revealed that there is rather more to the relationship between him and his child, and that he is terrified of her.

Rather strangely, the final story of the collection, *The Cloak*, is played for broad comedy as arrogant horror movie star Paul Henderson discovers that vampires, represented by the voluptuous Ingrid Pitt, are his biggest fans. The story has a lot of possibilities but is somewhat thrown out of balance by the performance of Jon Pertwee, who was at the time still playing his signature role of Doctor Who on BBC television. In that part, the actor surprised many by giving a fundamentally serious performance, but here, Pertwee reverts to his previous style of mugging and physical comedy. It seems rather odd to end the film on such a light note, but perhaps this reflects a fundamental truth; due to repetition, the traditional figure of the vampire was losing its sexual danger and was close to becoming a figure of fun.

The House that Dripped Blood proved an international success, despite the fact that, in what may well be a unique case, Amicus had to appeal to the BBFC in order that the censorship rating for the film be changed from 'A' (meaning children could attend if accompanied by adults) to 'X' (which by 1970 meant over eighteens only). Ironically, not a single drop of blood is to be seen in the entire film, but for marketing purposes, as Hammer found back in 1955 when they made *The Quatermass Xperiment*, an 'X' certificate was vital for a horror film.

Amicus were firmly back in the horror business and Subotsky and Rosenberg set about finding new subjects. Their next horror project, *I, Monster*, turned out to be not a very new idea at all, based as it was on Robert Louis Stevenson's 1886 classic *The Strange Case of Dr Jekyll and Mr Hyde*. For no apparent reason, Subotsky (who adapted the novel himself) changed the names of the main characters, thus Jekyll became Dr Charles Marlowe and his alter ego Edward Hyde became Edward Blake. This was not to be the strangest thing about *I, Monster* as the decision was made to shoot the film in an experimental 3-D process. The disadvantages of this approach were apparent to all of the experienced directors Amicus approached to direct the film, each of whom turned the job down.

One person willing to give it a try was twenty-two-year-old Stephen Weeks, who had in 1968 made the First World War-themed short film *1917* for Tony Tenser at Tigon. Despite his youthful enthusiasm, the 3-D process proved to be impractical, slowing down the filming for an effect, which apparently did not even work for most people. The decision was made to abandon the 3-D shooting part-way through production on *I, Monster*, a film that bears the hallmarks of its troubled production on screen for all to see. This is evident in its truncated running time of only seventy-five minutes, which in 1971 was barely long enough to be described as feature length.

The film is something of a struggle to sit through in many ways, the end result being murkily photographed, cluttered with extraneous foreground details and long, pointless tracking shots. This is a real shame as Christopher Lee had been attracted to play the lead role of Marlowe/Blake, giving him a chance to play one of the classic parts in the horror canon that had been denied him when Hammer made its disappointing *The Two Faces of Dr Jekyll* in 1960. Lee is excellent in both roles, aided by very good make-up effects by Harry Frampton, which become more extreme as Blake becomes more degenerate. By the end of the film, Blake's make-up looks much like the startling and iconic style that Lon Chaney wore for his 1920 silent version of the tale.

Peter Cushing was kept in employment here in what was a very difficult period for the actor. Following the death of his wife, Helen, in 1971, Cushing worked almost constantly, appearing in twenty-three films and television episodes in the period between then and 1974. His role here as one of Marlowe's pals is not exactly rewarding, spending most of his time in his club talking to Marlowe or their mutual friend Enfield. The latter was played by Mike Raven, who was at the time making a somewhat desultory attempt to become a star of British horror films. Despite a family background in acting and having made his name as a radio DJ, Raven was far from being a natural performer; most surprisingly of all is how unsuitable for acting his lisping, rather inexpressive voice is. At least we got to hear Raven's voice here—in his previous outing in Hammer's *Lust for a Vampire* (1971), he suffered the indignity of being overdubbed by the *basso profundo* old stager Valantine Dyall.

What Became of Jack and Jill was so grim and nihilistic that it was barely released in 1972, some two years after it was made and is an extremely difficult film to categorise. The film takes place in a Britain where it is widely thought that humanity has only a few years of existence left (shades of David Bowie's *The Rise and Fall of Ziggy Stardust and the Spiders from Mars*, which was also released in 1972). Johnny (Paul Nicholas) rejects all personal responsibility, which results in him and his girlfriend Vanessa Howard trying to get their hands on the house and money of Johnny's grandmother (Mona Washbourne) by convincing her that the young are plotting to overthrow and murder the old. There was certainly some talent involved here: Bill Bain, here directing what would be his only feature film, was an excellent television director who died in 1982 aged only fifty-two.

A Box Office Bonanza from the Crypt

One might have been forgiven for thinking that both the inspiration and market for portmanteau horror films had been thoroughly tapped out by 1972. Such thinking was proved wrong in March 1972 when *Tales from the Crypt* became Amicus's biggest hit to date. The film was made for almost twice the company's normal budget thanks to co-production financing from American International Pictures, which had by this point moved almost all its horror film production to England. Freddie Francis was convinced to return to the director's chair and the increased budget also ensured that a very starry cast was assembled of actors whose name value was at this point rather larger than their fee. This included Joan Collins who was in the midst of a career lull that only lifted when she had an unexpected hit with the softcore sex drama *The Stud* in 1978. Also starring was Richard Greene, who was a superstar to a generation of children thanks to his 1955–59 hit television series *The Adventures of Robin Hood*, but by the end of the 1960s, he was reduced to appearing in moth-eaten *Fu Manchu* sequels for Jess Franco. Ian Hendry had a shot at being a big star in the early 1960s when he quit his television series *The Avengers* (which got along just fine without him) to take up a film contract. Hendry's acting style was probably too low key and naturalistic for 1960s film stardom and an over-fondness for drink had started to erode his career by 1972. Also good value for older audiences was Nigel Patrick, a popular British leading man of the 1940s and 1950s, as well as the almost inevitable Peter Cushing, who as we shall see was particularly keen to appear. Ralph Richardson, playing the crypt keeper in the linking footage, was still at the top of his professional career in 1972, and in typical Amicus fashion, he filmed his entire role in a single day.

Key to the success of *Tales from the Crypt* was the fact that Milton Subotsky, whose screenwriting was not always the most subtle and skilled, was working from stories originally published in the infamous EC horror comics of the 1950s. This gave the proceedings an edge of mordant, sardonic wit, which lifts the film above the standard of previous Amicus productions. With five tales crammed into ninety-two minutes, each story is short and snappy, making its point and then making way for the next one. The first story, '…And All Though the House', is a case in point: Joan Collins murders her husband at home on Christmas Eve, only to be visited by a homicidal Santa Claus. She cannot phone the police for help as the murder she has just been committed would be uncovered.

This is followed by 'Reflections of Death' in which Ian Hendry leaves his wife and family to start a new life with his girlfriend, but as they leave, the pair are involved in a car crash. Staggering from the wreckage, he eventually discovers that two years have passed since the accident and worse news is still to come. 'Poetic Justice' is the highlight of the film, with Peter Cushing giving a lovely, heartfelt performance as a harmless old widower being forced out of his beloved home by local worthies as his somewhat dingy presence is bringing down the local house prices. Cushing's performance is nothing short of heart-breaking, especially when he talks to his dead wife's picture—he really was a wonderful actor.

'Wish You Were Here' is an entertainingly gory, which cheerfully acknowledges pinching its plot from W. W. Jacobs' famous horror story *The Monkey's Paw*. Ruthless, somewhat dishonest, and near bankrupt businessman Richard Greene dies soon after wishing on a jade statue that his financial problems be solved. When his body is returned for the funeral in an open casket, his wife (Barbara Murray) realises that the statue will still allow two more wishes, but if she gets the wording wrong, the consequences will be horrific.

Finally comes 'Blind Alleys' in which Nigel Patrick plays the cruel new director of a very uncaring care home for the blind. While the inmates suffer freezing cold and poor food, he lives in luxury with his beloved German Shepherd dog, but leader of the inmates, Patrick Magee, is plotting an intricate and clever revenge. The story is somewhat predictable, but this is its strength as delightful anticipation builds towards Patrick getting what he deserves.

The unexpectedly major success of *Tales from the Crypt* spurred Rosenberg and Subotsky to plan further multi-story films, the first of which was *Asylum*, a collection of Robert Bloch stories scripted by the author and directed by Roy Ward Baker. So fast were Amicus' production methods that the film was in cinemas by mid-November 1972. The basic story was very clever and a departure from the norm for Amicus with Doctor Robert Powell going for an interview at a remote psychiatric clinic to discover that he has been set an unusual test. The director of the clinic is hopelessly insane and is now one of the patients, convinced that he is another person entirely. Powell must hear the strange stories of four patients and decide which of them is the former director.

Unfortunately, Bloch's stories are somewhat weaker that the ones used for *Tales from the Crypt* and the film often lapses into silliness, but there are still bright spots. The first story, 'Frozen Fear', features Richard Todd unhappily married to Sylvia Sims and wishing to go off with his mistress Barbara Parkins. This being an Amicus horror film, instead of getting a good lawyer, he murders her and cuts up the body, neatly wrapping the pieces in brown paper and putting them in their chest freezer in the cellar. Unfortunately for the adulterous pair, Sims had practised voodoo and Todd is soon assailed by the brown paper parcels. It is all a rather slight variation on the disembodied hands horror trope that had been a staple of the genre since Conrad Veidt starred in the 1924 German silent film *The Hands of Orlac*.

Rather better is 'The Weird Tailor', in which Barry Morse (a superb actor underused in film who would soon become one of the stars of the television series *Space: 1999*) plays an old European tailor facing financial ruin. His prospects improve when Peter Cushing promises a large amount of money for him to make a suit from a special white cloth he provides. When Morse discovers the purpose the suit is to be used for he is horrified. Again, the story crosses over into silliness, which is a real shame as both Morse and Cushing (who is top billed for a role that took him two days to shoot) are simply marvellous, making this story the pick of the bunch almost despite itself.

The last two stories are disappointments. 'Lucy Comes to Stay' features Charlotte Rampling as Barbara, recently released from a mental asylum and staying with her brother (James Villiers). Events begin to spiral out of control when Barbara's friend Lucy arrives and begins to influence Barbara. The twist ending is so hugely obvious it can be seen from outer space. The final story has more of the element of surprise about it, but 'Mannikins of Horror' can best be described as daft. Herbert Lom plays an inmate of the asylum who has developed the ability to transfer his soul into a miniature robot, which contains organic matter on its inside. This is the silliest story of the lot, but it ties in with the overall linking story in quite an interesting way.

A decided improvement on these shenanigans was the sequel to *Takes from the Crypt*, which took its title, if not its stories, from another of EC Comics' '50s titles, *The Vault of Horror* (1973). AIP were not involved this time, although they retained a relationship with Amicus as well as making films in England under its own subsidiary company. Otherwise, the mixture was very much as before, with a group of strangers meeting in an enclosed environment, in this case a comfortable lounge complete with a stock of drinks in the basement of a building. Each one has a strange story attached to them; here, a series of recurring dreams, and at the end, it is revealed that—as usual for an Amicus portmanteau—they are all dead. Roy Ward Baker returned from *Asylum* (as it were) to direct, Freddie Francis not wishing to return at this point to the multi-story format—though he would soon do one for World Film Services, the incredibly misjudged *Tales that Witness Madness*.

For *Vault of Horror*, writer Milton Subotsky still had a rich vein of scarily humorous EC Comics tales to work with, none better than the first, 'Midnight Mess', in which Daniel Massey tracks down his long-estranged sister (played by his own sister, Anna Massey) and murders her so that he will inherit the family fortune. Stopping off at a nearby restaurant for a meal, he discovers why the locals do not go out at night and that he is on the menu, resulting in an unforgettable final image.

'The Neat Job' is more overtly comedic, as Terry-Thomas's successful businessman marries late in life to a younger woman, played by Glynis Johns. At twelve years younger than the sixty-two-year-old Terry-Thomas, Johns was perhaps a little old for the role of inexperienced *ingénue*, but she plays the role with a beautifully manic air. Thomas, it transpires, is set in his ways, pathologically neat and something of a martinet about the house, while Johns is a total klutz. This being an EC Comics story, the only possible solution is murder, but you can be sure it is done neatly.

'This Trick'll Kill You' is the weakest of the tales, featuring Curt Jurgens as a stage magician on holiday in India with his assistant and wife, Dawn Addams. While there, he witnesses a woman in a bazaar performing the legendary Indian rope trick, and the pair kill her to learn how the feat is performed. Only then do they learn, to their cost, just how dark the magical powers are that bring the rope to life. 'Bargain in Death' is rather more fun as Michael Craig plays a horror author who arranges to be buried alive, then dug up to claim the insurance money. His partner in this fraud (Edward Judd, last seen by horror fans in Terence Fisher's *Island of Terror*) runs off with the money, but salvation appears to be at hand when a pair of medical students arrange to have his corpse dug up in order to practice their anatomy studies—but fate plays a rather unlikely hand in the proceedings. The most notable aspect of this story to British audiences was the casting as the rather overage medical students of Robin Nedwell and Geoffrey Davies who at the time were the stars of ITV's highly popular 'Doctor' sitcoms (which changed format and titles every few years).

'Drawn and Quartered' ends this collection of stories very strongly, largely due to the felicitous casting of Tom Baker in the lead role, shortly before he was chosen to replace Jon Pertwee in the title role of *Doctor Who*. Baker brings a highly effective blend of intensity and menace to the part of an artist, living in poverty in Haiti, who learns that the paintings he has sold for a pittance are selling in London for thousands of pounds. Plotting his revenge on those responsible, Baker gains the voodoo power to have whatever happens to portraits he paints also happen to the subjects of the paintings. Unfortunately, before he gained this power, he began working on a self-portrait, with predictably messy results.

From Beyond the Grave was put into production soon afterwards, but such was the glut of horror productions on the market that despite it bearing a 1973 copyright date, the film did not gain a UK circuit release until February 1974 and its US release was delayed until November 1975. Despite appearing so late in the cycle of British horror, and after Amicus had made seven previous portmanteau movies, *From Beyond the Grave* was surprisingly fresh and enjoyable. A few changes had been rung, including a new director in former editor Kevin Connor, directing the first picture in what would be a long career, including several more for Amicus. The scripts also came from new hands, with stories by R. Chetwynd-Hayes being adapted by Raymond Christodoulou and Robin Clarke. The new writers introduced a clever new linking format with Peter Cushing giving a charming and light-hearted performance as the proprietor of antique shop Temptations Limited. A series of customers enter the shop, and if they cheat on the transaction, a terrible fate awaits them.

David Warner stars in 'The Gatecrasher' as a customer who fools Cushing into believing that a valuable antique mirror is a reproduction. The story is not completely unlike *Dead of Night*'s antique mirror tale from back in 1945, but this mirror draws Warner into another dimension where he is placed under the influence of a sinister figure who demands to be fed with blood so that it can free Warner from its control and enter our world. The second story, 'An Act of Kindness', is a magnificent example of seedy, bleakly comedic domestic British horror, boosted immensely by its cast. Ian Bannen plays an ex-military office worker trapped in a dead-end office job and a loveless marriage to shrewish Diana Dors. He strikes up a friendship with street match-seller Donald Pleasence, later stealing a military medal from Temptations Limited in order to impress his new acquaintance. Bannen is invited to the Pleasence household, where he is pushed into a relationship with Pleasence's daughter, who is played by none other than Angela Pleasence, displaying her uniquely creepy, disturbing sexuality. The Pleasence father and daughter team is an absolute delight, clearly having a lot of fun and displaying razor sharp comic timing.

The more obviously comic episode of this collection is 'The Elemental', starring Ian Carmichael, star of many British film comedies as well as being BBC Television's Bertie Wooster and Lord Peter Wimsey. Carmichael makes the dishonest mistake of switching the price labels on two snuff boxes in Cushings' establishment, which seals his fate. On the train home, he sits opposite clairvoyant Madame Ofloff (Margaret Leighton) who announces that he has an especially nasty elemental on his shoulder. This unseen force begins to cause violent chaos in the Carmichael household and almost kills his wife, Nyree Dawn Porter. Madame Orloff is called in to exorcise the spectral force before it is too late.

Finally comes 'The Door', in which Ian Ogilvy (in his second Amicus movie in a row after *And Now the Screaming Starts!*) buys an ornate door from Cushing, but when it is fitted to a cupboard in his flat, he finds that beyond the door, he and his wife (Lesley-Anne Down) can see the ancient room the door was formerly attached to. It also puts them in contact with evil occult practitioner Sir Michael Sinclair who uses the door as a portal between his time and the present day in order to trap the souls of anyone who enters. This was an unusual role for Jack Watson, more usually seen as gruff Regimental Sergeant Majors or sad-faced old men, as in Peter Walker's 1976 effort *Schizo*.

As will be clear by now, the gentle old Yorkshireman who runs the Temptations antique shop is not who he seems, as a ne'er-do-well type who tries to stage a hold-up at the shop discovers to his cost in the film's climax. The ending of the film works splendidly for a film that, whether it was meant to be or not, was a wonderful send-off to what proved to be the end of the line for the Amicus portmanteau film. Considering that Amicus had produced four in two years, it was probably time for something different.

And Now the Screaming Stops!

The company still continued with horror productions for a while, each one in its own way trading on nostalgia. *And Now the Screaming Starts!*, released in April 1974, demonstrated that Subotsky and Rosenberg still had a way with a catchy title (the story's original title was the rather less prepossessing *Fengriffin*). A period piece set in 1795, this was written by an outside writer, the excellent and very prolific television scriptwriter Roger Marshall. The film was at heart both a disembodied crawling hand movie—a horror sub-genre that had been around since Conrad Veidt starred in the German production *The Hands of Orlac* in 1924—and a traditional old dark house gothic story. Ian Ogilvy stars again as a newlywed husband who returns to his ancestral home with wife Stephanie Beacham. Beacham is soon scared out of her wits by apparitions of an eyeless, handless man who bears a strong resemblance to local woodsman Geoffrey Whitehead.

The film managed the familiar Amicus feat of featuring a starry cast, most of whom appear in relatively small roles. Patrick Magee does not show up for over twenty-five minutes and it is almost an hour before Herbert Lom drops by in what turns out to be a cameo role in a flashback sequence (vital though it is to the plot). Peter Cushing finally appears after forty-five minutes, wearing his *Frankenstein and the Monster from Hell* wig and taking over the film's narrative.

Madhouse had an even stronger air of self-reflective nostalgia and can be regarded as a sort of British equivalent to the 1956 American film *The Black Sleep* (the last film Bela Lugosi completed during his lifetime). This was a nostalgia exercise reuniting old and in some cases half-forgotten stars made while younger filmmakers were busy creating new horrors more relevant to the modern age.

American International Pictures again co-produced and supplied Vincent Price, making the last film of his AIP contract, starring as Paul Toombes. Toombes is at the peak of his career as the star of the Doctor Death series of horror films when his fiancée is found beheaded at a swanky Hollywood party. The resulting scandal and mental breakdown destroys Toombes' career, which he attempts to resurrect with a Doctor Death television series to be made at an English film studio. This is being produced by an old enemy,

Oliver Quayle (played by the new horror star on the block, *Count Yorga, Vampire* star Robert Quarry), and written by his old friend Herbert Flay, who wrote the original Doctor Death films. Production on the series is beset with on-set accidents and murders until Toombes begins to doubt his own sanity. Directed by Jim Clark, who was far better known in the film business as an editor, *Madhouse* trades heavily on Vincent Price's back catalogue of AIP horror pictures, sequences from which are shown as being from Doctor Death movies. In truth, *Madhouse* has a very tired air about it—it is not awful or even particularly bad, it just lacks conviction and enthusiasm. Some of the films being mined for nostalgia were less than ten years old by the time *Madhouse* was being made, which is an indication of how much times had changed by between 1964 and 1974.

The final Amicus horror movie of all was a very strange horror movie mash-up indeed. *The Beast Must Die* was, of all things, a horror movie inspired by Agatha Christie's *And Then There Were None*—specifically, as the film turned out, the 1965 movie version directed by George Pollock under the title *Ten Little Indians*. Calvin Lockhart, an impressive Bahamian actor born under the rather less imposing name Bert Cooper, played a wealthy businessman and big game hunter whose latest quarry is a werewolf. To this end, he invites a group of suspects to stay at his country mansion.

The grounds of the mansion are peppered with cameras and microphones, controlled by Anton Diffring wearing a horrible checked sports jacket, while the suspects include Peter Cushing as a Scandinavian werewolf expert, complete with dodgy accent, and Charles Gray, who, as ever, plays Charles Gray. This being a low-budget production even by Amicus standards, the werewolf is played by a big hairy dog.

Paul Annett, a director who mainly worked in television, directed with little style and the film is paced very deliberately, far more like a mystery than a horror film until finally a werewolf appears forty-five minutes in. Considering that *The Beast Must Die* has a great title (Amicus were brilliant at thinking up catchy titles) and blends elements of horror, mystery, and Blaxploitation, the film is remarkably dull. The whole thing is simply too staid, desperate for an injection of something outlandish, a view which seems to have been shared by Milton Subotsky who added the idea of a 'Werewolf Break' near the end of them film. This was a thirty-second pause in the film, during which the audience could try to work out who the werewolf is (an idea taken lock, stock, and barrel from the 1965 film *Ten Little Indians*). This became the key selling point of the film, announced at the beginning of the film in a voiceover by Valentine Dyall and emblazoned on the film's posters. Except in the US, that is, where the film was retitled *Black Werewolf* and the 'Werewolf Break' removed. One can only imagine that the patrons of the sort of grindhouse cinemas that would screen a film entitled *Black Werewolf* would have been left disappointed.

This last-minute flourish of showmanship from Amicus could not disguise the fact that their horror films were running into the ground. With AIP no longer making horror pictures and the market for British horror rapidly running out of steam, a new approach was needed. The answer came in the form of Subotsky and Rosenberg's love of pulp science fiction when AIP agreed to fund Amicus' production of Edgar Rice Burroughs' 1924 novel *The Land that Time Forgot*. Co-written by famous British SF author Michael Moorcock, this First World War-set fantasy adventure began a cycle of proto-steampunk movies, which ultimately outlasted Amicus.

The Land that Time Forgot was released in the summer of 1975 and was Amicus' biggest hit in years. Further Edgar Rice Burroughs adaptations followed with the first film's star Doug McClure returning the following year in *At the Earth's Core*, this time opposite the very welcome presence of Peter Cushing. This was successful enough for *The People that Time Forgot* to go into production, a direct sequel to *The Land that Time Forgot*, this time starring John Wayne's son Patrick. The relationship between Subotsky and Rosenberg had become strained, however, and Amicus ceased to be an entity before *The People that Time Forgot* was released on 27 August 1977. As a result, the Amicus name did not appear on the film, but there was still some life in the format, even in a cinematic landscape altered considerably by the overwhelming success of *Star Wars* (1977).

After Amicus

Amicus producer John Dark continued the series along with Kevin Connor, who had directed the previous films, and star Doug McClure with 1978's *Warlords of Atlantis*. This really was the end of the road for this line of period fantasy adventure films, though Dark and Connor went straight into production with *Arabian Adventure* for release in the summer of 1979. This *1001 Nights*-inspired adventure top-billed Christopher Lee as an evil magician and starred Oliver Tobias as the film's hero.

Subotsky and Rosenberg stayed in the movie business, and interestingly, both men initially decamped to Canada. Rosenberg's first feature was the SF-Western *Welcome to Blood City* (1977), starring Keir Dullea and Jack Palance, while Subotsky continued with the portmanteau format. *The Uncanny* (1977) had the linking theme of Peter Cushing as a stressed writer trying to convince publisher Ray Milland that cats are an evil presence trying to take over the world of humans. How frightening the proceedings are depends to an extent on how cute or otherwise the viewer finds cats, but the three stories presented were dismal stuff. It is a shame as an impressive cast was assembled, including Donald Pleasence, Samantha Eggar, and Joan Greenwood.

Rather better was Subotsky's possession drama *Dominique* (1979), produced by his company Sword and Sorcery Productions (the name of which gave some indication as to the sort of films Milton Subotsky planned to make). This featured a starry cast including Cliff Robertson, Jean Simmons, and Jenny Agutter, and he followed this film with a high-profile, three-part mini-series based on Ray Bradbury's *The Martian Chronicles*. The final Sword and Sorcery production was another portmanteau horror production made in England for Chips Productions, an offshoot of Lew Grade's ITC production and distribution empire. This was the 1981 release *The Monster Club,* and most surprisingly of all, at a stage when the traditional British horror movie was all but dead, it was very good indeed.

Grade was at this point in the midst of a doomed attempt to turn ITC from a television concern into a major Hollywood studio. This would run aground on the back of two enormously expensive flops, *Raise the Titanic* (1980) and *Honky Tonk Freeway* (1981). ITC's involvement meant that *The Monster Club*'s director Roy Ward Baker had considerably better production values at his disposal than had been available in Canada for *The Uncanny*.

The Monster Club retained the three-story format of that film, but rang the changes with its linking story. This time around, horror author R. Chetwynd-Hayes (John Carradine) is bitten by starving vampire Eramus (Vincent Price). So grateful is Eramus that he invites the writer to visit The Monster Club, a nightclub for the local population of werewolves, vampires, zombies, and other assorted undead creatures. Between musical interludes by acts including B. A. Robertson (then at the peak of his success as a solo performer) and gnarly old stagers The Pretty Things (still around thirteen years after featuring in Tigon's 1969 *What's Good for the Goose*), Eramus relates three tales of strange creatures.

These three tales are based on stories by Chetwynd-Hayes himself and directed with real style and verve. The first story, 'The Shadmock', is the melancholic tale of Raven (James Laurenson), a Shadmock. This is a sad and lonely individual with the ability to kill by whistling, who hires a young woman (Barbara Kellerman) to help him in his rambling mansion. Raven falls in love with her and proposes marriage, but, at the urging of her crooked boyfriend (Simon Ward), her real aim is to rob his house.

The next segment of the film, 'The Vampires', is the film's comedy story, and for probably the only time in a portmanteau film, it is actually charming and funny—quite the highlight of the movie. Richard Johnson, clearly enjoying himself, plays a mid-European vampire living a quiet suburban existence with his wife (Britt Ekland) and young son. Their happy family life is interrupted by the attentions of civil servant vampire hunters Donald Pleasence and Anthony Valentine, both of whom give the distinct impression that they were having a whale of a time.

Finally comes 'The Ghouls', in which Stewart Whitman plays a grumpy horror movie director looking for a location for his latest production who stumbles across a village of ghouls led by Patrick Magee (appearing in his final British horror picture). That is about it with regards to plot, as the whole things quickly turns into a virtual zombie apocalypse movie, but Roy Ward Baker shoots the whole thing with such pace and kinetic style that the whole thing rolls along in fine style.

Sadly, like most of ITC's film output, *The Monster Club* failed to find its audience and a chapter in British cinema history closed, along with the horror film directing career of Roy Ward Baker. Although he continued directing for television for another eleven years, most notably *The Masks of Death* (1984), produced by Kevin Francis' Tyburn Productions and featuring Peter Cushing as an elderly Sherlock Holmes coming out of retirement.

Milton Subotsky continued in the film business until the very end, his later career consisting of co-producer credits to a set of Stephen King novels that he had the foresight to buy the movie rights to. Most notable of these was *Maximum Overdrive* (1986), which King himself wrote and directed, and *The Lawnmower Man*, which King had his name taken off as nothing but the title remained from his original story. By the time the film was released in March 1992, Subotsky had been dead for almost a year. Somewhat appropriately, this lifelong fan of the horror genre found that his career continued from beyond the grave, with the direct-to-video release *Sometimes They Come Back... Again* appearing a full five years after his death.

Max Rosenberg died on 14 June 2004 at the ripe old age of eighty-nine, retiring in 1997 after a post-Amicus career that included *The Incredible Melting Man* in 1977 and work on Paul Schrader's big budget remake of *Cat People* in 1982. Although the Amicus partnership ended with a degree of animus, even when they could no longer work together, it was clear that both men absolutely loved making movies and the genre in which they were working. Two cultured, literate men spending their lives doing the things they enjoyed the most. There can be little better epitaph.

7

Tony Tenser and Michael Klinger: Two Guys From Another Part of Town

The administrative base of the British film industry has traditionally been split from its famous production centres such as Elstree and Pinewood, close to plenty of countryside locations. Instead, the organisational and publicity functions of British-based film production companies were grouped together in the central London district of Soho.

In the eighteenth century, developers had attempted to make the area more attractive. The well-heeled and wealthy were not convinced, and instead, Soho was inhabited by a less wealthy population of artists and writers, immigrants and bohemians, and hard-working artisans and louche nonconformists. This marked the character of Soho for the decades and centuries to come, as the area became known for all forms of entertainment, from theatres to pubs to brothels. By the mid-twentieth century, Soho was famous for two things: its drinking culture, which attracted a diverse crowd including many of the most famous writers, artists, and actors of the day, and sex.[1] This meant that by a historical coincidence, the movie making centre of Britain, on which the fate of millions of pounds worth of investment routinely depended, lay cheek-by-jowl with London's sex industry.

The film production partnership of Tony Tenser and Michael Klinger, out of which grew Tigon-British, one of the great names of Britain's post-war horror film boom, came from precisely this accidental clash of cultures. Two movie-mad showmen were thrown together by chance, both of whom wanted to make their own films.

Tony Tenser was born in London on 10 August 1920 of Lithuanian immigrant parents. Although he was plainly a clever child, Tenser was just one of a large family of slender means. Higher education was out of the question, but he was hard working and determined with a tendency to excel at whatever trade he took up. By the time of the outbreak of the Second World War on 1 September 1930, he had risen from labouring in a lumber yard to being the manager of the premises. Tenser had always nurtured a love of movies, however, and after wartime service in the RAF, he became a trainee manager for ABC, the major cinema chain owned by Associated British Picture Corporation.

He proved to be a natural showman, particularly at the publicity side of the cinema trade, and within four years, he had been named ABC's Cinema Manager of the Year. His ambitions outgrowing the cinema exhibition sector, Tenser eventually became head of publicity for Miracle Films, a company that imported European films to the UK. As the expression goes, this would often involve 'selling the sizzle, not the steak', making mildly salacious material appear wildly permissive. Among the properties Miracle handled were the early films of Brigitte Bardot, who became an international star after appearing in Roger Vadim's 1956 film *Et Dieu...Crea la Femme*. On its British release in February 1956 the film was retitled *And Woman Was Created*, presumably because of a desire to remove any prospect of religious objections from a film that became better known by the more direct translation it was released under in the US, *...and God Created Woman*.

Placed in the unusual position of Miracle handling a release featuring a genuine star, Tenser was inspired to invent the term 'Sex Kitten' for Bardot, which immediately caught on. The publicity drive for the Bardot films also put Tenser into the orbit of Michael Klinger, a Soho strip club owner of a similar East End Jewish background to his own who was keen to break into the movie business. The same age as Tenser, Klinger had spent the war working as a government inventor working in munitions. Afterwards, he worked as a market trader before being given the chance to invest in Soho cinemas and strip clubs. The closeness to the movie trade meant that film executives could be seen in his clubs and his ability to provide attractive showgirls quickly meant that he was often asked to provide a pretty face or two for movie publicity shoots. This was how Klinger met Tony Tenser, the two men getting along well and finding that they had a lot in common besides their shared Eastern European Jewish background. Both were keen movie fans and were keen to deepen their involvement in the film trade.

Compton Films: Members Only

Interested in forming a partnership, the pair had to put some thought into exactly how they might achieve this as, by the late 1950s, when these events were taking place, British movie production was undergoing a major crisis, squeezed almost out of existence by the twin threats of television and big, colourful American productions. Producing their own films or setting up as independent distributors represented too much of a risk for the two men's comparatively meagre capital. The solution was for the pair to set up a private cinema club where films that could not otherwise be easily seen due to BBFC restrictions could be screened on a members-only basis.

Thus was born the Compton Cinema Club. In other hands, this enterprise might have become a thinly veiled excuse to screen pornography, but with committed film fans Tenser and Klinger in charge, the Compton showed a mixture of nudist movies, which were undergoing something of a boom as an excuse to show as many naked women as possible on cinema screens (and which were spoofed to great effect in 1969's *Carry On Camping*), and adult-themed arthouse cinema from Europe, Scandinavia, and the US. Such was the success of the venture that the Compton Cinema Club's membership included none other than John Trevelyan, secretary of the British Board of Film Censors.

Yet the club soon found that it struggled to find enough films to fill its schedules. This pushed an all-too-willing Tenser and Klinger into the film distribution sector. Compton Film Distributors imported a range of risqué and adult-themed subjects, screening uncut versions at the Cinema Club and offering BBFC-approved versions to the independent cinema sector. The films tended to be available cheaply, as the major cinema chains showed very little interest in buying this type of film. The still-large independent sector, which comprised up to half of Britain's cinemas was, by definition, made up of small chains of theatres that were unable or unwilling to come together to combine their buying power.

As in Tenser's days with Miracle Films, the pictures were sold with imaginative poster art, which made the films appear more salacious than they really were, and wild publicity stunts were perpetrated in an attempt to gain free newspaper publicity. With other small distributors active in the same market, such as the venerable Butchers Film Service, Eros, and Gala all chasing the same films as Compton, it was not long before the logical next step for Compton was for them to enter film production, where the risks were greater, but so were the potential rewards. Needing a cheap, easy to sell product, Tenser and Klinger hired photographer George Harrison Marks to make a nudist movie, released in 1961 under the title *Naked as Nature Intended*. This was initially rejected as unsuitable for release by the BBFC, which was great publicity for this type of film, and Compton outmanoeuvred the censorship board by having the film screened on a district-by-district basis, cleared by local council censorship committees. The BBFC changed their mind and allowed the film to be screened with some cuts, but *Naked as Nature Intended* still carried the *cachet* of being forbidden fruit among the audience for nudie movies.

This type of film was clearly just a passing fad, and the attempt to supress *Naked as Nature Intended* was symptomatic of a realisation that what started out ostensibly as educational films had become, to the surprise of absolutely nobody, a semi-respectable outpost of the porn industry. Tenser and Klinger's film empire was growing, and soon became known as Compton-Cameo after as merger with the Cameo cinema chain. If it was to develop in the film production business, the company would have to graduate to more mainstream fare. Their production company Tekli next made *That Kind of Girl* (1963), a genuine drama with the luridly sold subject matter of venereal disease. This was followed later the same year by *The Yellow Teddybears*, a tawdry tale based on a real-life case in which schoolgirls advertised the loss of their virginity by the wearing of Robertson's Marmalade golliwog badges.

Both films did good business, and this financial success encouraged Tenser and Klinger to further expand their horizons. Next they produced *Saturday Night Out* (1964) a slice-of-life comedy that did not lose money but failed to excite a huge amount of interest. Still a small company with limited capital, Compton-Cameo were still thinking in terms of popular genres with built-in audience interest. With this in mind, it had not escaped the notice of Tenser and Klinger that Hammer were still pulling in big audiences and attracting the interest of American studios and foreign distributors with their horror films some seven years after the breakthrough success of *The Curse of Frankenstein*. Thus it was that Compton-Cameo got into the horror movie business.

The production company now renamed Compton Films, their regular team of writers Donald and Derek Ford and director Robert Hartford-David fetched up at Shepperton Studios, Britain's traditional home for the more 'respectable' end of low-budget film production, to begin production on *The Black Torment*. Produced in colour on a much larger budget than the previous Tenser-Klinger productions, this was a costume melodrama not too different at heart than the sort of things Gainsborough had been making with great success in the 1940s, with added horror trimmings, colour photography, which was now expected by audiences for this type of production, and a splendidly lurid title.

The resulting film made a lot of money, despite its lack of star names (Heather Sears, at one point tipped to become a major star but now seeing her career dwindling to a halt, was top-billed), partially because it contained a measure of the raw edge that Hammer's mid-1960s horror titled tended to lack. Tenser and Klinger remained true to their exploitation roots though, and continued making other types of films, next making the salacious documentary *Primitive London* and following this with *The Pleasure Girls* (1965), a 'Swinging London' drama made for the tiny sum of £30,000 with what would a few years later be regarded as a very starry cast (Francesca Annis and Ian McShane in the lead roles) with a cameo by Klaus Kinski who at this stage in his career was willing to appear in almost anything due to his always pressing need for money.

Repulsion: Polanski and the Terror of the Psyche

When the company did return to the horror genre, it was with something startlingly different, in the form of Roman Polanski's first English language film *Repulsion*. Polanski had recently defected from Poland, at that time behind the Iron Curtain, which for artists meant severe restrictions on their creative freedom. Armed with a great artistic reputation thanks to his 1962 film *Knife in the Water*, which was nominated for a Best Foreign Language Film Oscar, Polanski nonetheless found himself struggling to find backers. In France, he had only been allowed to make a few short films, and his prospects in England looked little better, which is how he found himself at the door of a small exploitation film company looking for work.

Michael Klinger was willing to talk to Polanski and was taken with the idea of Compton making a film with him. *Repulsion* was conceived by Polanski and his co-writer Gérard Brach expressly for Compton's requirements for them to make some kind of horror picture. It is interesting to compare Tenser and Klinger's two-film association with Polanski to Hammer's dalliance with another exile director with more artistic motives than their normal run of films, Joseph Losey. Compton's association proved to be rather more successful, with *Repulsion* proving to be a big success for the company, performing well at the box-office and considerably raising the profile of Compton. The film also served its purpose for Polanski, launching him as a maker of English language films in a career which continues to this day.

Repulsion is a fascinating psychological horror film (if it can be categorised within the horror genre at all) about the slide into madness and murder of a young make-up artist afflicted with a deep-seated fear of men. The film attracted by far the most famous cast of any Compton film to date: Catherine Deneuve playing the protagonist Carol Ledoux, while Ian Hendry, John Fraser, and Patrick Wymark also appear, along with a guest star, billed as Yvonne Ferneaux. This represented the pulling-power of the Polanski name among an acting fraternity keen to work with the famed Polish director, but also the growing reputation of Compton as a filmmaking entity expanding and on the rise at a time when independent British filmmaking was struggling.

A Study in Terror, Cul-de-Sec, and the end of Compton-Cameo

Compton's production schedule at this point can best be described as schizophrenic. *Repulsion* gained the company a measure of respect and both the reputation and the cash to attempt a move to a much larger scale of production. The first result of this, released five months later in November

1965, was, of all things, a Sherlock Holmes film. Unlike Hammer's 1959 attempt at bringing the Baker Street detective to the screen in *The Hound of the Baskervilles*, Compton's writers Donald and Derek Ford came up with an original story. *A Study in Terror* had the idea, which might seem a little obvious now but was highly novel in 1965, of marrying two icons of late Victorian crime into a single narrative by having Holmes investigate the Jack the Ripper murders. By a fortunate coincidence the chronology of the fictional detective and the real-life serial killer meshed, with Arthur Conan Doyle's first Holmes story, *A Study in Scarlet*, being published in 1887, while the five murders most commonly attributed to the Ripper took place between August and November 1888.

John Neville, a renowned actor on the classical stage since the 1950s who in 1960 had played another figure of late Victorian infamy, Lord Alfred Douglas, in Gregory Ratoff's film *Oscar Wilde*, was contracted to play Holmes. Neville was by far the biggest star to appear in a Compton film to date and was supported by Donald Huston, an intelligent Welsh actor who had become a solid supporting player after a youthful career as a leading man; Huston was cast as Watson. This somewhat underrated film is of some interest in the history of Holmes adaptations as previous films had struggled to find a satisfying purpose for the character of Doctor Watson. In the stories of Sir Arthur Conan Doyle, Watson serves as the observer of Holmes and narrator of the stories, a function made redundant by the visual nature of film.

Previous Holmes films had either side-lined the character (occasionally the poor doctor was omitted entirely) or, in the case of the famous Basil Rathbone/Nigel Bruce film series, turned him into pure comic relief. By the mid-1960s, some twenty years after Rathbone called an end to his portrayal of the great detective for fear of typecasting, Rathbone and Bruce's reading of their roles still cast a long shadow across any filmic interpretation of the parts. Donald and Derek Ford's script and Donald Huston's playing of the role therefore made something of a refreshing change, with Watson largely coming across as a capable man of action instead of a dense buffoon.

James Hill was drafted in to direct the film. Hill was a stylish director who had been working on action series *Gideon's Way* and *The Saint* for Lew Grade's ITC company, and would soon score a major feature film hit with *Born Free* (1966) as well as directing for the crown jewel of British adventure television shows, *The Avengers*. With his television experience, Hill was used to working quickly on film to create results more expensive-looking than the money available would indicate as being possible. This made him perfect for Tenser and Klinger's purposes. Even more so than Hammer's *Hound of the Baskervilles*, *A Study in Terror* was sold in its home market every bit as much as a blood-curdling horror film about Jack the Ripper as it was a Holmes movie. Taken on these terms, it is rather more successful than

Robert S. Baker and Monty Berman's 1959 film *Jack the Ripper*. Somewhat bizarrely, the US market distributor Columbia Pictures sold the film with an advertising campaign aimed at fans of the big television hit of the season, ABC's camped-up *Batman* series ('Here comes the original Caped Crusader').

Compton's next few films were perhaps an overly eclectic bunch, reflecting the conflicting filmmaking aims of the company's proprietors. *Secrets of a Windmill Girl* (1966) referred to that venerable institution of British striptease the Windmill Theatre, where in the post-war era, naked women were arranged in various tableau but not allowed to move lest they attract the ire of the police and the Lord Chamberlain, then the official censor of theatrical performances. Featuring a young (and fully clothed) Pauline Collins in the lead role, this was another film designed to look more daring and risqué than it actually was, and it quickly became so dated as to gain the status of a period time capsule.

It is hard to imagine a greater contrast than Compton's next release, *Cul-de-Sac* (1966), another Roman Polanski movie, but this time more in the absurdist black comedy vein than *Repulsion*. In the film, two crooks on the run, Lionel Stander (making a return to English language filmmaking following a long period working in Europe after becoming a victim of the 1950s Hollywood blacklist) and the injured Jack MacGowran, hide out in a castle on a remote island belonging to the eccentric and mismatched couple Donald Pleasence and Françoise Dorléac (the real-life sister of *Repulsion*'s Catherine Deneuve). The resulting story of paranoia, isolation and madness bears interesting similarities to *Repulsion*, but is told in a completely different way. This made the film something of a hard sell for Tenser and Klinger, who were unable to promote it as a horror film, as they had Polanski's previous effort. British film critics struggled to get a handle on the film, but it did much better in Europe, where *Cul-de-Sac* won the top prize of the Golden Bear at the 1966 Berlin Film Festival.

Roman Polanski did return to the horror genre one more time, for his 1967 production *The Fearless Vampire Killers or, Pardon Me, But Your Teeth are in my Neck*, by which time, the director had begun to attract the backing of major Hollywood studios. The silly title and the film's promotion promise broad comedy, which Polanski's mid-European Jewish nineteenth-century vampire fairy tale never intended to deliver. Polanski himself starred in the film as Alfred, the young, nervous apprentice to elderly vampire hunter Professor Abronsius (Jack MacGowran), who comes up against Ferdy Mayne as vampire lord Count von Krolock. Some fun is had at the expense of the clichés of the vampire film, but Polanski is not really a comedy director and it helps not to go into the film imagining another *Carry On Screaming*. The original title of the film had been *Dance of the Vampires*, and if taken in the spirit (and the version) in which it was intended, is a fascinating, rewarding film.

By this point, it had become clear that Tony Tenser and Michael Klinger were very different types of film producers, and Tenser withdrew from the Compton group of companies. Klinger had ambitions to make large-scale productions, and by the early '70s, he succeeded with two films starring Michael Caine and director Mike Hodges, the legendary gangster thriller *Get Carter* (1971) and *Pulp* (1972). Between 1974 and 1977, as the British film industry collapsed around his ears, Klinger became probably the most successful movie producer in the land, being responsible for the *Confessions of...* series of cheerfully smutty comedies and for a pair of spectacular adaptations of Wilbur Smith novels starring Roger Moore, *Gold* (1974) and *Shout at the Devil* (1976).

Michael Reeves: *The Sorcerers*

Tony Tenser, meanwhile, started making horror movies. Before he left Compton, he agreed for the company to co-finance a science fiction horror being produced by Richard Gordon, who had made *Fiend Without a Face* and *First Man into Space* back in 1958–59; this was *The Projected Man*, shot at Merton Park Studios during the winter of 1965. The little production facility, based in the London suburb of Wimbledon, opened in 1930 and had most famously been the home of the Edgar Wallace Mysteries. The production of the film was somewhat troubled, with credited director Ian Curteis being replaced before the end of production, the remainder of the film being shot by co-producer John Croydon.[2] The resulting film is surprisingly entertaining, despite its plot regarding a matter transportation machine gone wrong being not exactly original, having seen service in *The Fly* (1958) and its two sequels, the last of which, *Curse of the Fly* (1965), had only just been filmed at Shepperton.

As a solo producer, Tony Tenser proved willing to give new talent a chance, especially when the talent, in the form of Michael Reeves, had an agreement with none other than Boris Karloff to star in a film. Reeves had worked as an assistant and production runner on various international co-productions before gathering together enough money to direct a horror film of his own in Italy in 1965. This was *Revenge of the Blood Beast*, starring Reeves' old school friend Ian Ogilvy, who had appeared in his earliest attempts at amateur filmmaking, and Barbara Steele. Steele was an English actress, formerly under contract to Rank, who had made her name as the leading female star of Italy's burgeoning horror movie scene after starring in Mario Bava's *Black Sunday* (1960). Bava made full use of Steele's unconventional beauty—all wide forehead, high cheekbones, and, most of all, huge eyes. As the witch Asa Vajda, her face punctured by holes from being placed into an iron maiden torture device, Steele was the visual centrepiece of the film and was instantly transformed into an icon of European horror.

Contracted for a day's filming on *Revenge of the Blood Beast*, Steele was expecting to spend a pleasant few hours in the Italian countryside shooting a cameo in yet another horror movie. Instead, she was horrified to discover that she was the female lead in the film and all her scenes would be shot in an exhausting twenty-two-hour period. Perhaps not surprisingly, Steele refused to speak to producer Paul Maslanky for many years afterwards.[3]

Back in England, Tony Tenser's first film as a solo film producer under the banner Tony Tenser Pictures Ltd turned out to be Michael Reeves' second film as director and his first acknowledged classic: *The Sorcerers*. Reeves had been set to direct of project called *The Devil's Discord* for Compton, a gothic horror with a contemporary setting that was to have starred Peter Cushing, but Michael Klinger was far less interested in horror than was Tenser and cancelled the entire project only weeks before filming had been due to commence.

Reeves' schedule being unexpectedly clear, Tenser and his production partners Curtwel—a production company owned by Raquel Welsh and her husband Patrick Curtis who owned the rights to Michael Reeves' scripts *The Devil's Discord* and *Crescendo*, which was later reworked by Jimmy Sangster for Hammer—set to work on a new project for Reeves, which it was hoped would have much-prized youth appeal.

Based on a story by John Burke, king of the film and TV novelisation, this would become *The Sorcerers*, scripted by Michael Reeves and his writer friend Tom Baker (no relation to the *Doctor Who* actor), the film was designed from the start to have easily exploitable elements. Being 1967, this meant a youth background, violence, and car/motorbike chases in a fast-paced narrative. Ian Ogilvy returned as Mike Roscoe, a young man hungry for kicks who agrees to be experimented on by elderly hypnotist Dr Marcus Monserrat and his wife Estelle. Curtis and Reeves were able to convince Boris Karloff to return to England to appear as Monserrat. By 1967, Karloff was seventy-nine years of age but still had a leading man's *cachet* and his presence in a horror film was a guarantee of international distribution.

Cathleen Lacey, whose career stretched back to Hitchcock's 1938 classic *The Lady Vanishes*, was cast as Estelle Monserrat. Her role was considerably strengthened at the suggestion of Karloff, who thought that Reeves and Baker's original script made his character too evil, so instead, a battle of wills was set up between Dr Monserrat and Estelle. Marcus Monserrat has been rejected and disgraced by the scientific establishment, but his years of suffering and hard work finally come good when he invents a machine that allows the user to feel what another person does. Not only this, it is discovered that the user of the machine can actually control the actions of another person. Marcus wants to use this discovery for good, but Estelle becomes drunk on the power this gives her after a lifetime of suffering alongside her husband.

Roscoe becomes a puppet, forced to fight, steal, and even murder under the influence of Estelle, until Marcus fights back in a psychic battle for Roscoe's soul. Made on a very low budget using cheap studio space that would normally have been used for making commercials, *The Sorcerers* presents the dingiest possible picture of Swinging London, with the elderly Karloff limping along the streets—a lifelong sufferer of back problems, the actor by now had problems walking—like a dapper, bearded ghost from another era.

Aided by experienced producer Arnold Louis Miller, *The Sorcerers* was shot guerrilla style, the crew snatching the shots they needed without asking for permission the disappearing before the police arrived. The results had a real semi-documentary style to them, the film's air of verisimilitude aided by the casting of Leeds-born actor Victor Henry as Roscoe's friend Alan. His Yorkshire vowels were as rarely heard in the British cinema of 1967 as they are today, and Henry's performance helps ground the film in reality. This makes it all the more tragic that the actor was unable to build upon his career's strong beginning, as he suffered brain damage following a freak bus accident in 1972, after which he remained in a vegetative state for thirteen years until his death in 1985.[4]

Susan George, playing Mike Roscoe's unfortunate girlfriend Audrey, was only seventeen when *The Sorcerers* was made, but is actually very good and clearly has star quality. Her career never really developed as much as it should have, but her part in *Straw Dogs* gave her a lasting notoriety. George also appeared in some other films of interest, including Peter Collinson's slasher movie *Fright* and Peter Walker's horror-tinged psychological thriller *Die Screaming, Marianne*. Like *Straw Dogs*, both were released in 1971.

Sadly, not all of Tigon's horror productions were of the same standard as Michael Reeves' work. *Curse of the Crimson Altar* (1968) was blessed with an incredible cast, with Christopher Lee, Barbara Steele, and Michael Gough joined by Boris Karloff, who was by now seriously ill and confined to a wheelchair. It is genuinely sad to report that the results of their efforts were a dull mess, directed in an incredibly flat manner by Vernon Sewell. By the time the film was released in the US, under the title *The Crimson Cult*, Karloff had died, having never recovered from a chill he caught on the film's night shooting. This at least gave *Curse* a certain notoriety when it was publicised as Karloff's last film, though it later transpired that the incredible old trooper had subsequently acted in scenes for four films in Mexico, which were completed after his death.

Vernon Sewell was not new to Tigon, having directed the previous year's *The Blood Beast Terror*, a film that Peter Cushing described as the worst he had ever appeared in.[5] In a somewhat refreshing change of pace, Cushing here plays the policeman investigating a series of murders that lead to the local scientific expert and his lovely daughter. The daughter, in a plot development best described as 'daft', transforms when sexually aroused into her true form, a murderous Death's Head Moth. Unfortunately, the film had nothing like the budget to either portray or dispatch its monster with any degree of realism. What had been intended were some acting fireworks as Cushing had been cast opposite none other than Basil Rathbone as Dr Mallinger. Tragically, the screen's most famous Sherlock Holmes died some two weeks before he had been due to travel to England to make the film. Last-minute recasting gave the role to Robert Flemyng, who was perfectly adequate in the role, but *The Blood Beast Terror* was a film that sorely needed star power in order to offset its baggy script and threadbare production values.

Witchfinder General and the School of Rural Horror

While *The Blood Beast Terror* was completing its troubled journey to the bottom half of cinema double-bills, Michael Reeves' next Tigon production was shooting, the somewhat better-remembered *Witchfinder General*. Reeves was very keen to cast Donald Pleasance in the role of Matthew Hopkins, but was overruled by AIP who were putting up the American funding for the picture. With its popular Edgar Allan Poe series of films winding down, the studio saw the lead role as being perfect for its major horror star Vincent Price. Thus was born the combative relationship between director and star, which has made the shooting of *Witchfinder General* the stuff of legend.

The location shoot in East Anglia saw Michel Reeves and his crew break boundaries, despite the director's admitted inability to deal with actors. Finding himself in a position he had never been in before—of having a leading man forced upon him whom he genuinely thought did not suit the material—Reeves made the best of the situation. The script had been written for Pleasence and treated Hopkins as a somewhat absurd, ineffectual authority figure, which was not such an unusual idea in an era when authority figures were routinely lampooned on film. Price and Reeves got along extremely badly on the location shoot, as Price's standard performance had by this point more than a hint of camp about it. This had proved perfect for Roger Corman's stylised, studio-bound Poe adaptations, especially his wonderful, Ireland-shot *Masque of the Red Death* (1964), but would have been entirely wrong for Reeves' harsh, bleak look at British history.

The script was adjusted for the new leading man and Reeves got a subtle, powerful performance from Price—eventually. The director had neither the people skills nor the authority of an old pro to explain clearly to the actor what was required, so reining Price in became a painful, if ultimately worthwhile, process. As in *The Sorcerers*, the unleashing of man's base desires, either by electronic means or through religious fanaticism, leads to madness and death, both for Matthew Hopkins and for his opponent in the film, Roundhead soldier Richard Marshall (Ian Ogilvy returning to action for Michael Reeves). Ultimately, Marshall gets his violent revenge on the man who has destroyed the family life he had planned for himself, but he is himself driven insane in the process.

If there was a sign that Hammer's approach to horror was becoming dated, it was shown in *Witchfinder General*, released in May 1968, while *Dracula Has Risen from the Grave* was in production over at Pinewood. While Christopher Lee's Dracula wasted his sexual magnetism and star power getting involved in yet another pointless vendetta in Hammer's fairyland middle Europe, *Witchfinder General* was terrifying audiences with more realistic horrors. Hammer, with its Hollywood studio collaborations, were no longer defining the outer limits of horror acceptability in the way it had been ten years earlier.

The film represents an interesting artistic point of view from Reeves and his writer Tom Baker (returning from the pair's previous film The Sorcerers) in an era when the flip, consequence-free violence of the James Bond series and the stylised mayhem of Sergio Leone and other directors of spaghetti westerns was starting to become the dominant style in action cinema. Real-life violence has consequences for everyone involved, and *Witchfinder General* reflects this to a disturbing and effective degree.

As in *The Sorcerers*, we see displayed the corrosive, corrupting effects of violence and its often misogynistic nature. Matthew Hopkins travels England during the Civil War, dispensing arbitrary punishment for the illusory and victimless crime of witchcraft. We see no evidence in the world depicted in the film that witches are real or have any actual supernatural influence, which help to frame Hopkins' actions as exercises in power and pointless brutality. It helps enormously that Vincent Price plays the role in as low-key a manner as possible, his powerful and physically imposing presence is such that his moody silence as another helpless woman is burned to death is infinitely more powerful than any theatrical display of emotion.

AIP, expecting just another cheap exploitation product for drive-ins and grindhouse double-bills, were very pleasantly surprised when *Witchfinder General* was delivered to them. Retitling the film *The Conqueror Worm* after Edgar Allan Poe's 1943 poem, the studio decided to use the film to reboot their moribund Poe film series. The film proved influential in other ways, beginning a cycle of middle-ages horror films such as *Cry of the Banshee* (a faux Poe movie from AIP), the German-produced *Mark of the Devil* and *The Bloody Judge* (the latter starring Christopher Lee), all released in 1970, and Tigon's excellent *Blood on Satan's Claw*, released the following year.

In the hands of a cinematic artist like Michael Reeves, or even a lesser but very real talent such as *Blood on Satan's Claw*'s Piers Haggard, this school of rural horror was capable of interesting things. Along with the aforementioned themes of power and misogyny, a theme also of Gordon Hessler's *Cry of the Banshee*, a rare opportunity opened up to examine Britain's pagan history and its suppression at the hands of puritan Christianity. By 1970, however, exploitation producers aiming at the European film market had become aware that violence towards women was not only a saleable commodity, but was able to be shown in more detail than ever before.

Mark of the Devil was a West German directed film, written by Michael Armstrong who, as we shall see, would soon direct *The Haunted House of Horror* for Tigon. As with that film, Armstrong found control of the production being wrested from him, this time by the film's producer Adrian Hoven. Hoven had planned a cash-in copy of *Witchfinder General*, and shot his own scenes behind Armstrong's back to ensure that the film was more of this type than Armstrong's more complex, politically charged vision of a film dealing with state violence. *Mark of the Devil* was made to a very high standard on Austrian locations, with a cast including name actors Herbert Lom and Udo Kier. It was sold, however, on its over-the-top depiction of violence towards women, the film's poster featuring the key visual image of the film: a woman having her tongue torn out by torturer Reggie Nalder. Famously, audiences in American cinemas showing *Mark of the Devil* were handed aeroplane-style sick bags.

The film proved highly successful, so much so that an in-name-only sequel was released in 1973, co-written by Armstrong but this time directed by Adrian Hoven. Entitled *Mark of the Devil 2* for its English language release, West German audiences queued up to see the follow up under a startlingly prosaic title, which translates as *Witches are Violated and Tortured to Death*. Reggie Nalder returned as a different character, but apart from that, it was rather more a remake than a sequel.

Beast in the Cellar and *Blood on Satan's Claw*

Tigon's quality control was sometimes overridden in the interests of making a good deal and giving a chance to new talent. Michael Armstrong was a budding writer-director who had made an experimental short film with a pre-stardom David Bowie. Tigon and their American production partners AIP were keen on his youth-oriented horror story *The Dark*, but to Armstrong's dismay, his script was rewritten into incoherence. AIP insisted on writing in a major role for their contracted star Boris Karloff, who then proved to be too ill to fulfil the role and had to be replaced by Denis Price. Worse still, fading star of AIP's *Beach Party* film series Frankie Avalon was cast, looking absurdly out of place with his 1964 hair and clothes among the fashionable English teens. Many of Armstrong's own casting suggestions, including giving a major role to David Bowie, who was still at this point to have his breakout hit with 'Space Oddity', were vetoed.

The first cut of the film was rejected by the AIP executives and new scenes were written and shot by hands other than Michael Armstrong, whose original vision of the film was becoming an increasingly distant memory. These added a new red herring in the form of George Sewell as the older lover of Gina Warwick. The result was by now retitled *The Haunted House of Horror*, which had a certain ironic appropriateness as it bore as little relation to the dull and illogical end result as it the film bore to Armstrong's original script.

Tigon continued to make non-horror films between their now more famous genre productions. Tony Tenser's eye for a good script was starting to desert him though, as can be seen in hindsight by most of the horror films the studio released that did not feature Michael Reeves' involvement. *The Beast in the Cellar* was Tigon's next horror film, and a very strange clash of styles it is too. Released to UK cinemas in August 1970, the film mainly demonstrates what strange times it was made in—only during the British horror boom of the early 1970s could distinguished actresses such as Beryl Reid and Flora Robson find themselves top-billed in a low-budget horror picture.

The Beast in the Cellar is more of a blackly comic psychodrama than it is any kind of conventional horror film. Writer-director James Kelley's story revolves around the relationship between two elderly sisters, Ellie (Reid) and Joyce (Robson), who are mixed up with a murder investigation while army manoeuvres go on nearby. It is a film that is more effective the less you know about the story, and as most reviewers tend to give away the ending, I will stop there.

Full value is obtained from the two stars who really do earn their top billing, and some of their scenes together are very entertaining. At times, *The Beast in the Cellar* really is very talky, and one wonders if the two stars were fully aware of the nature of the film they had signed up to. Most of their scenes are entirely separate from the horror content, which seems to have been tacked on afterwards to enliven the proceedings, the basic story struggling to sustain a film of roughly ninety minutes in length.

Blood on Satan's Claw (1970) performed no better than *The Beast in the Cellar* at the box office, but was artistically a considerable improvement. The film makes a very interesting companion piece to *Witchfinder General*, which turns out to be no coincidence. The film's time frame was moved back by about 150 years from its original Victorian setting, partially because nineteenth-century horrors were becoming a little too common, but mainly because of a desire by Tigon to recreate the success of *Witchfinder General*.[6]

Robert Wynne-Simmons' original notion was to have the narrative comprise of three linked stories, but when director Piers Haggard was hired, he worked with the writer to rework the plot strands into a single narrative. Although most of the thirty-one-year-old Haggard's experience had been on television, it included some of the best written and performed programmes being produced at this time, including *Callan*, *Man at the Top*, and *Public Eye*. Haggard clearly knew his way around a script and was used to working with talented actors. What came as a pleasant surprise, given that much of Haggard's TV work was shot in studio confines, was that *Blood on Satan's Claw* made highly effective use of location filming in Oxfordshire and Buckinghamshire. Dick Bush's cinematography adds to the rural atmosphere of a film in which evil is literally ploughed up from the ground.

The story revolves around a farming community, the young people of which are infected by a demonic evil when Barry Andrews, previously seen in Hammer's *Dracula Has Risen from the Grave*, digs up part of a skull, with eye eerily intact. Led by Linda Hayden, the teenagers of the village reject the authority of their elders and engage in sexual perversions and murder, opposed eventually by the local judge (Patrick Wymark in his final performance before his death at the tragically young age of forty-four). The film was also released under the title *Satan's Skin*, while *Blood on Satan's Claw* was sometimes prefaced with '*The*'—multiple titles indicate that the film did not meet with the roaring success of *Witchfinder General*, which is a real shame.

The two films approach similar material in markedly different ways: one might say *Blood on Satan's Claw* asks the question 'What if Matthew Hopkins was right?' While the influence of the devil is seen here to be real, the script makes allusions with two then-recent and very human manifestations of evil—the murders committed by Charles Manson and his hippie 'family' (the victims of which included Sharon Tate, rising actress and girlfriend of Roman Polanski), and the eleven-year-old English murderer Mary Bell.

Diversification and Decline

Aware that the future prospects for a small film studio producing only horror pictures was limited, given the increasing number of such films being produced, Tigon kept on with their efforts to diversify. They scored a hit in late 1971 with a family friendly Anglo-German adaptation of Anna Sewell's classic children's novel *Black Beauty*, and gained a lot of attention with the Spanish-shot Western *Hannie Caulder*. This starred Raquel Welsh at the peak of her career, but the film proved both an artistic and box office disappointment (it sold a lot of posters of Welsh dressed in only cowboy hat and poncho, however). Comedy was also tried, which certainly must have seemed a wise investment at the time with Hammer's cheap as chips adaptation of the TV sitcom *On the Buses* having proved the hit of the year. *The Magnificent 7 Deadly Sins*—a sort of comedy equivalent of an Amicus portmanteau horror—was packed with star names from the big and small screen including Bruce Forsythe, Harry H. Corbett, and Leslie Phillips, but audiences showed little interest.

Television adaptations were still the fashion though, and Tigon next embarked on a horror-film version of the BBC's apocalyptic SF series *Doomwatch*. The series began very brightly in 1970 as a sort of *Doctor Who* for adults (sorry Whovians, but you know what I mean) featuring a government agency with a remit to investigate and prevent ecological and scientific disasters. By the time of the show's third series in 1972, the cutting edge appeal of the show had started to wither away and the series was cancelled by the BBC. Although the main stars of the series, John Paul and Simon Oates, were featured, the main roles were taken by new characters played by Ian Bannen, Judy Geeson, and George Sanders. Whatever the reasoning behind this, cinema audiences proved unwilling to turn out for a film version of a series in which its popular stars hardly appeared.

As with Tigon's rival Hammer, a blizzard of activity in the early '70s was the prelude to collapse, and the studio was to produce only two more horror-themed pictures. *Neither the Sea nor the Sand* was a very odd proposition scripted by British newsreader Gordon Honeycombe from his own 1969 novel, which is part zombie movie and part love story. Susan Hampshire plays Anna, who comes to the island of Jersey to escape her unhappy marriage. There she falls in love with lighthouse-keeper Hugh (Michael Petrovitch), who spoils the budding romance by dropping dead. Although the actual mechanics of the process are never explained (which would have spoiled the mood of the piece entirely), it seems that so pure and deep is the love of Anna for Hugh that he returns from the dead.

Quite an effecting tale of doomed love, *Neither the Sea nor the Sand* is a story that would bear remaking in the current environment when zombie movies have gone beyond the confines of pure horror. At the time, however, the film was seen as being about as uncommercial a proposition as can be, which actually says volumes about the approach of Tigon and Tony Tenser at the time. At a time when popular cinema was seen in some quarters to be genuinely struggling for its very existence, the studio was making unusual projects instead of going over old ground. While neither *The Beast in the Cellar* nor *Neither the Sea nor the Sand* proved to be big financial successes, at least they were trying to make some films with class that were trying to expand the borders of the horror genre.

The Creeping Flesh, on the other hand, was probably the most traditional horror film Tigon had made since *The Black Torment*. What turned out to be Tigon's farewell to horror cinema was still, while hardly perfect, a solidly carpentered film that united, for the first time in the studio's history, the two great British stars of horror cinema, Peter Cushing and Christopher Lee. By this time, the personal struggles Peter Cushing had undergone following the death of his wife in 1971 were clearly etched on his face and emaciated body, giving the actor a grey, haunted look that fed back into his work in interesting ways.

Freddie Francis returned to direct, taking over at short notice from Don Sharp. This means that *The Creeping Flesh* is largely missing the creative visuals that were a hallmark of Francis' best work. In fact, the film is somewhat dogged by a cheap look, but the narrative develops in unexpected ways that make it constantly interesting and watchable. Cushing's scientist/explorer discovers a skeleton on one of his expeditions, the makeup of which disproves all previous theories of man's evolutionary progress. The obsessed Cushing's expeditions have used up much of the family's fortunes, much to annoyance of his half-brother Christopher Lee, who runs a mental hospital and has been overshadowed by Cushing for his whole life.

This has an interesting real-life parallel as Lee was by now a bigger star than his friend Cushing, who had been given the star roles and better billing by Hammer throughout the previous decade. Lee's performances were becoming deeper and more magnetic and he was starting to outgrow the opportunities provided by the horror genre. It is illustrative to note that Lee was given top-billing on *The Creeping Flesh* for a role that was rather smaller than that of Cushing.

The skeleton, it turns out, regrows its flesh when it gets wet and from this point you can be excused for thinking that you know exactly how the film will progress. Happily, you (and I, when I first saw it) would be wrong, and the film takes a major left turn partway through. For reasons I struggle to follow, Cushing reckons that the skeleton represents undiluted evil—a conclusion he reaches only after he has injected his daughter with a solution taken from it in an attempt to cure her mental health problems. She escapes from their home and goes on a murderous rampage across London, in scenes that open out the film visually and give the film some much-needed pace. These scenes also give roles to the likes of Tony Wright, an actor who once looked like he might become a big star but here is reduced to a non-speaking role and looks ten years older than his then-forty-eight years of age.

Eventually, we get to see what we have paid for, as the film returns to its central plot for the last twenty minutes and the skeleton finally gets soaking wet. The whole thing is actually not a bad romp, but there is a real feeling, as with Hammer's *Frankenstein and the Monster from Hell*, of the end of the line rapidly approaching. Tony Tenser left the film business soon after *The Creeping Flesh* was filmed and the company collapsed soon after. Had Tigon bought out Hammer instead of Michael Carreras, which had been a real possibility, it is hard to see how matters would have turned out very differently for either party.[7] Tigon carried on for a while, retreating from horror into softcore sex and comedy, but the writing was on the wall and the company had a very short future.

8
Pete Walker: Suburban Horrors

Retirement from the movie business did not sit well with lifelong film fan Tony Tenser, and in 1974, he returned to filmmaking one more time to produce Pete Walker's grizzly cannibal movie *Frightmare*. Thus, the producer of *Witchfinder General*, probably the most discussed and interesting British horror film of the 1960s, linked up with the producer-director of the most thematically interesting British horror films of the 1970s.

Peter Walker was a former stand-up comedian from a show business family who got into movie directing via same route as Tony Tenser: softcore sexploitation pictures cheerfully pushing the edges of the censorship restrictions of their day. Walker also knew how to make a film look good on a small budget, one of his secrets from the start being to hire the best actors he could afford. Classically trained character actor Derek Aylward appeared in early Walker sexploitation movies such as *School for Sex* (1969) and proved an enthusiastic participant, being surrounded by half naked women all day proving a compensation for his very small fee.

Walker was keen to break out of making sex films, his first step being *Cool it Carol* (1970), a comedy-drama with copious amounts of nudity in which naïve young couple Janet Lynn and Robin Asquith try their luck in London and become involved in the sex industry. The London portrayed here is determinedly unglamorous in a way not seen since Michael Reeves' *The Sorcerers*, and the effect is, whether by accident or design, somewhat melancholic. This was Robin Asquith's introduction to the British softcore sex movie, a genre we would bestride like a pimply-bottomed colossus four years later when his starring role in *Confessions of a Window Cleaner* became a huge success.

Cool it Carol was a good-looking film, the first feature photographed by Peter Jessop, who would go on to become Walker's regular cinematographer for most of the director's career. Another newcomer to full-length films was writer Murray Smith, who would work on several other Pete Walker films but is best known for his television work, including creating the television series *Strangers* and its follow-up *Bullman*. *Cool it Carol* was followed up by a crime thriller, *Man of Violence* (1971) which is quite good fun within its limits and was attractively photographed on location in Walker's native Brighton.

Brighton locations were also featured in Walker's next film, *Die Screaming Marianne* (1971), but most of the film was shot on the Algarve in Portugal. This was a very strange film with a Murray Smith plot involving two sisters, an inheritance, and murder that, in the finished film, borders on incoherence. Relations between the younger members of the cast and the director were apparently somewhat fraught, but the film, as ever with a Pete Walker production, is filled with talented and well-known actors. Susan George stars alongside sitcom star Barry Evans (who had made a big impression a couple of years earlier in the film *Here We Go Round the Mulberry Bush*) and a painfully thin-looking Judy Huxtable, almost unrecognisable even from her appearance in *Scream and Scream Again* the previous year. Always fond of using reliable old pros, Walker cast Leo Genn in the key role of the Judge, his performance proving one of the highlights of a rather eccentric film.

Some parts of *Die Screaming Marianne* were very Hitchcockian in tone, while other parts, perhaps with hindsight, suggested that the direction of travel in Walker's films was heading towards horror. Walker continued making sex-themed films in this period, including *The Four Dimensions of Greta* (1972), a sex comedy, again written by Murray Smith, which holds the distinction of being Britain's first film to be shot in 3-D.

The Flesh and Blood Show, released in the UK in October 1972, continued Walker's experiments with 3-D and saw a more decisive move towards horror. Writer Alfred Shaughnessy (who had directed *Cat Girl* back in 1957) came up with a script that was at heart a version of Agatha Christie's *And Then There Were None*, updated with higher levels of violence and a quite incredible amount of gratuitous full-frontal nudity. As ever, an excellent cast was assembled with Robin Asquith returning alongside Luan Peters, who had appeared in *Man of Violence*. New blood was added including Ray Brooks and Patrick Barr, who would become part of the unofficial stock company appearing in future Pete Walker films. As with most of Walker's films, *The Flesh and Blood Show* was shot entirely on location, in this case in the coastal resort of Cromer, largely on a theatre on the resort's pier. The story involved a group of young, horny actors hired to take part in a semi-improvised stage show in a creepy, deserted theatre by a mysterious impresario. Members of the cast are murdered until a terrible secret regarding the theatre's wartime past is discovered in an extended flashback sequence, which original audiences saw in 3-D.

This was followed up by *Tiffany Jones* (1973), which again featured Walker's fellow Brightonian Ray Brooks, this time alongside Anouska Hempel in the lead role. *Tiffany Jones* was a comic strip comedy based, for once, on an actual comic strip that featured the adventures of the eponymous heroine, a young fashion model. The strip ran from 1964 to 1977, beginning in the *Daily Sketch* and transferring to the *Daily Mail* after that newspaper ceased publication in 1971.

Causing Trouble at the *House of Whipcord*

None of the above suggested the fireworks that were to follow when Pete Walker and David McGillivray began their film partnership. *House of Whipcord* began as a project to be written by Alfred Shaughnessy, but he was forced to withdraw when production was bought forward on the latest series of ITV's hit TV series *Upstairs Downstairs*, on which he was story editor and chief writer. Instead, David McGillivray was drafted in to produce the final script, which began one of the most fascinating collaborations in seventies cinema.

Pete Walker was a kind of one-man show, producing, directing, and arranging finance for his pictures himself, which meant that he remained somewhat semi-detached from the mainstream of the British movie business—or what was left of it by 1974. In its turn, the movie business was happy to keep Walker at arm's length. This meant that by the time of *House of Whipcord*, Walker, with the willing assistance of David McGillivray, had the twin aims of producing movies that would attract an audience while also causing trouble and rubbing people up the wrong way.

This meant making films that engaged with issues of the day. This had the practical advantage that illustrating points of social importance allowed the films to be given a somewhat easier ride by the censors. *House of Whipcord* was widely read as poking grim fun at the moralisers and censorship advocates personified by the hectoring form of Mary Whitehouse. Her National Viewers and Listeners Association, with its roots in evangelical Christianity, protested against what they saw as the permissive society being portrayed on screen. Amused that his film had been read in this way, particularly by Secretary of the British Board of Film Censors Stephen Murphy, Walker added the following dedication to the opening credits of *House of Whipcord*: 'This film is dedicated to those who are disturbed by today's lax moral codes and who equally await the return of capital and corporal punishment'.

The film opens (in difficult to see day-for-night shots) as a traumatised young woman is picked up by a truck driver on a rainy night. We then flash back to how she got into this position, and we learn that she is young French fashion model Ann-Marie De Vernay (played by Penny Irving) who has been picked up at a party by the splendidly diabolical-looking Mark E.

Desade (Robert Tayman from Hammer's *Vampire Circus*). Instead of the kind of action that Walker would have presented in *The Four Dimensions of Greta*, however, Desade takes his date to an old house that turns out to be a private prison, whose owners are dedicated to punishing young women who have broken the moral codes they have laid down—Ann-Marie has recently been arrested for taking part in a nude photo shoot in a local park.

This horrifying establishment operates a three strikes rule: if an inmate breaks the prison rules once, they are put into solitary confinement; for a second infraction, they are stripped naked and whipped; and for a third breaking of the rules, the inmate is executed by hanging. The prison is run by Margaret Wakehurst (a ferocious performance by Barbara Markham), a former prison governor dismissed for brutality, and the blind, dementia-struck former high court judge Justice Bailey. The latter is played by Walker regular Patrick Barr, a mainstay of low-budget British film production since the 1930s days of quota quickies. Bailey hardly knows what is going on around him and is used to rubber stamp the decisions of the homicidally vindictive Wakehurst, who persecutes Ann-Marie because she reminds her of a young French woman, the death of whom ruined her career.

Effective though Barr and Markham are, the star turn is Head Warden Walker, played to icy perfection by Sheila Keith. This late-middle-aged Aberdeen-raised actress was previously best known for comedic roles, and she used the comedian's fearlessness to throw herself enthusiastically into a run of sadistic roles in Walker's movies, becoming something of a talisman for his productions. In *Whipcord*, her character smartly sums up the hypocrisy of the prison authorities, promising to Ann-Marie that she will 'Make [her] ashamed of [her] body' while simultaneously thoroughly enjoying stroking said body.

House of Whipcord is basically an attempt at a British version of the woman in prison pictures that were popular around this time thanks to the popularity of *The Big Doll House*, which took over $10 million on its 1971 release, which was pretty good going for a movie that cost $125,000 to make. *Whipcord* also represents Pete Walker's final break with sex films—despite the film's advertising being aimed at the tits and whips audience, the film presents a bare minimum of nudity and flagellation. His film's sympathies are solidly on the side of the abused female prisoners, who are presented in unglamorous fashion.

At a time when popular cinema was beginning the process of being overrun with right-wing urban vengeance fantasies—*Dirty Harry* received its British release in March 1972, while *Death Wish* was released in the UK in October 1974—it is interesting to note that a film such as *House of Whipcord*, sold on its perceived sex and violence, was able to act as a stinging, brutal corrective. Walker claims in interviews that his priority was to make profitable exploitation pictures as quickly as possible, but it remains difficult to believe that such a skilled director was unaware of the powerful subtext of his own films.[1]

Suburban Cannibals and Killer Priests

House of Whipcord was very successful at the box office, and Walker and McGillivray immediately began to plan a sequel, with the writer suggesting the subject matter of cannibalism. *Frightmare* was the result, with Sheila Keith boosted up the cast list to co-starring status in a film that can lay claim to being the most grimly deranged film to be made in Britain during the 1970s.

Today, *Frightmare* has long since attained the status of cult classic, but on its release in December 1974, the film completely failed to match the performance of its predecessor. There are several possible reasons for this. Firstly, 1974 saw the height of the IRA's campaign of terrorism with the Christmas of 1974 seeing London suffer a series of bomb attacks. A night out at the pictures suddenly dropped down the list of priorities for many people.

A second factor was that the film had less obviously exploitable aspects than its predecessor. While the British poster for *House of Whipcord* accentuated the grim horror of the film, the American release poster is something of an exploitation classic ('The story of a strange hobby and its victims, whose only crime was to be young and beautiful!'). For an exploitation movie, particularly one directed by Pete Walker, *Frightmare* lacks sex to such an extent that no publicity department in the world would have the cheek to advertise it with a girl in a bikini.

What the poster presents instead is the film's key image: a deranged, grinning Sheila Keith aiming a blood-soaked electric drill at the viewer. Some, though not all, British newspaper reviewers were outraged by *Frightmare* and made sure to tell their readers in no uncertain terms how disgusted they were. Pete Walker was delighted by this turn of events and filled half of the poster space with excerpts headed by the tag line: 'Dare you see the film that shocked the critics?'

Sheila Keith played the central role in the film of Dorothy Yates, a tarot card reader who had been locked up in a mental institution two decades earlier along with her husband Edmund (Rupert Davies) after being convicted of multiple charges of murder and cannibalism. With the pair now pronounced cured and, in the words of psychiatrist Gerald Flood 'as sane as you or I', we all know it is just a matter of time before Dorothy begins her murderous activities once more. The film is, as much as anything, about suburban horrors created by the ultimate dysfunctional family, as Dorothy murders with various household objects anyone who comes through her door. Edmund assumes an ever more sad countenance as he realises his beloved wife has started murdering again—Rupert Davies' expressive face a study in resigned horror.

Davies may not have relished appearing in low-budget horror pictures, roles he was forced to accept after his starring role in the BBC's 1960s *Maigret* television series left him hopelessly typecast. Yet he always gave his best, and with *Maigret* today a faded memory due to a lack of repeat screenings, it is these humane, sympathetic performances for which the actor is best remembered.

Frightmare is, to this writer at least, a difficult film to love. Compared to other Pete Walker movies it lacks well-constructed suspense sequences and the overall effect is extremely grim and nihilistic. It also lacks the satirical edge of *House of Whipcord*, save for a few half-hearted swipes at what it portrays as a complacent psychiatric establishment. The film comes across as technically proficient—with one exception, which we will come to later, Walker always put together good-looking movies—but lacking heart.

Walker and McGillivray's next film, *House of Mortal Sin*, addressed these issues, and if it did not prove to be Pete Walker's biggest hit, it remains this author's favourite of their pictures. *House of Mortal Sin* was known as some point in production as *The Confessional*, which eventually became the films alternate title. The *House of...* name suits the film quite well though, and helps forms a loose connection to *House of Whipcord*. The idea this time was to break boundaries and cause friction by presenting a sexually repressed, multiple-murdering Catholic priest. On the film's release in February 1976, however, Walker and McGillivray found that pretty well nobody was shocked by this idea and the film totally failed to create the same level of attention that *House of Whipcord* and *Frightmare* had.

The film did prove somewhat difficult to find a suitable actor for its lead role of Father Xavier Meldrum. Peter Cushing turned down the part and a host of late-middle-aged character actors were considered from Harry Andrews to Stewart Granger. In the end, perhaps reflecting what a hot potato the part was considered, the character actor, writer, and director Anthony Sharp was cast. Sharp was a capable performer, but one who had never got within a mile of a movie leading role in a career that stretched back to 1938. Despite his lack of star power, Sharp was an experienced and skilled player and a good fit for the role. His stock in trade in his screen career was playing authority types such as politicians and military officers, which suited *House of Mortal Sin*'s theme of a killer who can act with impunity because of the authority and trust his office creates.

McGillivray's script (from Pete Walker's story) is well-constructed, representing perhaps the writer's best work in the horror field. Walker, having saved a few quid by being unable to attract a star name in the lead role, was able to attract a very talented supporting case. Susan Penhaligon, about to become a well-known television name via the series *A Bouquet of Barbed Wire*, plays heroine Jenny, upset over the breakdown of her relationship with the loutish Terry (Stewart Bevan, who audiences previously saw an awful lot of in the nudity-filled flashback scenes of *The Flesh and Blood Show*). She has the misfortune to enter the confessional box of Father Meldrum, who seems rather too interested in learning the details of her sexual activities with Terry. To make matters worse, Meldrum has recorded the conversation and attempts to blackmail Jenny, threatening to reveal that she has had an abortion.

The other major cast members include the excellent Norman Eshley (previously seen in Richard Fleisher's 1971 blind girl in peril film *See No Evil*) as a youngish Catholic priest who falls in love with Jenny's sister Vanessa, played by the former Jessica Van Helsing and Pete Walker regular Stephanie Beacham. Another favourite of Walker's returned as Father Meldrum's sour-faced, one-eyed housekeeper Miss Brabazon, which saw Sheila Keith's return. Here she gives a performance of range and, at times, warmth despite the hateful nature of a character who tortures Meldrum's elderly mother.

The script sees Meldrum use the objects of his priestly faith to kill—a burning censer, rosary beads, and, in a very well-done touch, poisoned sacramental bread. Part of the impulse was beyond doubt to make each murder more potentially shocking and offensive than the last, but *House of Mortal Sin* remains a very solidly constructed thriller/horror movie, featuring some of Walker's most stylishly shot sequences.

Artistically, this was to be the high-watermark of Walker and McGillivray's work, and in November 1976, their final picture together was released, a misbegotten attempt at a Hitchcockian horror movie entitled *Schizo*. The film is a genuine attempt to do something different and expand what the Walker films were doing. This makes sense as *House of Mortal Sin* demonstrated that there were a finite number of ways of shocking people without simply upping the violence levels to an extent where censorship restrictions became a real problem. Also, Walker's ability to produce a polished product for very little money had finally got him noticed, even if the higher reaches of the British filmmaking establishment proved unwelcoming—*Schizo* was distributed by Hollywood major Warner Brothers.

The film starts off as quite an interesting psychological thriller in the manner of Hitchcock's darker works. Lynne Frederick stars as Samantha, a young woman mentally scarred by memories of her mother's brutal murder who finds herself pursued by the hulking, sad-faced Jack Watson. Watson keeps putting reminders of her mother's stabbing in Samantha's way, including placing a huge, bloody knife by the cake at her wedding. Meanwhile, people around Samantha are being murdered.

This all reads promisingly, but *Schizo* loses its way disastrously. After a bright opening, the narrative starts to meander and lose focus until, finally, characters start getting bumped off to retain audience interest. John Fraser, who had starred in Roman Polanski's *Repulsion* a decade earlier, is a welcome presence as Samantha's psychiatrist friend Leonard. It is something of a shame when he is killed in his own car while waiting at traffic lights, in a sequence that steals outrageously from *The Ipcress File*. To pull things further off track, Samantha goes to see a medium recommended by her housekeeper Queenie Watts, who turns out to be an actual medium, eyes bulging out like grey fried eggs when she is possessed by spirits. Things go downhill still further from here on until a bloody climax, which is more likely to provoke giggles than gasps of horror.

Walker and McGillivray's working relationship did not survive the making of *Schizo*, on which the director called in Murray Smith to do rewrites. McGillivray continued writing horror scripts, however, moving on to working on the even lower budgeted work of Norman J. Warren, which we shall come to later. Pete Walker, meanwhile, moved on to his own next horror project, *The Comeback*, which was released in the UK in June 1978. This would be his largest-scale project to this date, featuring international singing star Jack Jones as pop star Nick Cooper, who is making a comeback after years out of the spotlight due to a failed marriage.

His manager, Webster Jones (David Doyle, between seasons on *Charlie's Angels*, on which he played the regular role of Bosley), arranges to have Cooper stay in a huge old manor house staffed by an elderly couple (Sheila Keith and Bill Owen) in order to work on his lyrics and vocals in a studio especially set up there. Cooper is kept awake at night by strange sounds from somewhere in the house, and he does not know that his ex-wife has been horribly murdered by a mysterious figure in a dress and rubber mask, her body decomposing at his London apartment. As Cooper develops a close relationship with Jones' assistant (Pamela Stephenson, around a year before *Not the Nine O'Clock News* made her a major comedy star) he begins to doubt his sanity as people close to him start to disappear and he begins to see horrible sights in the house which then vanish.

The Comeback lacks the neo-Hitchcockian visual flourishes of Pete Walker's best work, but it is far from a disaster, being tightly plotted, good looking, and consistently interesting. The film is of particular interest for the way it plays with gender roles. The whole story is a sort of gender-reversed version of a traditional gothic tale in which a male protagonist finds himself in a scary old house with secrets in the attic (shades of *Jane Eyre*). In another reversal of traditional roles, the reason singing star Nick has not made an album in six years because his wife had him stop work when they got married. Among the suspects is Nick's creepy, sexist musical assistant who shows instant hostility towards Pamela Stephenson's Linda in the manner of a masculine variation of *Rebecca*'s Mrs Danvers. Finally, the film presents the killer as a possible cross-dresser in a lacy black dress, rubber mask, and wig for no real reason other than to disguise the identity of the murderer.

To throw a spoiler into the discussion, another character is revealed to be a secret cross-dresser (or possibly transgender), which turns out to be a red herring but is a scene that stays in the memory. Once it is revealed that this character is not the murderer, what remains is a cameo portrait of someone unable to reveal their true selves and suffering heartbreak as a result, which is an unusually humane attitude for any film of the era to take. Other examples of the era are generally unpleasant portrayals such as the killers in *Freebie and the Bean* (1974) and *Dressed to Kill* (1980).

The Comeback also benefits from being intelligently constructed. To make up for only having one murder in the opening hour, the film keeps returning to the body, allowing us to see it in various stages of decomposition. The idea works better in practice than it reads on the printed page and also serves as a visual indication of the passing of time. Marred only by a sudden and silly climactic scene, the film shows, despite the gory murder at its centre, Walker gravitating towards a more traditional style of horror.

Keen to try something different, Walker, with his writers Murray Smith and Michael Armstong (who, back in 1970, had written and directed *Mark of the Devil*), came up the following year with *Home Before Midnight*, a straight drama about a successful rock songwriter who finds himself in legal trouble when it turns out that his new girlfriend is aged fourteen. Decently made, this is a very odd film with an extremely troubling attitude towards sexual activity between adults and minors. The film seems to be broadly on male protagonist James Aubrey's side, and portrays characters we are supposed to think are aged fourteen in leering full-frontal nude scenes.

At this point, Pete Walker retired from the movie business, moving into property development instead. Opportunities in British exploitation filmmaking were becoming ever more difficult to find as the introduction of affordable home video ate further into a cinema audience which had been shrinking since the mid-1950s. He was tempted back when, for the first time in his life, Walker was approached to direct a film for someone else.

That someone else was Cannon Films. Cannon had originally been set up in the US in 1967 as a producer and distributor of low budget, mainly exploitation films. Along the way, they scored one breakout hit, the 1970 John Avildsen film *Joe*, which gained an Oscar nomination for Best Original Screenplay. By the end of the decade, the company was close to bankruptcy and was bought up by Israeli cousins Menahem Golan and Yoram Globus, who had been in the movie business, initially in Israel, since the early 1960s. In 1969, Golan had directed and co-written the Norman Wisdom comedy *What's Good for the Goose* for Tigon British. Having turned Cannon's finances around with its selection of grindhouse movies updated for the VHS generation, Golan and

Globus wanted to expand the company's UK operations and they asked Pete Walker to make a low budget horror movie for them.

Walker and Michael Armstrong came up with a SF horror story about an alien foetus, with the idea of causing mischief with a horror movie about abortion. Golan and Globus rejected the idea immediately, telling Walker in no uncertain terms that they wanted a good old fashioned horror film of the type Bela Lugosi and Boris Karloff used to make. Walker and Armstrong certainly gave the customer what they wanted, with an adaptation of Earl Derr Biggers' 1913 novel *Seven Keys to Baldpate*. The story was retitled *House of the Long Shadows*, meaning that Walker could finally claim to have made a *House of...* trilogy.

This was the seventh time the novel had been filmed, if one counts a 1946 TV version, but the first since 1947. This indicates that not only were the rights to the story cheap to obtain, but that Walker and Armstrong had decided to go all-out for nostalgia. They certainly succeeded in this, treating 1983 audiences to the first ever teaming of Christopher Lee, Peter Cushing, Vincent Price, and John Carradine. By this point, Carradine was seventy-seven years old and not in good health after a career that stretched back to being an unbilled extra in silent films of the 1920s. He was also, of course, one of the actors who played Count Dracula in the Universal Pictures horror film series, in *House of Frankenstein* (1944) and *House of Dracula* (1945).

The rest of the leading players were of a similar vintage, giving *House of the Long Shadows* the deliberate air of a tribute to an era now passed. Vincent Price was seventy-two, Peter Cushing was seventy, while Christopher Lee was a mere sixty-one years of age. What is remarkable is how much vim and energy Price, Cushing, and Lee put into their performances (sad to report that John Carradine did not have much energy left by this point in his career). Price hams it up gloriously, while Cushing puts together a fascinating, atypical characterisation of a frightened little man with a distinctive lisp. Christopher Lee demonstrates how much depth he had added to his screen performances over the years. He had always been perfectly capable of playing severe, humourless characters, and in years gone by, this is exactly what he would have delivered. Here you can see Lee's added confidence, range, and depth—a comparison to his performance in 1968's *Curse of the Crimson Altar* is quite instructive.

Sadly, *House of the Long Shadows* is a considerable disappointment. The plot involves a successful author (Desi Arnaz Jr) who accepts a bet with his publisher (an excellent Richard Todd) that he can write a novel in twenty-four hours in a creepy old house. Once there, he finds that the house is the ancestral home of the Grisbane brothers (Price, Lee, and Caradine) and their sister (Sheila Keith, naturally), all of whom turn up to interrupt Arnaz's work, along with the house's new owner Corrigan (Lee). Murder, of course, ensues.

The older members of the cast really give their all and it appears that a lot of fun was had on set, but the production looks so cheap that Pete Walker, who was more than capable of putting together suspense and horror sequences, is defeated.

House of the Long Shadows does serve a purpose, however, waving a fond farewell to both the Universal horrors of the 1930s and '40s and to the British horror boom. This had continued in various forms from the mid-1950s for twenty years, but was now a source of nostalgia itself. Pete Walker had carried the genre on when the studios that had made their name in horror, Hammer, Amicus, and Tigon British, had found it impossible to continue. Before the classic era of British horror was entirely extinguished, however, one more filmmaker emerged to produce some of the most extreme and quirky productions of the mid-to-late 1970s—Norman J. Warren.

9
Norman J. Warren: Horrors from Beyond

Born in 1942 in London, Norman J. Warren was a young film buff, stricken by polio as a child. Having made his own short films, he entered the film industry in 1959, working as a runner, the lowest rung on the filmmaking ladder, but one in which an ambitious and clever young man can gain a working knowledge of all levels of productions. He worked on films such as *The Millionairess* and *The Dock Brief*, while working hard on making his own opportunities. In 1965, he wrote and directed the ten-minute short film *Fragment*, the credits for which showed that Warren was moving in some interesting circles. *Fragment* starred and was produced by actor Michael Craze, who would achieve fame the following year when he was cast in *Doctor Who* as the Doctor's companion Ben. Executive Producer on the film was Ronan O'Rahilly, the founder of the famous offshore pirate radio station Radio Caroline and later manager to George Lazenby; O'Rahilly is credited with giving Lazenby the disastrous advice to give up the role of James Bond after appearing in the 1969 production *On Her Majesty's Secret Service*. He also assisted Antony Balch, the future director of *Horror Hospital*, on his short film *Towers Open Fire* with William Burroughs.

The dialogue-free *Fragment* was a very smartly directed piece about a young women contemplating suicide after discovering that her boyfriend is married. It was clear from this that Warren really knew how to frame a shot and the film sounds fabulous thanks to a subtle jazz score by John Scott. As a direct result, he was hired to direct two sexploitation movies in 1968 and 1969. This was not a field in which Warren wished to remain, however, and instead he began the long process of putting together the funding to direct his own independent horror movie. Meanwhile, he worked as an editor and came close to getting a project off the ground for Amicus, and later a Vincent Price picture for AIP.

The eventual result of this activity was *Satan's Slave*, finally released in 1976 and produced for an initial investment of £15,000, the eventual cost being around £35,000 once deferred payments for equipment were included, though the film looked far more expensive.[1] This was written by Pete Walker's collaborator David McGillivray, and was, particularly in its export version, far more explicitly violent than anything Walker had attempted. Of course, this also meant that even in the heavily cut version released to British cinemas, it made the products of the declining Hammer and Amicus studios look like very mild fare indeed. The story sees Catherine (played by seventies British horror regular Candace Glendenning) being driven by her parents to see her uncle, Alexander (Michael Gough), a journey interrupted by an amusingly badly staged car crash that sees both parents die. This saw a lovely old Rover being driven by cinematographer Les Young (*in lieu* of a stunt driver) into a tree at around 4 mph. Alexander takes Catherine in to live at his enormous country house, where she meets his son, Stephen (Martin Potter), and his secretary, Frances (Barbara Kellerman), who share a disturbing, abusive relationship. Catherine discovers that she has a terrible fate in store if she cannot escape the house.

Satan's Slave was mainly filmed at Pirbright, Surrey, using the very same country house that had been used for *Virgin Witch*. To backtrack slightly, the rather interesting sex and violence epic *Virgin Witch,* based around a modern coven of witches, starred sisters Vicki and Ann Michelle along with the reliably excellent Patricia Haines, and had been filmed in 1972. It was directed by Ray Austin, the former stuntman and director on *The Avengers*. Such were the multitudes piling in to the British horror picture scene by his point that *Virgin Witch* had been written, of all people, by Hazel Adair, co-creator of the legendarily terrible Birmingham-set soap opera *Crossroads*, who also co-produced along with TV wrestling commentator Kent Walton. Sadly, it was almost the last feature film Patricia Haines would appear in— she made *The Fast Kill* for the notorious Anglo-Canadian director Lindsay Shonteff (whom you might recall from the excellent *Devil Doll* and amusingly incompetent *Curse of Simba*) at around the same time—before her death at the age of forty-five in February 1977.

By 1976, the going was considerably rougher for anyone wanting to make a British horror film (or indeed any other sort of British film), but *Satan's Slave* made a huge profit for its investors on its release in December of that year. The film looks like a much more expensive production than was actually the case, partly due to the attractive but cheap-to-use locations—the use of a huge country house is a great asset to anyone making a horror movie—and partially due to some excellent performances. Michael Gough as Uncle Alexander is a study in classy malevolence and Candace Glendenning, previously seen in 1972 in both *Tower of Evil* and Pete Walker's *The Flesh and Blood Show*, gives probably her best screen performance as Catherine. Also memorable is Barbara Kellerman as the abused Frances, landed with one of the worst employers in film history in the shape of Martin Potter's Stephen.

The success of the partly self-funded *Satan's Slave* had made Norman J. Warren a viable proposition as a movie director, able to attract funding. This was, however, in the straightened circumstances of the mid-1970s British film industry in a horror genre that had been worked almost to exhaustion by UK producers. Less than a year later, Warren's next production, *Prey*, was released. This was from a story by publicist Quinn Donoghue, but much of the film was written by Max Cuff, partially during shooting.[2] The shoot itself took a mere ten days, with post-production completed just five weeks later—an amazing achievement on a tiny budget.

Here, Warren entered interesting new territory for low-budget British horror of the era by taking on an SF-horror theme. An alien lifeform kills and takes over the body of Anders, played by Barry Stokes, whose previous career had included being part of the Skydiver submarine crew in Gerry Anderson's *UFO* back in 1970 and more recently in the title role of *The Ups and Downs of a Handyman* (1976), possibly the worst British sex comedy ever made, which was quite an achievement. He is taken in by a lesbian couple, played by Glory Annen and Sally Faulkner (previously been seen in 1974's *Vampyres*), the latter of whom is capable of murderous rages, but nothing on the same scale as the sharp-toothed, animalistic beast that Anders reverts to when he needs to feed.

There is clearly intelligence operating in Warren's work beyond just finding excuses to present sex and violence: *Prey* and *Satan's Slave* both feature couples where one party is domineering to the point of violent abuse. There was space in the narrative of *Prey* for a sequel, but this never happened. Instead, Norman J. Warren's 1978 release was the prosaically entitled *Terror*, which saw the return of writer David McGillivray. The central idea behind the film was hardly original, as the ancestors of a royal personage are struck by a curse laid by a witch he had burned at the stake in medieval times. A more original touch is that the series of bloody murders that punctuate the film begin after the screening of a movie based on the story.

Terror remains a fascinating curio for a few reasons: from the perspective of forty years in the future, it is interesting to see a British horror picture that reflects the changes of fashions that happened at this time. We are finally past the era of flared trousers and huge collars, as reflected not only by the wardrobe of the main cast members, but also by the presence of a very punky stripper featured in a sequence in a sex club. Considering that *Terror* is a film that exists in order to murder its characters in memorable ways, it is actually pretty good fun and quite visually arresting. It is certainly quite a thing to see the film's star James Aubrey being attacked by a huge mass of 35-mm film, which envelops him like some huge, tentacled monster.

The film was a deliberate tribute to the work of Dario Argento, in its hanging of the narrative on a series of spectacular, visually impressive murders, and an odd-dreamlike feel, which is not really meant to make conventional narrative sense. *Terror* is hardly in the same league as Argento's incredible *Suspiria* (1977), but Warren's intentions are certainly honourable. Instead of *Suspiria*'s setting of a girls' school, Warren and McGillivray largely set *Terror* in a film studio, which allows them to have some fun at the expense of the sex and horror exploitation film sector both were more than familiar with. As well as the horror picture at the centre of the plot, we also see the production of a spectacularly dreadful sex picture entitled 'Bathtime for Brenda'.

Starring the aforementioned James Aubrey, who must have been wondering what his career was coming to in a year when he also appeared in Pete Walker's *Home Before Midnight*, *Terror* gets full marks for being interesting, quirky, and at least trying to do something different. The film was also a box office hit, the number one film in the UK on its release, and also very popular with American audiences. This is more than can be said for Warren's next film, released in 1979 and released under the titles *Outer Touch* and *Spaced Out*. This bizarre SF sex comedy was mainly notable for using stock footage from Gerry Anderson's *Space: 1999*.

Warren seems to have had SF on his mind as a popular subject, as his directorial career reached a peak with the heavily *Alien*-influenced *Inseminoid* (1981). This was co-produced by Richard Gordon and was that old stager's final picture, making for a nice link back to the British SF-horrors such as *Fiend Without a Face* and *First Man into Space*, which he made in the late 1950s. £1 million was put together to make the film, with funding coming from the major Hong Kong studio Shaw Brothers, plus American and South African backers. This still represented a tiny amount of money for what *Inseminoid* was trying to achieve and the fact that a coherent and decent-looking film emerged was a major achievement.

In the far future, a group of astronauts and scientists are taking part in an archaeological expedition on a freezing, desolate planet. A force on the planet make a member of the expedition attack the others, then Sandy (Judy Geeson) is raped by a horrific alien creature, which results in her undergoing an extremely rapid pregnancy. Now with superhuman strength and entirely under the influence of the alien force, Sandy becomes cannibalistically murderous in protecting her unborn child.

Judy Geeson really throws herself into her part, impressively selling the concept of the put-upon, unwillingly impregnated mother to alien monsters with a uniquely intense performance that does her great credit. Some of other cast members are also very impressive, particularly Stephanie Beacham, who had racked up quite an impressive horror CV over the previous ten years, and Victoria Tennant. Rather less impressive are the American cast members recruited for the sake of international sales. Not to put too fine a point on it, Robin Clarke and Jennifer Ashley are absolutely terrible, especially in comparison to the array of British stage actors who fill the rest of the roles.

Somewhat unexpectedly, given the upward trajectory of his career and the profitable international release of *Inseminoid*, which was also popular as a VHS release, Norman J. Warren's career as a horror director virtually ended here. After making *Gunpowder* in 1986, a cheap and not all that cheerful comedy spy movie, he returned for one last attempt when he was approached to make *Bloody New Year* (1987), a sort of time-warp horror about a group of teens trapped on an island who find a hotel decked out for a new year's party. It is all a far cry from the cheap, effective horrors Warren had made in the 1970s, but it might just be the best horror film ever made on Barry Island. The movie business had changed almost out of recognition and it was becoming ever harder for independent producers to raise finance as major Hollywood studios were by now, in essence, making big budget exploitation films.

Norman J. Warren is a filmmaker to his bones and made documentaries and dramas for the BBC and other companies as well as commercials while continuing his efforts to get new productions financed. At time of writing, he has completed another film, this time a Chinese co-production, and is attempting to arrange distribution.

10

The Haunting of Harry Bromley Davenport

Harry Bromley Davenport's career in British horror films is short, and produced two films that could not be more different, one being one of the most bizarre and fondly remembered British movies of the decade among horror fans. Davenport's first film as writer-director was the little-seen 1976 feature *Whispers of Fear*, after which he adapted novelist Peter Straub's 1975 novel *Julia* for the screen, the finished screenplay being credited to Dave Humphries. Directed by Richard Loncraine, the film was completed in 1977 and released under the title *Full Circle*. It failed to get an American release for some years, before being rediscovered and retitled *The Haunting of Julia* for US release in 1981.

Although the film failed to attract a large audience under either title, *The Haunting of Julia* is an intelligent and well done film that is worth seeking out. Mia Farrow and Keir Dullea star as an American couple in England whose marriage breaks up after the accidental death of their daughter. As Farrow tries to rebuild her life in her new London home and begins a tentative romance with her neighbour, friendly long-haired lighting shop owner Tom Conti, her grief allows her to become haunted by the vengeful spirit of another child who died in the 1950s and people around her start to die in mysterious accidents.

The film is well cast and made with subtlety and intelligence, avoiding the sudden bangs to make audience members jump out of their seats so commonly use in more recent productions. Instead, attention is paid in both script and direction on keeping the audience guessing. Mia Farrow is excellent in the lead role, a far stronger and more independent figure than she had been at the start of the decade in Richard Fleischer's *Blind Terror*. In that film, she had been so annoyingly victim-y that one almost wished the knife-wielding maniac would find her. Keir Dullea, never the most expressive of performers, is dubbed by another actor, which does his performance no favours, but he is actually quite good as Farrow's unsympathetic, stuffed shirt ex-husband.

Davenport returned in 1982 with the extremely odd SF horror *Xtro*. Philip Sayer stars as Sam, a father who is abducted by aliens while in the garden of his farmhouse playing with his young son. Three years later, the alien presence returns to Earth, this time as a monstrous creature that kills a couple whose car collided with it. It then attacks and impregnates a young woman in her home, and in a touch reminiscent of *Inseminoid*, it results in a very rapid pregnancy, the subsequent birth revealing the fully grown Sam returned to Earth. Sam seeks his out his wife, Rachael (Maryam d'Abo), and son, Tony (Simon Nash), resulting in an extremely uncomfortable family drama as Rachael has moved on with her life and has a new boyfriend who is not exactly pleased at the missing husband's reappearance. In an extremely disturbing sequence, Sam abducts Tony and drinks his blood, imparting in the child special powers that he struggles to control. In one of the oddest and most memorable scenes in all of 1980s cinema, Tony produces a life-size, living version of his Action Man toy to kill a neighbour who has killed his pet snake.

Xtro is a very strange film and the proceedings from this point are much better seen than described. While in some respects it has similarities to *Inseminoid*, it is partially a twisted family drama, partially a particularly bloody body horror film, and partially a horrific reworking of the paternal alien visitor theme, which was at the centre of Steven Spielberg's *E.T.* Taken on its own terms, and provided the viewer is willing to overlook the occasional poor acting performance—Philip Sayer is excellent, however—or underfunded special effect, *Xtro* really works.

Harry Bromley Davenport subsequently moved to America, where he made a sequel to *Xtro* in 1990, but mainly worked outside of genre cinema, making music documentaries. His contribution to British horror history is idiosyncratic but very real: a very strange little film that is among the key productions of the 1980s.

11

Eurohorrors: Italy, Germany, and Spain

The 1970s saw the withdrawal of large-scale American funding from British film production, with the country generally seen as being far less fashionable to mainstream sensibilities. There were still European directors working within the horror genre who found Britain an attractive place to set their films.

In Germany, the long-running Edgar Wallace film series had continued to be set in England throughout the 1960s, while rarely looking anything other than Central European. There were exceptions, such as the Anglo-German co-productions *The Devil's Daffodil* (1961) shot at Shepperton in separate English and German-speaking versions with different leading actors and *The Trygon Factor* (1966) directed by Cyril Frankel, also at Shepperton in bright colour with a starry cast including Stewart Granger, Susan Hampshire, and Robert Morley. These were both whodunits, but the Wallace films veered increasingly into horror territory, and in 1969, they were being produced as Italian co-productions. The first of the Italian Wallace films, *A Double Face*, was directed by Riccardo Freda largely at Rome's Cinecitta Studios but with some location work featuring very recognisable Berkshire road signs.[1] The film was not a financial success and the series thereafter looked even more towards Italy, eventually abandoning the British settings altogether and throwing its lot in with the new wave of *giallo* horror mysteries.

These became a popular European genre with the enormous success of Dario Argento's *The Bird with the Crystal Plumage* in 1970, which made Argento's early reputation and was the first part of his 'animal trilogy' along with *Cat O'Nine Tails* (1971) and *Four Flies on Grey Velvet* (1972). For the rest of the 1970s murder mysteries featuring increasingly bloody and violent killings were a staple of European cinema release schedules. As their horror content increased, Argento, the director who had almost single-handedly created the genre, moved on to revolutionising the horror film with 1977's bizarre, dreamlike masterpiece *Suspiria*.

Among the first wave of *giallo* horror thrillers was *The Iguana with the Tongue of Fire* (1971), another Riccardo Freda picture, this time shot extensively in Dublin. A wonderful opportunity to see what the Irish capital looked like in the early '70s, the film also demonstrates just how violent these films very quickly became, with its opening scene of a woman having acid thrown in her face before her throat is cut. The sequence reads more horrific than it plays on screen, thanks to some truly laughable effects work. Freda himself was so unhappy with the finished product that he used a pseudonym, Willy Pareto, on the opening credits. The largely Italian cast featured one name familiar to fans of British horror (and also war) movies in the shape of Anton Diffring, Hammer's television Baron Frankenstein.

Spain

Spain had its own popular horror film industry in the 1970s, most famously the *Blind Dead* series of films about a murderous band of long-dead Knights Templar. The country even had its own horror superstar in the form of Paul Naschy, aka Jacinto Molina Alvarez, who played most of the classic horror movie roles during his career, but was most famous for his Wolf Man films. One of the best-known products of the '70s Spanish horror boom was *The Living Dead at Manchester Morgue* (1974), an Italian co-production mostly filmed in Italy, but featuring location footage shot in Cheadle, Manchester, and in the Derbyshire countryside. This British-set zombie movie was released under a confusing array of titles during 1974 and 1975 and was directed by the Spaniard Jorge Grau, responsible the previous year for the splendidly luridly titled *The Legend of Blood Castle*. Grau's film was clearly influenced by George A. Romero's *Night of the Living Dead*, the 1968 film that had revived the long-dormant zombie film genre. *The Living Dead at Manchester Morgue* featured levels of violence and gore that took it out of contention for a wide British release, but which sold well in continental Europe and helped ensure that the film has remained an object of fascination to British horror fans. The sole 'name' actor in the mainly Italian cast for international audiences was the sixty-year-old American character actor Arthur Kennedy, who spent most of his career from the late 1960s appearing in various genres of popular Italian cinema. Even the film's star, Ray Lovelock, was born in Rome, though this was his real name, as his father was English.

A more sustained run of low-budget British horror films were made in Britain in the early 1970s by the anglophile Spanish director Jose Ramon Larraz. Although they were made with Danish money, Larraz filmed his first two features, *Whirlpool* (1970) and *Deviation* (1971), in England. Perhaps because of their Danish funding, these films were a heady, if grubby looking, mixture of drama, bloody murder, and enormous amounts of nudity (to be fair, the murky available prints of these films available for viewing probably do not fairly represent the work of Larraz and his cinematographers).

Both feature his regular leading man of the period, English actor Karl Lanchbury, who was to feature in four of Larraz's five British horror movies. Lanchbury generally played unhinged killers with pronounced misogynistic tendencies—his sleazy photographer Theo in *Whirlpool* stages rape scenes in the woods with an entirely unwilling female victim. *Deviation* certainly lives up to his title, with Lanchbury returning as a young man obsessed with embalming who is part of a sex and murder gang. The recurring visual motif of Larraz's British films is murder during or after the act of sex, usually committed by one of the sexual participants.

Despite the salacious material and some terribly wooden acting in these initial two films, there is some evidence of an interesting filmmaker trying to get out from beneath the crushing weight of nihilism. Also, it is hard to completely dislike a film with dialogue such as 'No one's going to make you eat a lizard if you really don't want to'—one is occasionally reminded that Larraz's ear for dialogue is not that of a native English speaker. After returning to Spain for a period, in 1974, Larraz made the two British films on which his reputation as a director rests: *Vampyres* and *Symptoms*.

Symptoms surprised everyone, probably including its own makers, when it was chosen as one of the official British entries to the Cannes Film Festival. Angela Pleasence brings her uniquely off-kilter screen persona to the role of Miss Helen, a young woman living alone in a rambling old house who takes in female lovers. The latest of these is Anne (the excellent Lorna Heilbron), who finds herself increasingly worried by a strange presence in the house. This could be creepy handyman Peter Vaughan, or it could be Helen, who is becoming increasingly unhinged but hiding it from the few people she interacts with.

Although there are occasional scenes of gore, this represents Larraz at his most subtle, creating a languidly oppressive atmosphere that turns into a 1970s variation on Roman Polanski's *Repulsion*. The whole house of cards might easily have collapsed without a strong central actress, but fortunately Angela Pleasence gives an absolute *tour de force* performance as Helen, increasingly tortured and losing touch with reality but never losing the sympathy of the audience.

Vampyres took the creepy old house location and offbeat sensibility of *Symptoms* and added huge amounts of violence, nudity, and lesbianism—clearly Larraz was not planning on a career in arthouse cinema in the wake of his Cannes success. Naturally, this meant that while the critically lauded *Symptoms* lapsed into obscurity for many years, *Vampyres* almost instantly became a cult classic. This is not to denigrate *Vampyres*, which remains an interesting and intelligent work in which not everything is explained to the audience. The plot is quite simple, as two female vampires, Fran (Marianne Morris) and Miriam (Anulka Dziubinska), lure passing male motorists to their large house (Oakley Court, home to many Hammer films, which was at this point derelict and available for any film company to use). We never see how they have become physically dependent on blood—in the opening sequence, the pair are shot to death in their bed during sex, which is hardly the traditional method of creating vampires. A couple of holidaymakers staying in a nearby caravan observe the strange goings on and are drawn in to Fran and Anulka's world of sex and death.

A far more direct film than *Symptoms*, *Vampyres* still manages to be full of subtle touches among the blood and breasts and is a world away from the crude exploitation of Hammer's *The Vampire Lovers*, despite comping across at times like a softcore porn film (it was heavily cut on its original UK release). Fran and Miriam's existence is suffused with sadness and desperation, and as with Angela Pleasence in *Symptoms*, Larraz never has us totally lose sympathy with the vampire pair.

It is a pity to report that the unique mixture of art and sleaze represented by the British horror career of Jose Larraz basically ended here. His horror career largely relocated to Spain, though he did make two films that were widely shown in British cinemas (if not widely seen—audiences were getting sparse in the late 1970s). One of his Spanish softcore dramas was dubbed and charmingly retitled *The Violation of the Bitch*, doing the rounds of the seedier type of British cinema in 1979 on a double bill with the Mary Millington sex film *Playbirds*. Bizarrely, Larraz's final British film was a cheap attempt at a female James Bond adventure, *The Golden Lady*. This was another 1979 release complete with a disco-funk soundtrack, a theme song by The Three Degrees, a terrible script, and a budget that did not live up to the ambitions of the film's story.

Larraz continued working into the early 1990s, largely operating in the exploitation end of the Spanish film industry, sometimes using the pseudonym Joseph Braunstein, and occasionally making more artistically minded work for Spanish television. He died in 2013 at the age of eighty-four, two years before a Spanish-made remake of *Vampyres*, his best-known film by far, was released.

12

American-British Gothic Horror

By the late 1960s, British producers of horror films were under threat from the same source as every other British movie maker, the US, and this manifested itself in two ways. Firstly, a new approach to horror was developing, which used the tropes of the gothic horror tradition, but put them into a contemporary American context. Roman Polanski, who had begun his English-language film career at Compton Films in 1965 with the claustrophobic horror of *Repulsion*, used some of the same themes of mounting paranoia in an apartment setting in his 1968 breakthrough American hit *Rosemary's Baby*. This added the new ingredient of Satanism, which had also been used increasingly in British horror film plotting, most notably in Hammer's *The Witches* (1966) and *The Devil Rides Out* (1967).

This pointed the way forward for the horror genre, with the enormous success of *The Exorcist* following in 1973 and launching a new wave of gothic horrors. On top of this came group of new horror directors from outside the mainstream of American cinema whose productions suddenly made what the likes of Hammer had been making seem positively cosy and parochial. The future of the entire horror genre, in retrospect, can be seen to have been created with films such as *The Last House on the Left* (1972) and *The Texas Chainsaw Massacre* (1974), intense contemporary horrors that took the blood and horror that audiences craved and placed them into an American setting at a time when US audiences were far more interested in America than they might have been ten years previously in seeing films set in England or Italy.

These contemporary set horrors tended not to be supernatural in nature. The monsters in these films were not the suave, fanged Dracula or the grey-faced manmade Frankenstein monster, but looked like ordinary people, or perhaps had no face at all. If the face of 1960s horror was Christopher Lee with sharp teeth and widow's peak, the faces of the genre in the 1970s and '80s were blank: Leatherface from *The Texas Chainsaw Massacre*, Jason

Voorhees in his hockey mask from the *Friday the 13th* films, or the literally blank face of the Michael Myers character from the *Halloween* films.

Back in 1968, British horror producers had another emerging problem. Earlier British horror films were proving popular on television, but they had such serious censorship problems and had to be so severely edited by network censors that extra scenes had to be shot in order to ensure the resulting film would remain at a useable length. Films including Hammer's *The Evil of Frankenstein*, *Kiss of the Vampire*, and *The Phantom of the Opera* had extra scenes shot in America that did not advance the plot but padded the film's length.

Occasionally, a young American director would come to Britain to make a horror film of his own. Chicago native Gary Sherman was directing adverts and other commercial films on London when he managed to get backing for his debut feature film *Death Line*, which was released in 1972. This revolves around the clever and unusual idea that London's underground system contains a group of cannibals descended from workers trapped after a cave-in when the tunnels were being constructed. The last remaining member of this tribe has been living by capturing and eating commuters, but attracts the interest of the authorities when he kills a senior official at the Ministry of Defence. Sherman certainly gets the most from his meagre budget, including a visually stunning ten-minute slow-tracking shot around the lair of the cannibalistic killer known as The Man. Hugh Armstrong gives an intensely moving performance in the role, which is especially remarkable considering his dialogue consists of the words 'Mind the doors', the only words he knows. The mood of what could have been an unbearably bleak film is lifted by the welcome appearance of Donald Pleasence, who carries the film's narrative weight as a sarcastic and mordantly amusing police inspector investigating disappearances and killings on the underground.

One solution was that American producers began to make their own gothic horrors in Britain, cutting out middlemen such as Hammer and Amicus and making an end result that used British studios, technicians, and actors, but which conformed entirely to American specifications. One of the earliest producers to use this approach was Dan Curtis, the producers of *Dark Shadows*. This was a daytime television soap opera that was suffused in a gothic atmosphere from its very beginning in June 1966. The series became a pop culture phenomenon when, ten months later, on the verge of cancellation and with nothing to lose, Curtis and his writers added vampire Barnabas Collins to the cast. *Dark Shadows* lasted until 1971, producing 1,245 episodes and two feature films before finally running out of steam.

The literate and talented Curtis was keen on producing other gothic horror tales, and in 1968, he produced a splendid version of Robert Louis Stevenson's *The Strange Case of Dr Jekyll and Mr Hyde* in Canada but with such a strong British cast that it earns a mention here. This was shot on videotape, which is probably a major reason why this version is today rarely seen, and was directed by Charles Jarrott, a British director who would spend most of the rest of his career in America. A top-flight British cast was assembled, including Billie Whitelaw and Denholm Elliott, in support of American star Jack Palance, who gives a performance of great power and subtlety. The burly actor, with his unique, high-cheekboned and broken-nosed physiognomy, was a natural for the monstrous Mr Hyde, but his gentle, conflicted Henry Jekyll is a revelation and this production is ripe for rediscovery.

Palance and Curtis reteamed in 1973 for a new version of *Dracula*, this time shot on 35-mm film in England with Curtis directing. The film was made to be screened by CBS as a television special in the US and to be shown as a feature film in Europe. EMI film distributors, who had been backing Hammer's productions until early 1973, were happy to handle this production at precisely the time in which they had lost confidence in Hammer under that studio's new ownership of Michael Carreras.

Curtis's *Dracula* is a handsomely mounted production, benefitting from a degree of location photography that would have been outside Hammer's financial reach, the production travelling to Yugoslavia and (for the first time in a production of Stoker's story) Whitby. An excellent cast was also assembled, including Nigel Davenport as Van Helsing and Simon Ward, who got his first credited movie role in 1969's *Frankenstein Must Be Destroyed*. Palance is both fierce and tortured in the title role, which makes efforts to position the Count as a ruthless but tragic anti-hero.

Rather less worthy was a bizarrely misconceived musical version of *Dr Jekyll and Mr Hyde*, shot on videotape at Shepperton and premiered on American television network NBC in March 1973. This had a chance of working—after all, *Sweeney Todd* would later make a highly successful stage musical. Talented artists were assembled, with none other than Lionel Bart, the writer of *Oliver!* providing the music and lyrics. The cast is variable, with Donald Pleasence providing good value as Fred Smudge, a sneak thief employed by Hyde, and Stanley Holloway as Jekyll's butler Poole was a reliable old hand at this kind of stuff. Even Susan George proves more than capable as Anne, a music hall singer Hyde keeps locked up in an apartment.

Bart's songs are by some distance not his best work, but the factor that sinks the whole enterprise is a wildly miscast Kirk Douglas in the lead role(s). He had the physical menace Hyde requires, but at the age of fifty-six, he was far too old for the role of Jekyll as written here. Screenwriter Sherman Yellen appears to have envisaged a much younger man for the role of the recently engaged to be married Jekyll. Interestingly, Yellen's next script was for a musical version of Dickens' *Great Expectations*, made by Lew Grade's ITC. This time, wiser heads prevailed and the songs were cut from the film prior to its delivery to NBC Television in 1974.

Also in 1973 came *Frankenstein: The True Story*, a mammoth production made by Universal as a two-part, three-hour television 'event' and shot at Pinewood Studios. Universal certainly threw the kitchen sink at this one, the production values of which made Hammer's *Frankenstein and the Monster from Hell*, which lay unreleased on the shelf at distributors EMI, look more than somewhat poverty stricken. The script was commissioned from Christopher Isherwood—newly famous after many years writing in relative obscurity thanks to the 1971 hit movie *Cabaret*, based on his *Berlin Stories*—and his domestic partner Don Bachardy.

Publicity for *Frankenstein, The True Story* made great play of its being a faithful adaptation of Mary Shelley's original novel, to the extent of making a short publicity film in which top-billed James Mason is filmed at her grave. It was not her real grave and the Isherwood/Bachardy script veers from Shelly quite considerably, but compared most other versions, it is remarkably close to her spirit and, to a degree, her plot. Director Jack Smight assembled an absolutely stellar cast of British thespians, many of whom were stars of another era entirely. To further impress audiences, names appearing in the film, such as Michael Wilding and Margaret Leighton, are listed at great length at the production's opening. The action is shifted from the traditionally unspecific middle-Europe to Regency period England, and Smight makes a positive fetish of the English locations used by his ravishing-looking production, which is matched by some very impressive large-scale interior sets

So much about the production is so splendid that it is sad to report that Leonard Whiting makes an uncharismatic Victor Frankenstein, which is especially frustrating as he spends much of the film opposite two actors performing at the absolute top of their game. The first of the two parts is dominated by David McCallum as Henry Clerval, who acts as mentor to the young Doctor Frankenstein in his attempts to construct a human being. In the second half, Mason takes over as Dr Polidori, a character not in Shelley's novel and who is similar to *Bride of Frankenstein*'s Dr Pretorius—in a nice literary reference, the character is named after John Polidori, who was present at the famous soirée at which Mary Shelley first conceived the story of *Frankenstein* and who was himself author of *The Vampire*, the first ever vampire novel. Mason more than earns his top billing with a highly entertaining display of subtle, purring malevolence.

Michael Sarrazin is very affecting as The Creature (the script uses the same name as Jimmy Sangster did for Hammer's *The Curse of Frankenstein*), an astonishingly beautiful blank canvas when he is first created, slowly reverting to physical ugliness as the process used to make him reverses itself. Sarrazin's performance cannot be praised enough, retaining our sympathies right to the end despite the horrific things The Creature does in the course of the narrative.

13

The Omen: Hollywood from Bust to Boom

By the mid-1970s, Hollywood's major studios had adapted and changed from the days of the late 1960s when they came close to bankruptcy. By 1969, many of the majors were close to collapse having almost completely lost track of what the shrinking cinema audience actually wanted to see. The mid-1960s vogue for big-budget musicals produced hits such as Disney's *Mary Poppins* and Warner Brothers' *My Fair Lady* (both in 1964), both of which were topped by the unprecedented success of 20th Century Fox's *The Sound of Music* in 1965. The unfortunate result of this was that Hollywood then proceeded to bankrupt itself and try the patience of audiences by making enormous musicals that not enough people went to see. The vast sums spent on films such as *Doctor Dolittle* (1967), *Finian's Rainbow* (1968), and *Paint Your Wagon* (1969) did not result in the anticipated box office bonanza.

When even the James Bond film released in that year, *On Her Majesty's Secret Service*, struggled to turn a profit, it became clear that studio executives no longer had an idea of what a general audience—if such an entity still existed—wanted to see. The hippie biker film *Easy Rider*, costing a mere $360,000 to make, took an incredible $60 million after its release in July 1969 and it was clear that all bets were off.

Part of Hollywood's response was to radically change the types of movies it made. As already noted, American studios had begun to produce their own horror movies, both in Britain and America. This was part of a process over the course of the '70s by which major American studios colonised the types of exploitation genre movies that had previously been made by independent film-makers and distributed by smaller concerns. Naturally, they had the ability to make these films on much larger budgets than audiences had seen before, which created the phenomenon of the summer blockbuster. In the '70s, this meant that audiences were treated to *Jaws*, a 1950s giant animal monster movie updated for 1975 sensibilities, and *Star Wars*, which in 1977 cost

20th Century Fox $11 million revisiting the *Flash Gordon* and *Buck Rogers* movies of the 1930s (one cannot imagine that Fox executives regretted the investment). The previous summer, Fox had a major financial success making their own British gothic horror film in the form of *The Omen*.

Largely set in England and with a mostly British cast, David Seltzer's script for *The Omen* cleverly fused various ideas then current in horror, used in films like *Rosemary's Baby* and *The Exorcist*, adding a much higher level of crowd-pleasing showmanship to the mix. Thus we see Satanism, the domestic horror of parents discovering their child may be evil, and an apocalyptic element seen in many '70s films as the hope of the '50s and '60s ran aground on the rocks of oil shortages, wars, and economic crises. Gregory Peck starred as the American ambassador to Britain, who discovers that his son Damien—who is adopted, unbeknown to his wife Lee Remick—may be the Antichrist.

The Omen proved that, following *Rosemary's Baby* and *The Exorcist*, A-picture horror was not a passing fad. The boost that sixty-year-old Gregory Peck's career received, near-dormant by the mid-1970s, also did not go unnoticed. An older generation of Hollywood stars was suddenly much keener on appearing in a new wave of major-studio horror films. In America, British director Michael Winner cast fifty-five-year-old Hollywood legend Ava Gardner in *The Sentinel* (1977), while the following year, Tony Curtis, a competitively youthful fifty-three years old, but experiencing a serious career slump, got his first lead role in years in *The Manitou*.

Some of this new wave of horror pictures were at least partially British. Kirk Douglas found himself rather better cast than his previous turn as a singing Dr Jekyll in Alberto de Martino's *Holocaust 2000* (1977). This was an Anglo-Italian co-production, with funding from Joseph E. Levene's Embassy Pictures. Levene had made a fortune in the late 1950s when he bought the rights to the 1958 Italian production *Hercules* for a small amount, gave the film massive publicity, and scored a major hit. *Holocaust 2000* is an undeniably entertaining exercise in producing as close a copy as possible to a major hit film without getting sued. Thus Douglas, who is building a new design of nuclear power plant in the Middle East, becomes aware that he is the subject of a biblical prophecy that he is the father of the Antichrist. The trouble is, he has both an adult son, Angel (Simon Ward), and a much younger pregnant girlfriend. The whole thing is utter tripe but very watchable, and it did not seem to put Kirk Douglas off the horror genre—his next stop was Brian De Palma's splashy telekinesis picture *The Fury* (1978).

The same year also saw the release of *The Legacy*, co-written by Jimmy Sangster (who had long-since decamped to Hollywood) and directed by Richard Marquand, the tragically short-lived Welsh director who went on to helm the *Star Wars* sequel *Return of the Jedi* (1983). This was a pleasingly old-fashioned update of some old dark house horror tropes in which a group of mid-level stars—including Katherine Ross, Sam Elliott and Roger Daltrey joined by the ever-welcome presence of Charles Gray—are either threatened or die in various horrible and visually arresting ways, which had become *de rigueur* in post-*Omen* horror films. Although *The Legacy* lacked the star power and originality to become a breakout hit, it was a good-looking film and made a healthy profit on its estimated £2,500,000 budget.

In 1979, there was a feeling of the wheel having turned full circle when *Dracula* was the subject of a big budget remake by Universal pictures, the very studio that had made the first sound version of Bram Stoker's tale with Bela Lugosi back in 1931. Like that version, the new film was based on Hamilton Deane and John L. Balderston's 1924 stage adaptation rather than directly from Stoker's novel, the new script having been written by W. D. Richter. Interest in *Dracula* had been sparked by a hit Broadway stage version of the Deane and Balderston play, which ran from 13 October 1977 to 6 January 1980, racking up 925 performances. The original leading man of this revival, Frank Langella, was cast as Count Dracula for the new film by Ango-American director John Badham.

Badham had previously been something of a journeyman director working in American filmed television, which in the early to mid-1970s was producing a surprising amount of genuinely worthwhile and creative work. He was catapulted into the front rank of Hollywood directors when his second feature film, *Saturday Night Fever*, became the hit of 1977. This was a small-budget, gritty New York drama that gained worldwide attention for its disco sequences; it also made John Travolta the biggest male star in the world for a couple of years. Badham's follow up was immediately categorised as a 'Disco Dracula' by some lazy newspaper headline writers, but proved instead to be a lush, romantic, beautiful-looking film with a real understanding of gothic imagery.

Langella is nothing less than excellent in the title role of a film, which is less explicit and more romantic than previous versions, and the film shows an interesting contrast to the nudity and violence of major studio horror films made at the beginning of the 1970s. The film boasted attractive Cornwall locations standing in for Whitby and magnificent sets by Peter Murton erected at Shepperton Studios—Carfax Abbey is a particular visual treat. Langella plays the Count with an air of loneliness and melancholy, which is very effective, certainly more so than the overplaying of Laurence Olivier as Van Helsing, who lays on his Dutch-Jewish accent rather thickly. Other roles work a lot better, especially Donald Pleasence as Dr Seward, father of Dracula's target Lucy (Kate Nelligan) and custodian of the local madhouse. Interestingly, Badham had the colour balance of his film desaturated when it appeared on laserdisc in the early 1990s, the scenes at Carfax Abbey in particular looking virtually monochrome. Colour only returns fully to the film in the final scene, after the dispatch of the Count. This bears comparison to Freddie Francis' work in 1968 on *Dracula Has Risen from the Grave*, in which coloured filters were used to suggest that the very presence of Dracula brought a sickness to the atmosphere.

The 1979 *Dracula* did not prove a major financial success and was largely forgotten for many years, but there is a great deal to enjoy and it retains a loyal cult following.

14

Art Horror and the New Screen Violence

As horror was increasingly regarded as a safe bet by film financiers and distributors in the 1970s, filmmakers who might ordinarily not have made horror pictures increasingly began to co-opt the genre and bend it into different forms. This was part of a general trend at the beginning of the '70s for filmmakers in America, Britain, and mainland Europe to test the fast-retreating limits of censorship restrictions with ever more graphic depictions of nudity and violence. In Germany, the long-running series of Edgar Wallace horror mysteries morphed into the violent Italian *giallo* genre, while in America, Sam Peckinpah brought new levels of violence to the Western with his 1969 masterpiece *The Wild Bunch*. The Italian spaghetti westerns had a reputation for over-the-top violence, but in retrospect, the subsequent American Westerns that tried to emulate the Italian films were far more brutal—see Michael Winner's 1971 production *Lawman* for a good example of this trend.

Genre filmmakers had been able for some years to gradually increase the levels of violence in their productions, but the 1970–71 period can be seen as the period when screen violence came of age. As the optimism of the 1960s slid into the uncertainties of the 1970s and censorship restrictions began to crumble, mainstream directors began to use cinematic depictions of violence, often in highly controversial ways.

Ralph Nelson's Western *Soldier Blue* was released in August 1970 in the US, but the film did not see a UK release until April 1971. The film was widely read as making points about American brutality in the Vietnam War, but its more explicit agenda was to highlight crimes against Native Americans. This it achieved via a shockingly violent recreation of the Sand Creek Massacre of 1864, which would struggle to be released uncut even today. Even in the heavily cut form in which the film was released, *Soldier Blue* was a smash hit in the UK and around the world, though it proved far less popular in America.

Later in 1971, both British censors and audiences were confronted with *Straw Dogs* and *A Clockwork Orange*, both of which featured highly controversial depictions of rape—censor-imposed cuts to the former made the scene look even worse than director Sam Peckinpah had originally intended. The censorship battle surrounding *Straw Dogs* was a relatively minor skirmish compared to the furore created by Ken Russell's *The Devils*, released later the same year.

Russell was most famous in 1971 for his television film biographies of classical composers and for his ahead-of-its-time spy movie *Billion Dollar Brain* (1967), a highly underrated film that unfortunately killed the Michael Caine Harry Palmer movie franchise. He then rebuilt his commercial reputation with the D. H. Lawrence adaptation *Women in Love* (1969) and *The Music Lovers* (1970), before causing a national scandal with *The Devils*, a no-holds-barred adaptation of Aldous Huxley's 1952 historical novel *The Devils of Loudun*.

Thus, with typical Ken Russell contrariness, the most effective, brilliant, and disturbing British horror film of the 1970s was hardly a horror film at all, more an angry religious fever dream. Thematically, *The Devils* picks up on a much larger scale some of the themes explored in Michael Reeves' *Witchfinder General*. Popular fears of witchcraft and demonic possession are used for political reasons to increase the power of the wealthy and well-connected and control the general population. Oliver Reed stars as Urbain Grandier, a seventeenth-century priest who is in temporary charge of the French walled city of Loudun. He becomes politically inconvenient to the power-hungry Cardinal Richelieu, who sees the self-governing city as standing in the way of his control of the entire region. Thus Grandier finds himself the victim of the Catholic inquisition, in the form of the crafty, ruthless Baron de Laubardemont (the marvellous Dudley Sutton) and deranged witchfinder Father Barre (Michael Gothard). He is aided in this by Vanessa Redgrave, Mother Superior of the local nunnery, who has been driven insane by her own unfulfilled sexual desires and physical deformities. Sexually obsessed by Grandier, whom she has never met, she accuses him of coming to her at night in the form of a demon. Grandier, who has spent his life as an amoral sexual adventurer, knows he is doomed, but refuses to submit to forces perverting religion for political ends.

The Devils is visually ravishing, Production Designer Derek Jarman recreating the white-tiled walls of Loudon on the Pinewood backlot to stunning effect, while Russell and his Cinematographer David Watkin conspire to create a beautiful, bizarre spectacle. While at times the film is a lot of fun, it is also angry, political, and heartfelt, a treatise on the misuse of religion, written and directed by an artist of the Catholic faith (which Russell would soon renounce). The latter half of the film, in which Redgrave's order of nuns desecrate their church with a riot of sexual depravity while Reed is tortured and put to death by fire, paints a very convincing picture of hell on Earth.

Sections of the British press took against *The Devils* even while it was being shot, salaciously reporting (largely imaginary) tales of sexual hijinks from the set. Both the studio that had financed the film, Warner Brothers, and the British Board of Film Censors, had serious problems with some of the film's more *outré* content. As a result, the film has never been released on home video in Ken Russell's intended version, and only screened in its full version at film festivals. Some countries banned the film altogether, while the film received a mixture of critical opprobrium (most famously from *The Evening Standard*'s Alexander Walker) and film festival awards. Today, *The Devils* is widely considered one of the most important films ever made in Britain.

Former cinematographer Nicolas Roeg established a reputation as one of Britain's most gifted and unusual directors with two films radically different from each other. *Performance*, shot in 1968 but not released by a reluctant Warner Brothers until August 1970, was co-directed with Donald Cammell. Its 1971 follow-up *Walkabout* was directed by Roeg solo and proved enduringly popular. In 1973, the director came up with *Don't Look Now*, an extremely difficult to categorise film that uses some horror imagery and themes. The main theme of the film is how a couple (Julie Christie and Donald Sutherland) deal with the emotional fallout caused by the accidental death of their daughter. During a working trip the couple take to Venice, Christie is contacted by a clairvoyant who claims to be in contact with the spirit of their daughter. Christie becomes obsessed with the idea that her daughter lives on in the spirit world, while Sutherland keeps seeing glimpses of a short figure wearing the same red coat their daughter was wearing when she died.

Don't Look Now is a film with much to praise about it. Especially praiseworthy is that it credits the audience with visual literacy, using a complex editing style that pulls backwards and forwards between different time frames, never once becoming confusing. The film also looks marvellous, but in a realistic way; Roeg shot in Venice during the winter, but avoided the common trap of prettifying the location. Crucially, Christie and Sutherland make a marvellously natural screen couple. With tedious predictability, press coverage of the film concentrated almost exclusively on the film's sex scene, which is unusually explicit for the era but in no way prurient. If *Don't Look Now* somewhat lacks suspense, the material in Daphne Du Maurier's short story struggling to maintain the film's near two-hour length, it certainly deserves to be remembered for more than this.

On its UK release in October 1973, *Don't Look Now* was on the top half of what was, in retrospect, an incredible double bill with one of the great *cause celebres* of British cinema—*The Wicker Man*. Based on David Pinner's 1967 novel *Ritual*, the film's pivotal role of Lord Summerisle was planned from the start by writer Anthony Shaffer and director Robin Hardy to be played by Christopher Lee. Shaffer was a very hot property at the time, having written the hit play and film *Sleuth* and Alfred Hitchcock's much feted return to form

Frenzy, both films being released during 1972. So keen were director, writer, and star to get *The Wicker Man* made that all three worked for no fee.

The story sees Edward Woodward's repressed, strictly Christian police sergeant Howie sent to the remote Scottish community of Summerisle to investigate the disappearance of a young woman. Here he meets Lord Summerisle and is shocked by the sexually free Pagan lifestyle practiced by the locals, who all seem considerably happier than the tightly wound Howie.

Location filming in Scotland was begun in October 1972, despite the film being explicitly set during the spring season. This was due to the film being backed by the production and distribution concern British Lion, which had recently been taken over by businessman John Bentley. During this era, it was not uncommon for Britain's film institutions to be bought by asset strippers (Shepperton and Elstree studios were lucky to survive this fate in the 1970s and 80s) and Bentley's motives were widely suspected. Therefore, *The Wicker Man* was rushed into production to demonstrate his good faith, but by the time the film was completed, he had sold the company on to EMI Films, the successor company to Associated British Picture Corporation.

The new company management took an instant dislike to the film, having Robin Hardy recut the film to a form some twenty minutes shorter than the original version he presented. What should have been a high-profile project was released by British Lion with no press screening on the bottom half of a double bill with *Don't Look Now* in late 1973. Despite the company's obvious dislike of the film, press reaction to *The Wicker Man* was very positive and the film won international awards. Robin Hardy almost immediately made attempts to salvage the cut footage so that he could reconstruct his original cut of the film, but some of the footage appears to have been lost—popular legend has it that it was used as ballast during the construction of a motorway flyover.

The Wicker Man is generally regarded as Christopher Lee's greatest film role, a judgement that the actor himself was in agreement with. Lee decried the studio-ordered recutting of the film, urging audiences to see it even in the mutilated state in which *The Wicker Man* was sent on general release. A cult film virtually from the moment of its original release, extensive searches have taken place for the missing footage over many years, with the result that the film has been released in various edits, representing not just the restoration of cut footage, but often substantially different versions of the film.

Interestingly, in 1973, Christopher Lee and former Hammer producer Anthony Nelson Keys produced a horror film of their own, the strange but interesting *Nothing but the Night*, which has some striking similarities to *The Wicker Man*. In this case, Lee himself plays the policeman who finds himself out of his depth while investigating the strange deaths of the trustees of a fund for orphan children. Director Peter Sasdy's film is not in the same league as *The Wicker Man*, but its final plot revelation is completely unexpected and unsettling.

The Fall of the House of Hammer: 1971–79

Return of the Prodigal Son

In January 1971, Michael Carreras was invited back into the Hammer fold by his father Sir James as the studio's Managing Director. Hammer was in a strange position by this point, with the studio's name having become a legend among audiences and being one of the very few in Britain to have actually increased its rate of production in the increasingly difficult circumstances the film industry found itself. *The Vampire Lovers* (1970) proved to be a false dawn and did not lead to further co-productions with American International, while the major American studios were all reducing their investment in British films. Sir James engineered a deal with Nat Cohen at Anglo-EMI (the successor company to Associated British Pictures Corporation) to keep Hammer going, but could see which way the wind was going and was increasingly keen to offload the company while it was still a going concern.

The first production in Michael Carreras' in-tray was *Blood from the Mummy's Tomb*, which was ready to start shooting at Elstree. The production was troubled from the start of filming, losing its leading man Peter Cushing after the first Monday of shooting when his wife, Helen, was taken seriously ill, dying on the Thursday. Cushing was utterly devoted to his wife and it was clear he was incapable of continuing. Andrew Keir, who had been a kind of substitute Cushing in 1966's *Dracula: Prince of Darkness*, and proved a highly effective Bernard Quatermass a year later in *Quatermass and the Pit*, was quickly drafted in to replace Cushing as Professor Fuchs. Then, a week before the end of shooting, the film's director Seth Holt died suddenly of a heart attack. Holt's health had been shaky for some time, a factor that had, in 1968, forced him to give up the direction of *If...* in favour of Lindsay Anderson. He was also known to be a heavy drinker, the same affliction that claimed his brother-in-law, the director Robert Hamer.

Michael Carreras stepped in personally to complete the filming schedule and make sense of the footage Holt had left behind. The resulting film was released at the bottom half of a highly entertaining double bill with *Doctor Jekyll and Sister Hyde*. One of the reasons behind Hammer's furious burst of activity from 1970 to 1972 was that the company was again producing its own double bills, something it had experimented with in 1966 with *Dracula Prince of Darkness/Rasputin the Mad Monk* and *The Reptile/The Plague of the Zombies*. *Taste the Blood of Dracula*'s UK release in May 1970 saw the film twinned with Jimmy Sangster's return to the psychological horror genre *Crescendo*. This had been a project originated by Michael Reeves, who eventually went uncredited, co-written by Alfred Shaughnessy (who, back in 1957, had directed the fascinating *Cat People* remake *Cat Girl*).

Scars of Dracula was made as a matched pair along with *Horror of Frankenstein*, going on British general release in October 1970. *Lust for a Vampire*, the sequel to *The Vampire Lovers*, was twinned in January 1971 with a very odd non-Hammer film, the biker movie *The Losers*, in which William Smith's biker gang battle the Viet Cong. The third film in what has become known as Hammer's Karnstein Trilogy, *Twins of Evil*, reached British cinemas in 3 October 1971 alongside one of the studio's more interesting productions of the period, *Hands of the Ripper*.

This saw Peter Sasdy return to Hammer for this third and final film, though he was to return for the 1980 television series *Hammer House of Horror* and its 1984 follow-up *Hammer House of Mystery and Suspense*. *Hands of the Ripper* was an attempt to bring a new twist to the subject matter of Jack the Ripper, with Angharad Rees starring as Anna, daughter of the Ripper, who witnesses her father murder her mother. In later life, this causes her to enter murderous trances, as Eric Porter, as the psychiatrist who takes her into his household, discovers to his cost. This was certainly one of the most violent and gory Hammer pictures of the period, but gets marks for trying something different, as does the studio's next production.

Straight On Till Morning was liked very much by Anglo-EMI's executives, who possibly saw similarities in Peter Collinson's film to Alfred Hitchcock's *Frenzy*, which came out to great acclaim a month and a half before Hammer's film. On its eventual release on 9 July 1972, *Straight on Till Morning* was twinned with another old Jimmy Sangster psychological horror script dusted off from the archives. *Fear in the Night* had been in development since 1963, titled either *Brainstorm* or *The Claw* at various times. The two films were released as a *Women in Terror* double bill, an unpleasant bit of packaging that failed to set the box-office tills ringing. In the case of *Straight on Till Morning*, this was definitely a loss to the film-going public as the film is one of Hammer's most interesting and artistically successful experiments of the 1970s. The film starts as kitchen-sink social realism as Rita Tushingham's immature dreamer Brenda leaves her working-class home to see the bright lights of London. There she meets the absurdly handsome and wealthy Peter (Shane Briant) a beautiful young man who hates beauty and whose subtle controlling tendencies are eventually revealed to be murderously psychotic. The film's slide from realism to a two-handed psychodrama is fascinating to watch, and the film's ending is both truly disturbing and inventively realised by director Collinson. It is not too much of a stretch to describe *Straight on Till Morning* as a lost classic of '70s cinema.

In retrospect, the low-budget *Fear in the Night* is most interesting for the fact that it is so defiantly uncinematic and small scale. Besides a fascinating time-capsule look at a 1972 Granada motorway service station, the film is largely set in a deserted boarding school, for which Piggot's Manor was used. Owned by ex-Beatle George Harrison, this house was subsequently donated to the International Society for Krishna Consciousness and was renamed Bhaktivedanta Manor. Writer-director Jimmy Sangster also arranged the film around a very small cast, most of the action featuring Judy Geeson, Ralph Bates, and Joan Collins. This helps give the story a similar feel to Hammer's subsequent television series *Hammer House of Horror*, a series format that the company began work on in 1973.

The series did not reach the screens until 13 September 1980, but the box office receipts for Hammer's recent cinematic horror output demonstrated the fact that the company needed to change direction if it was going to survive. The *Women in Terror* double bill did badly, as had the *Doctor Jekyll and Sister Hyde/Blood from the Mummy's Tomb* pairing the previous October, despite its representing some of Hammer's very best work from this period. The public's indifference to these films was in contrast to the stellar performance of the company's return to comedy for the first time in ten years: *On the Buses*. This had been released on 9 July 1971 and was still playing in cinemas at the end of the year, breaking attendance records along the way.

Old Horrors in New Clothing

This massive success of *On the Buses* helped to paper over the cracks, but Hammer's core business by this time was the production of horror movies, and their efforts to refresh old formulas are worthy of note. *Vampire Circus* certainly attempted to do something different with the genre, with (somewhat like *Brides of Dracula* back in 1960) the air of an adult fairy tale. The film's reputation has grown ever since its largely ignored release at the end of April 1972. In America, the film played on a double bill with *Countess Dracula*, another attempt by Hammer to present a new angle on the vampire myth. This had been released in the UK at the end of January 1971, having been shot at Pinewood the previous summer.

Demons of the Mind was a sort of gothic psychological horror picture, which had originally been written as a werewolf movie. The film's UK distributor was clearly unimpressed with the resulting film, failing to distinguish this unique movie from the glut of horror films by now being produced in Britain. A highly unusual tale of hereditary madness, Robert Hardy's Zorn is so terrified of his two children inheriting the family curse of madness that he locks them away from the world. Despite the attentions of psychiatrist Paul Jones, a series of grisly murders occur in the area. Interestingly, and perhaps reflecting the various rewrites Christopher Wicking's script went through, the reaction of the local villagers is very similar to that seen in vampire films, the film even ending with a quite splendid staking. Beautifully shot, *Demons of the Mind* was kept on the shelf for over a year after its completion by distributor EMI, director Peter Sykes' film eventually seeing the light of a projectionists lamp at the bottom of a double bill with the non-Hammer British horror film *Tower of Evil*.

Hammer was not the only company wanting to update tired horror formulas. Hammer's frequent production partner Warner Brothers had noted the success of *Count Yorga, Vampire*, a contemporary set vampire film that had originally been planned as a softcore porn movie called *The Loves of Count Yorga*, under which title the film still occasionally screens on TV. The film's tiny $64,000 budget was recouped many times over by distributors American International after its June 1970 American release. The word went to Hammer that Warner Brothers would look kindly upon a contemporary set Dracula picture.

Made under the title *Dracula Today*, *Dracula AD 1972* was released on 28 September 1972, having been seen earlier that summer in Europe and Scandinavia. The film was released to general derision, its clueless depiction of youth culture provoking general amusement. This was a shame as the film has a lot going for it, Christopher Lee's Dracula being invoked by Christopher Neame, a twenty-seven-year-old actor with just the right air of high-cheekboned, rock-star cool. Additionally, for the first time since Hammer's first *Dracula* movie in 1958, Christopher Lee was facing his most famous nemesis, Peter Cushing's Van Helsing, or for most of the movie, the character's grandson, Lorrimer Van Helsing.

Brian Clemens and Albert Fennel, who had produced *Doctor Jekyll and Sister Hyde*, were behind another Hammer project that had great promise, either as a television format or as a series of films. Clemens himself chose to direct his own script for *Captain Kronos Vampire Daughter* on location in April and May 1972. Clemens attempted to create a single figure, Kronos, around which the adventures would revolve in his profession as a vampire hunter, along with his associate Professor Grost. Vampires, according to Clemens, came in different species, each with their own hungers and weaknesses. German actor Horst Janson was cast as Kronos, though he was dubbed into English by Julian Orchard, somewhat muting the effectiveness of his performance.

Unfortunately, *Captain Kronos Vampire Hunter* took almost two years to find its way onto EMI's UK release schedule, creeping into cinemas briefly at the beginning of April 1974 with virtually no publicity of any sort beyond a fairly unprepossessing poster. With its genre-busting mix of vampirism and swashbuckling, the film has become a cult favourite with Hammer fans over the years and it can definitely be counted as a missed opportunity. The same fate befell *Frankenstein and the Monster from Hell*, which was pre-sold to Paramount outside the UK but struggled to make its way to British cinemas. Shot in September and October 1972, for economy's sake on a single soundstage in Elstree, this represented the comeback of director Terence Fisher, who had not directed a film since 1969's *Frankenstein Must Be Destroyed*, partially due to a series of road accidents.

Also returning for the occasion was Peter Cushing as Baron Frankenstein, replacing Ralph Bates after the failed black comedy experiment of *Horror of Frankenstein*. Both director and star were getting older by now: while Fisher's style was seen to be somewhat old-fashioned compared to younger talents like Peter Sykes and Alan Gibson who Hammer had been hiring of late. On screen, this particularly showed in the case of Cushing. Always a slightly built man, he was now positively bird-like, and looked to have aged ten years in the three since he had last played the Baron.

British movie audiences in 1974 would have gained a false idea of the health of Hammer Films. Firstly, *The Satanic Rites of Dracula* went on release on 13 January. This release date in itself gives a clue that all was not well, as the depths of the post-Christmas winter is traditionally when film distributors dump products that they think have very little chance of attracting audiences. To make matters worse, this was over a year after Christopher Lee's final appearance as Count Dracula for Hammer had completed filming. In America, matters were even more desperate, with Warner Brothers passing up the chance to release the film. They eventually sold *Satanic Rites* on to a third party, who released it in 1978 under the title *Count Dracula and his Vampire Bride*. Back in the UK, *Captain Kronos Vampire Hunter* saw its belated cinematic release on 7 April, while *Frankenstein and the Monster from Hell* went on general release on 2 May.

This flurry of releases hid the fact that not only had Hammer not filmed anything for most of 1973, since *The Satanic Rites of Dracula* wrapped on 3 January, but that the ownership of the company had changed. Sir James Carreras had been keen to sell Hammer for some time, and was on the point of selling out to horror rivals Tigon British, which was at that time attempting to turn itself into a mixture of distributor, exhibitor, production services company, and property empire, as well as a filmmaking concern. Keen to keep Hammer in the family, Michael Carreras offered his father better terms and took over the company, Sir James stepping down from Hammer's board at the end of January.

Hitting the Buffers: 1973–79

The younger Carreras immediately found himself in the midst of a crisis, as Hammer's major financial backer, Nat Cohen at EMI Films, chose this precise time to back out of their financing agreement. With EMI being the only large-scale backers of British film at this point, Carreras found himself spending most of his time in charge of Hammer chasing potential sources of funding round the world.

Initially, he found success with a two-picture deal with one of Hong Kong's two major films studios, Shaw Brothers. The first fruit of this was a continuation of the Dracula series that, after an extended pre-production period, finally went before the cameras at Shaw Brothers studios in October 1973. With the huge success of Bruce Lee's films, plus other martial arts films such as *King Boxer* and *Five Fingers of Death* (both in 1972), genre mash-ups had become all the rage, with kung fu vampire films jostling for space in film distributors' schedules alongside kung fu spaghetti westerns with titles such as *The Fighting Fists of Shanghai Joe* (a deliriously violent 1973 Italian production).

Although Peter Cushing was convinced to appear (the actor had maintained a furious pace of work in the years following the death of his wife, Helen), Christopher Lee had no intention of donning his vampire's cape again. Thus John Forbes-Robertson was cast in his stead for *The Legend of the Seven Golden Vampires*, albeit briefly before transforming into a Chinese vampire. The film was eventually released in the UK at the end of August 1974, the highest profile Hammer release in some time. Interestingly, while the trailers sold the movie firmly as a horror picture, the posters sold it as a martial arts film, with artwork not dissimilar to that of the posters for *Enter the Dragon*, which in 1973 had posthumously made Bruce Lee an international superstar.

This proved to be another false dawn for Hammer as the film proved popular in the UK and the Far East, but Warner Brothers again passed on the film. The film had to wait some five years to be released in America, retitled *The Seven Brothers Meet Dracula* and recut to near incomprehensibility for the drive-in and grindhouse crowd. The second Hammer-Shaw Brothers co-production fared even worse, with Michael Carreras firing both Producer Don Houghton and Director Monte Hellman, taking on both roles himself. The results of their efforts was *Shatter*, a dull, illogically plotted thriller with Stuart Whitman as the titular hitman seeking revenge on those who double crossed him. Ti Lung played the Chinese martial artist who helps him get revenge, though the film gives neither him nor us a reason to care what happens to Shatter.

Michael Carreras subsequently attempted to get various TV projects off the ground and travelled the world looking for finance for movie ideas such as *Vlad the Impaler* and the Indian-set *Kali-Bride of Dracula*. With very little funds of their own, Hammer needed multiple production partners, which generally proved impossible. In 1975, a deal was finally done with Anglo-German financing to make a version of Dennis Wheatley's *To the Devil... A Daughter*. This was to prove the last gasp of the original incarnation of Hammer as a producer of horror films, and ironically, it was perhaps the company's best film of the decade. Inspired by the success of *The Exorcist*, Hammer finally managed to produce a new film in sync with what was happening in the film world at the time. Peter Sykes' film remains bold and interesting right up until the most anticlimactic ending imaginable.

Led by Christopher Lee giving a ferocious performance, the cast is excellent, a wonderful selection of the British acting talent available at the time, including Honor Blackman, Denholm Elliott, and a teenage import from Germany, Nastassja Kinski. Perhaps the only weak link is a miscast Richard Widmark, who was hardly a box-office name by this point. It is interesting to note that Hammer should be once again dependent on the casting of a past-his-prime American star to secure funding, a return to the company's 1950s B-picture roots.

Despite *To the Devil... A Daughter* proving modestly successful in financial terms, the fact was that what is today known as the British Horror Boom was well and truly over, and if Hammer was going to survive, it was going to have to come up with some new ideas. Michael Carreras was not unaware of this fact, and *To the Devil... A Daughter* producer Roy Skeggs reported that Hammer's owner was notable by his absence from the set.[1] This was because the increasingly embattled executive was in America trying to raise interest and funds for what was hoped to be the film that would reintroduce the Hammer name to a hip, young audience: *Vampirella*.

This was based on a popular comic heroine created in 1969 by Forrest J. Ackerman (science fiction writer, literary agent, and long-serving editor of the magazine *Famous Monsters of Filmland*), along with artist Trina Robbins. She was a vampire heroine from the planet Drakulon, who dressed habitually in boots and an incredibly skimpy swimsuit which amounted to a few strategically placed strips of masking tape. Barbara Leigh was signed to play the role, after both Caroline Munro and Valerie Leon turned down the part due to the amount of nudity involved. The project was widely advertised and script, director, and budget finalised, but the parties concerned were unable to agree a deal to green light the film. American International were interested, but the final deal simply would not come together, with reported differences over the need to attract a major American star to the project, and merchandising rights preventing the film from being made.

After the long and frustrating saga of *Vampirella* had dragged on for over a year, Hammer's scanty finances were stretched still further by *Nessie*, the studio's other great hope for a big mid-1970s hit. By 1976, film producer Euan Lloyd had joined the board of Hammer, and along with Michael Carreras, they created the idea of a big-budget Loch Ness Monster film. Christopher

Wicking was engaged to put a script together and production partners were lined up in the form of television star David Frost's Paradine Productions and Toho, Japan's biggest film studio. The latter were the producers of the long-running *Godzilla* film series, which had begun what would be a nine-year hiatus after 1975's *Terror of Mechagodzilla*. In the wake of *Jaws*, which had become an enormous worldwide hit in the summer of 1975, one might have thought that a $7 million investment in a watery monster movie might be, if not a sure bet, certainly worth a punt. Intended backers Columbia eventually decided otherwise, despite preparations for the film being at such an advanced stage that Toho had constructed a Loch Ness Monster model. *Nessie* was dead in the water, but Hammer still showed signs of life.

The 1970s was a nostalgic time, and Rank Films return to film production near the end of the decade saw the studio back no less than three adventure films set in the country's imperial past. *The 39 Steps* was remade for the third time in 1978, this time in a version set in John Buchan's original time frame of 1914, which proved popular at the box office. The following year, this was followed up by a version of Erskine Childers' classic 1903 spy novel *The Riddle of the Sands*, which failed to repeat the success of its predecessor.

Michael Carreras, as part of his ambitions to diversify Hammer away from being a horror studio, had long harboured plans to remake Alfred Hitchcock's 1939 classic *The Lady Vanishes*. The process of getting the film before the cameras was every bit as tortuous as had been the aborted productions of *Vampirella* and *Nessie*. An interesting difference here was that, at each turn, what had been originally planned as a relatively frugal production for American television, mutated into a larger production. Eventually, co-producers AIP dropped out, leaving Rank as the sole producer of a film whose budget was getting ever larger as Hammer's creditors became ever more impatient.

During the film's shooting in Austria and at Pinewood studios, the budget for the film was exceeded, and eventually Carreras, and by extension Hammer Films, was removed from the production, and soon after Carreras was removed from Hammer itself. *The Lady Vanishes* was eventually released in May 1979 to a muted reception from audiences, which was a pity as it was a beautiful-looking film and pretty fair entertainment. Cybil Shepherd, Elliott Gould, and Angela Lansbury appeared in the roles originally played by Margaret Lockwood, Michael Redgrave, and May Whitty. They were upstaged, however, by Ian Carmichael and Arthur Lowe as cricket-obsessed Englishmen abroad Charters and Caldicott, proving surprisingly acceptable substitutes for the much-loved originals Basil Radford and Naunton Wayne.

Hammer was no more, but soon it would rise once more from the grave.

16

The 1980s: Raising Hell

The Video Era and the 'Video Nasties'

The almost total collapse of the traditional British filmmaking sector coincided with a huge drop in the numbers of people actually visiting their local cinema—if it had not been turned into a bingo hall or carpet warehouse by this point. Ironically, most people in the 1970s would have been watching as many films as audiences consumed during the post-war peak of British cinema-going, but they were watching them on television. As the '70s continued, this allowed new audiences to see British horror films produced during the 1950s and '60s, which gave an increasing impression that Hammer, desperately trying to stay afloat during the mid-1970s, was competing with its own past.

Further change was coming, though: home video recording systems were being developed, the first truly popular ones being Sony's Betamax, released in 1975, and VHS, from Japanese rival JVC, which was launched during the following year. While this allowed owners to record broadcast television, it was also a medium by which films could be distributed. Initially, this was via video rental libraries, as the retail prices of the films themselves were prohibitively high for most people to buy their own copies.

By the turn of the 1980s, home video had become a genuine social phenomenon, completely changing how films were consumed, so much so that there were fears that British cinemas would virtually disappear. The major film studios viewed this new medium as a threat rather than an opportunity and were loathe at first to release new films on video. This meant that there was a gap in a booming new market hungry for product, a gap that was filled by small companies releasing films that could be purchased cheaply. This often meant genre movies made outside of the Hollywood mainstream—which meant that, for the first time, large numbers of horror films from countries such as Spain, Germany, and especially Italy—could be easily seen by large numbers of people.

Italian genre films had been distributed in Britain previously: spy movies, swashbucklers, and sword and sandal movies, as well as horror pictures emanating from Roman film studios all made their way to British cinemas in the 1960s, but tended to be handled by smaller distributors such as Tigon and Eros. Shown in smaller cinemas, these tended not to have much cultural impact beyond the worldwide success of the spaghetti western, hundreds of which were made for about ten years from 1965. Far more of these were made than ever made their way to British screens, many of which being aimed largely at third-world audiences.

With this huge change in how films were being consumed, more than a decade's worth of low-budget, non-mainstream horror films were made freely available to anyone with a video recorder in the house. The potential embarrassment of being seen by the neighbours going into a run-down cinema showing a disreputable-sounding film was gone, as was the prospect of being turned away for being too young for the film's certification. One result of this huge change in the way films were consumed was that the next generation of British horror filmmakers had a very different set of influences. Italian horror directors such as Mario Bava and Lucio Fulci became just as big an influence as the output of Hammer and Amicus on emerging filmmakers of the 1990s and 2000s.

Another effect of the video revolution was the 'Video Nasties' scare. This was a perfect storm of pressure from Britain's tabloid press, along with that perennial nuisance to creative endeavour the National Viewers and Listeners Association and right-wing politicians, which eventually resulted in the passing of the Video Recordings Act 1984. Along the way, the people of Britain were treated to much uninformed comment linking the watching of horror films with real-life murders. While the addition of age ratings by the BBFC was hardly the end of the world, many films were heavily edited and some banned from release completely. Worse than this, perfectly harmless fans of horror movies found themselves the subject of the positively Orwellian attentions of the British state.

A list, popularly known as the Video Nasties, was prepared by the Director of Public Prosecutions, who claimed that the films may have violated the Obscene Publications Act 1959 and were therefore liable to 'deprave and corrupt' the viewer. Unfortunately, the list of films prepared by the DPP appeared to have been chosen almost at random, but was taken at face value by a general public who would be unlikely to have seen many of the films. Thus, as well as Italian cannibal movies and American slasher films, the police could confiscate and destroy your copy of 1974 Blaxploitation picture *Foxy Brown* and even Fred Schepisi's 1978 Australian new wave classic *The Chant of Jimmy Blacksmith*. Absurdly, quite a few films on the list had been passed uncut for cinema release by the BBFC. Even a few British films made the list, most notably 1976's *Exposé* (aka *The House on Straw Hill*) and the more recent SF horrors *Xtro* and *Inseminoid*.

Eventually, the parade moved on, but this archetypal example of a press-driven moral panic demonstrated that, while the respectable end of the 1980s British film industry was producing handsomely mounted 'heritage cinema' such as *Chariots of Fire* and *A Room with a View*, the atmosphere for anyone wanting to produce modern horror films was more than somewhat hostile. Despite such difficulties as the risk of audience members being raided by the police and the not-inconsiderable difficulties British filmmakers had in making large-scale films in any great numbers, the British horror film lived on.

Hammer: Afterlife

Hammer, its new management having apparently given up on the prospect of the studio making any further productions for theatrical release by the dawn of the 1980s, found some success in television production, firstly with the 1980 series *Hammer House of Horror*. This was an anthology series, though somewhat more even in tone and quality than Hammer's late 1960s attempt at the form, *Journey to the Unknown*. *Hammer House of Horror* was a very high profile series (in the British market, at least) and was popular with viewers, but the new Hammer retained the bad fortune of the old version of the company. The series was produced for Lord Lew Grade's ITC, which was suffering financial woes linked to Grade's attempt to turn the company into an international film distributor to rival the Hollywood majors. With ITC's funds being funnelled into feature film productions, a second series of *Hammer House of Horror* was not commissioned.

Undaunted, Hammer pressed on and signed a deal with 20th Century Fox, for whom Hammer had made *Journey to the Unknown*, for a series of thirteen feature-length productions for television. The horror content for these films was reduced considerably, as was reflected in the somewhat inelegant umbrella title for the series: *The Hammer House of Mystery and Suspense*. In America, the films were shown under the shorter, but rather unmemorable banner *Fox Mystery Theater*.

The series of films did the rounds of the regional ITV companies from September 1984, provoking little enthusiasm from Hammer's traditional fan base. This was to prove the last gasp for Hammer, at least during the twentieth century. Despite perennial rumours and attempts to revive the Hammer brand over the following decades, the most famous studio name in British cinema history remained dormant. New blood and new money was needed to bring its inert body back to life once more.

International Productions

As with *The Omen* in the 1970s, the new decade saw some large-scale Hollywood productions decamp to Britain in order to take advantage of British production facilities, personnel, or filming locations. The first of these to be released was *The Shining*, which was released in the US on 23 May 1980 in a 144-minute version, almost six months before a twenty-five-minute shorter cut was released in the UK and mainland Europe. Director Stanley Kubrick had long been based in Britain, and picked up on Stephen King's 1977 novel in the wake of the box office disappointment of his 1975 historical drama *Barry Lyndon*. Seeking a more commercial project, he took the basic structure of King's novel but rejected much of the detail, allowing himself almost two and a half hours to present a deliberately paced visual feast that allows the audience to do some of the work themselves, while including some genuinely terrifying and memorable scenes.

Jack Nicholson plays Jack Torrance, a would-be writer who is hired to look after an empty, secluded hotel over the winter, taking his wife (Shelley Duvall) and young son with him. The hotel is built on a Native American burial site and a previous caretaker murdered his wife and children. Torrance begins acting more and more strangely (scenes that Nicholson plays to the manner born) until he becomes violent towards Duvall. Their son, Danny, meanwhile, is revealed to have psychic powers, which he uses to call the hotel chef (Scatman Crothers) back to the hotel, which is cut off from all communication.

The film was a tough shoot for all concerned, despite the film being shot almost entirely on huge, incredibly detailed sets at Elstree Studios. That the film was not shot on location at a genuine Art Deco hotel is a genuine surprise, mainly because the film is convincingly designed and skilfully shot. This was one of the first films to use the Steadicam camera mount, which allowed a camera 'worn' by an operator to make incredible smooth and fast moving tracking shots. The Shining was only moderately well-received on its original release, fans of King's novel objecting to changes made to King's narrative, but the film quickly rose in critical estimation until today it is regarded as one of the most iconic horror films of the twentieth century.

Rather less well-received was director Mike Newell's *The Awakening*, which beat *The Shining* to British cinemas by a week. This was a stultifyingly dull version of Bram Stoker's 1903 novel *Jewel of the Seven Stars*, which Hammer had adapted in 1971 as *Blood from the Mummy's Tomb*. Lacking in incident and starring a miscast Charlton Heston (it is never entirely clear whether or not he is attempting an English accent), *The Awakening* came and went rapidly, attracting very little attention during its short cinema release.

Potentially more interesting was *The Watcher in the Woods*, directed by John Hough, who had brought stylish visuals to *The Legend of Hell House* seven years previously. The story concerns a couple (Carroll Baker and David McCallum) who move into a large English manor house. The old lady who owns the manor (Bette Davis) sees that the couple's daughter (Lynn-Holly Johnson, soon to be a Bond girl in *For Your Eyes Only*) is the double of her own daughter, who vanished thirty years previously.

This production was part of an attempt by Walt Disney Studios, at this point in time struggling to find an identity, to make films for an older audience than they had previously targeted. Unfortunately, Disney executives grew nervous at the dark nature of the material and had second thoughts. As a result, the film had at least three different endings at various points in its elongated filming schedule, two of which were completed and shown to audiences during the film's brief 1980 release and subsequent rerelease the following year.

While these two productions failed to set the box-office tills ringing, John Landis had huge success with *An American Werewolf in London*. Landis spent the best part of a decade trying to find funding for his idea for a werewolf movie before he developed into a bankable A-list director with his back-to-back hits *National Lampoon's Animal House* and *The Blues Brothers*. With *An American Werewolf in London*, Landis was able to mix his comic sensibilities with his love of gothic horror. The film is thus a unique mix of witty dialogue and subtle comedy touches, making the switch in the film's latter half to full-on scenes of carnage all the more shocking.

Besides the gallery of British acting talent on show, Landis chose for his leads two little-known American actors, David Naughton and Griffin Dunne, who shared a very pleasant line of smart, funny dialogue of the type now utilised by the likes of Quentin Tarantino and Joss Whedon. Frankly, it is hard to imagine that *An American Werewolf in London* was not influential on the writing styles of these two great talents. The plot sees Naughton and Dunne as two young Americans on a walking tour of Britain who are attacked on the moors by a werewolf. Dunne is killed, but keeps returning to warn his friend that he will soon turn into a ferocious monster and must kill himself. Naturally, the horrified Naughton does not listen and carnage ensues—lots and lots of carnage—but not before he starts dating the nurse treating him, played by Jenny Agutter, in a role that made her a legend among teenage boys in the early 1980s.

After decades without a high-profile werewolf movie and with Landis having worked for years to get his movie funded, it was ironic *An American Werewolf in London* arrived in the midst of a cycle of such films. *The Howling* utilised the werewolf transformation effects Rick Baker designed for *American Werewolf*, Baker having given up hope on Landis ever getting his film financed. An agreement was made where Baker left *The Howling*'s effects to his assistant Rob Bottin, while Joe Dante's much cheaper, B-movie-ish *The Howling* beat *American Werewolf* to the screen by around six months. By the time it was released in August 1981, Michael Wadleigh's troubled film adaptation of Whitley Streiber's novel *Wolfen* had finally made it to general release a month earlier. Starring Albert Finney as a New York City detective investigating a series of killings carried out by super-intelligent wolves, this had been the subject of major reediting and reshoots for sixteen months after Wadleigh had delivered his original cut of the film.

This revival of the werewolf genre cannot have harmed the prospects of ITC putting money into *The Company of Wolves* (1984). This offered a very different slant on the notion of human wolves along with a passable low-budget interpretation of the *American Werewolf/The Howling* transformation effects. Based on a story from Angela Carter's *The Bloody Chamber*, which offered feminist reworkings of popular fairy tales, *The Company of Wolves* was co-written by Carter and the film's Irish director Neil Jordan. Presented as the dream of a pubescent girl (in a piece of wish-fulfilment, her annoying older sister is immediately bumped off), the film's narrative is made up of a series of short stories told by different characters on the film, including the young girl herself and her granny (Angela Lansbury). The theme of the film is the dangerous path young girls face as they reach womanhood and face the wolf that lives within all men. In the final tale, she meets a charming, handsome huntsman who transforms into a wolf and she learns that even wolves have feelings.

Not a horror film in any conventional sense, *The Company of Wolves* certainly deserves discussion in a horror context, taking on as it does the iconography of the genre. It does so by taking place in a studio-bound, artificial fairy-tale woodland that brings to mind the mid-European setting of so many of Hammer's gothic horrors. This is a film clearly aware of the visual aesthetic of British horrors films, but not slavishly attached to the history of the genre, and using the genre for its own ends. Additionally, the film features some truly startling visuals, including one scene in which actor Stephen Rea tears his own skin off to reveal the wolf beneath.

The year 1985 saw three major British-made films made with international backing, *The Bride, The Doctor and the Devils*, and *Lifeforce*, the first two of which were highly influenced by classic gothic horror. *The Bride* seems to have been an attempt to produce a feminist-themed remake of *The Bride of Frankenstein*. The film certainly looks ravishing, the traditional Germanic, deep shadows of the Universal horrors replaced by a lush, bright colour palate. Sadly, not everything about the film works anything like as well as the photography. Jennifer Beals received terrible critical notices for her interpretation of the title role, which was a little unfair as, acting-wise, the film is mostly let down by director Franc Roddam's casting of non-actors in key roles. Sting, playing Charles, the latest film representative of the Frankenstein family, comes across as little more than a hairstyle and a costume, speaking his lines with all the enthusiasm of a man reading a shopping list. The film's artistic and financial failure is a real shame as the basic idea of Frankenstein creating a woman who outgrows him intellectually is an interesting one. The film's secondary plot strand, in which his original, male creation (Clancy Brown), leaves Castle Frankenstein, meets up with a midget (David Rappaport), and joins the circus, works far better.

The Doctor and the Devils saw Freddie Francis return with some style to the gothic genre in a film adapted from an unproduced script written in 1953 by Dylan Thomas. The rights to the script were bought by Mel Brooks, whose earlier successes *The Producers* (1967) and *Blazing Saddles* (1974) he followed up with a comedic love letter to the Universal horror film *Young Frankenstein* (1974). More recently, in 1980, he had produced *The Elephant Man*, a highly successful slice of Victoriana that has echoes in the late Victorian muck and filth of *The Doctor and the Devils*. As the title might suggest, this is another version of the Burke and Hare story, and is quite similar in its narrative to the 1960 version of the story, *The Flesh and the Fiends*.

The best film of the latter part of Freddie Francis' directorial career by some considerable distance; this is a handsomely mounted production featuring a terrific cast, headed by a pre-James Bond Timothy Dalton. Dalton plays Dr Rock, the Edinburgh anatomy lecturer who buys fresh corpses to work on from a pair of Irish criminals, Fallen and Broom (Jonathan Pryce and Stephen Rea), who have taken to murder in order to produce a steady supply. The reasoning behind the script's changing of the character names is a mystery, as is the film's failure at the box office. The main failing of the film (besides the acting of Twiggy as a local prostitute) is that the story of Dr Rock and his attempts to drag the medical profession into the modern age is kept rather too separate from that of Fallen and Broom. One of the points of the story is that Rock does not get his hands dirty, but Dalton is practically in a different movie to the rest of the cast.

Alien had shown in 1979 that horror and science fiction could be mixed to potent effect, being at heart a creepy old dark house horror picture featuring an alien monster. The success of this film allowed other big budget SF-horror hybrids to be made, including Tobe Hooper's remarkable *Lifeforce*.

Hooper had scored a massive and highly influential success in 1974 with *The Texas Chainsaw Massacre*, which was shot for around $300,000 and pulled in some $30 million at the box office. Eight years later, he broke into the mainstream film market with *Poltergeist*, co-written and co-produced by Steven Spielberg—controversy has reigned over the years over exactly how much of a hand Spielberg had in the actual direction of the film. For Hooper's follow-up to the hugely successful *Poltergeist*, the newly bankable A-list director made *Lifeforce*, the first of a three-film deal he signed with Cannon Films. Cannon, owned by the Israeli team of Menahem Golan and

Yoram Globus, was in the process of briefly becoming the largest force in British filmmaking, and in 1986, they would buy Thorn-EMI's ABC Cinema chain and Elstree Studios production facility via a deal with controversial Australian businessman Alan Bond.

At this stage, Cannon, which had gained a reputation for making crude but successful B-movies, wanted to upgrade the quality of its product and to its credit threw everything at this attempt to make a genuine, high-class blockbuster. Unfortunately, the result was a box-office disappointment, but with the distance of time, *Lifeforce* can be seen as one of the hidden gems of 1980s popular cinema. While author Colin Wilson's source novel *The Space Vampires* was heavily influenced by the work of H. P. Lovecraft, Hooper made a film that took the basic framework of that story and turned it into a very expensive love letter to Hammer Films.

Specifically, *Lifeforce* is very similar to Hammer's 1967 adaptation of Nigel Kneale's *Quatermass and the Pit*, and also to Kneale's fourth television *Quatermass* serial, which had been broadcast on British television in October and November 1979. Dan O'Bannon and Don Jakoby's script has a British-American space shuttle discovering a huge alien space probe hidden within Halley's Comet, which contains three naked, perfect humanoids, two male and one female. When the shuttle returns to Earth, the bodies are revealed to be a type of alien vampire that sucks the life-force out of people, eventually infecting the whole of London as it harvests the human population. The film is very well cast, featuring such luminaries as Michael Gothard, Frank Finlay, and Patrick Stewart in a cast led by Steve Railsback and Peter Firth. The trouble is that the film really lacks a star name—perhaps if a bigger name could have been attracted to the production, it might have made a difference to *Lifeforce*'s box office prospects.

Ken Russell, perennially described by lazy journalists of the '70s as the *enfant terrible* of British cinema, was not much of an *enfant* by 1986. Since the release of his quasi-horror masterwork *The Devils* in 1971, Russell had avoided horror, maintaining a career directing off-beat music biographies for cinema and television, and he was coming off the back of two controversial, high-profile feature films, *Altered States* (1980) and *Crimes of Passion* (1984). Now, American studio Vestron Pictures backed Russell's return to horror themes: *Gothic*. Here, the director went back to the very roots of the gothic genre, presenting a visually striking interpretation of the famous 1816 night at Lord Byron's Swiss chateau, which resulted in the writing of Mary Shelley's *Frankenstein* and John Polidori's *The Vampire*.

Gabriel Byrne plays Byron as cruel and manipulative, particularly towards his personal physician Polidori, brought to life in a standout performance by Timothy Spall (in one of his three horror pictures made during the 1980s, the others being *The Bride* and *Dream Demon*). Spall gives the best performance seen in the film, his Polidori seen as pitiable and self-hating, clearly in love with Byron, who treats him with ill-disguised loathing during this fateful night. Natasha Richardson and Julian Sands play the Shelleys, the former acting as the voice of reason, the latter as an enthusiastic acolyte of Byron's druggy vision of free love.

Audiences should not go into *Gothic* expecting much by way of conventional narrative. Here, Russell takes the viewer into the heart of a stormy, drug-fuelled night as the four participants experience a series of increasingly terrifying hallucinations. Visually, the film is a feast of wonderful, painterly images, which makes what was to follow from Ken Russell all the more disappointing.

Gothic was successful enough for Vestron to request another horror-themed picture from Russell, the results of which being possibly the director's most bizarre picture, and one which suggests that he was not taking the assignment entirely seriously. *The Lair of the White Worm* (1988) was based loosely on Bram Stoker's novel of the same name, the last full-length work the *Dracula* author published, released in 1911, the year before his death. It is often described as the lesser of Stoker's novels, and Russell's reimagining of it certainly lives down to this reputation. Flatly directed on what looks like a low budget, the film contains a group of simply awful performances (hang your heads in shame Hugh Grant, Peter Capaldi, and Sammi Davis). Only Amanda Donohoe and Stratford Johns really enter into the spirit of the thing, which is basically a wild and whacky *Carry On* picture, with a vein of humour rather ruder than even the later of those films attempted. Frankly, it is awful, but Peter Capaldi fighting off vampires armed with a set of bagpipes, a mongoose, and a grenade is something that deserves to be seen at least once.

Vestron also backed another British quasi-horror film in this era, which is rather more than a guilty pleasure: *Paperhouse* (1988). Based on the 1958 novel *Marianne Dreams* by Catherine Storr, which had been adapted in 1972 as the British children's serial *Escape into Night*, this new version was the first feature to be directed by Bernard Rose, who subsequently relocated to America and directed the hit horror film *Candyman* (1992). *Paperhouse* plays like *A Nightmare on Elm Street* for kids, as a young girl, convalescing from an illness, finds herself drawn into a dream world that is created from a drawing she had made of an unhappy boy looking out of the window of a house. The boy, it transpires, is a real boy who is dangerously ill in hospital, and anything she does to the drawing directly affects him. A fascinating and sympathetic look at childhood fears, *Paperhouse* got good critical notices and led to a long career for Bernard Rose, most notably a series of Tolstoy adaptations. He would return to British horror in 2005 with *Snuff-Movie*, before making further horror pictures in America.

Hellraiser: BDSM and Baggy Underpants

Without a doubt the key British horror film of the 1980s was *Hellraiser*, a UK production that gained a lot of its finance from the American company New World. New World had originally been founded in 1970 by the legendary B-movie producer/director Roger Corman and his brother Gene, after the former had grown frustrated with his former production partner American International Pictures interfering with his work. The experiment was a success, and throughout the 1970s, New World became the sort of exploitation movie hothouse for new talent that AIP had been in the previous decade. The Cormans sold their stake in New World in 1983, and by the time of *Hellraiser*'s production, it had been developed under its new ownership into a huge multimedia company, owning, among other things, Marvel Comics.

Hellraiser was written and directed by the thirty-five-year-old Liverpudlian Clive Barker, who had made a name for himself as a writer of contemporary set horror stories. He had co-written the screenplays for two previous film adaptations of his work, *Underworld* (1985) and the Anglo-Irish production *Rawhead Rex* (1986), both of which were directed by George Pavlou. Barker was unhappy with how the material was handled and *Hellraiser* represented his attempt to control his own work. For this project, he adapted his own novella *The Hellbound Heart*, which was first published in November 1986.

The story concerns Frank, who buys a puzzle box that we can see holds great significance to him from a North African market. When he returns home and solves the puzzle, hooks and chains immediately appear from the wall and tear Frank to pieces. When Frank disappears, his brother, Larry (Andrew Robinson), Larry's wife, Julia (Claire Higgins), and their daughter, Kirsty (Ashley Laurence), move into the house. When Larry gashes his hand badly, his blood seeps under the floorboards of the spare room, reviving the remains of Frank. Frank's resurrection is startlingly well done, both gory and oddly reminiscent of the effects work done in 1958 for *Fiend Without a Face*. Frank reappears as a skinned body, revealing himself to Julia, who he once had a passionate affair with. Frank needs more human blood to return to full existence once more, and Julia agrees to help.

Julia becomes a sexual predator, bringing men back to the house with the promise of sex before murdering them so Frank can absorb their blood. These scenes have a mordant wit, exuding a very British sense of seedy sexuality. Julia becomes a deadly siren dressed in a series of large-shouldered suits while her hapless pickups drop their trousers to reveal some quite stunningly grey and unattractive underwear. It helps the atmosphere of the film enormously that the house looks very real, appearing every inch a British 1930s terraced house. This makes a welcome change from the traditional settings of British horror of an impossibly grand country house or some ultra-modern dwelling.

Hellraiser's innovative mixture of body horror and domestic horror is thus grounded in an authentic setting, with one strange exception: the film at first looks and sounds entirely British with a few American cast members, but as the narrative develops, it becomes weirdly unclear exactly where it is meant to be set.

Hellraiser surprisingly became a major success, aided by a great script, some convincingly fleshy animatronic effects, and Pinhead, the Cenobite who became the visual mascot for the series, but who has a surprisingly small role in the first two films in the series. A sequel was inevitable, Barker's contribution to *Hellraiser II: Hellbound* (1988) being a story credit and as Executive Producer. Perhaps if Barker had had more direct involvement, the terrible mess that this follow-up makes of his characters and themes might have been avoided. At least the new film makes it clear that the action takes place in the US after an opening sequence made up of an abbreviated rerun of *Hellraiser*'s climactic scene. It then transpires that Kirsty, having survived the destruction of the family home on the first film, has been committed to a mental institution run by Dr Channard. It turns out that Channard actually believes what Kirsty is saying and has been searching for a doorway to the Cenobite dimension.

Channard has Julia resurrected and becomes a Cenobite himself, while Kirsty travels to the Cenobite dimension in the hope of freeing her father, Frank. Unfortunately, thanks to budget cuts imposed on the film by New World, the script bites off considerably more than it can chew and the results look absolutely dreadful. Tony Randel's direction and Peter Atkins' screenplay (rewritten when Andrew Robinson declined to return from the first film) conspire to suck every idea, every trace of wit and originality, from *Hellraiser*. What both films are good at is creating strong female characters, which is to be applauded in a genre in which women have often taken the role of passive victim.

The *Hellraiser* series continued after this low point for a very long series of sequels, their production leaving the UK with 1992's *Hellraiser III: Hell on Earth*, from English director Anthony Hickox. Doug Bradley's character of Pinhead, always the favourite of fans, moved from being the visual motif of the series to the central thread linking the films from this point onwards, often parachuted in (not literally, thankfully) to a story entirely unrelated to the events of the first two films.

Hellraiser: Bloodline followed in 1996, being a prequel to the previous films, which director Kevin Yagher had his name removed from after the producers ordered reshoots by other hands. *Hellraiser: Inferno* (2000) saw the ever-cheaper productions now be released straight to DVD. *Hellraiser: Hellseeker* saw an attempt to bring the series back to its roots, bringing back Ashley Laurence as Kirsty alongside the ever-present Pinhead, as well as some story input from Clive Barker. *Hellraiser: Deader* was filmed in Romania in 2003, but did not see a release for another two years, shortly before another Romanian-shot series entry appeared—*Hellraiser: Hellworld*—which featured Lance Henricksen and a young Henry Cavill.

The decline of *Hellraiser* from trailblazing originality to exhausted contractual obligation was completed with the release of *Hellraiser: Revelations* in 2011, a film hastily shot on a tiny budget, apparently so that production company Dimension Films could retain its rights to the franchise with the hope that a big budget remake of the original might ensue. Doug Bradley declined to appear as Pinhead, and thus far, the remake has failed to appear, despite Clive Barker delivering a script some years ago. Another micro-budget sequel has been produced in 2017, however, under the title of *Hellraiser: Judgement*, which at time of writing awaited a release date. Any remaining audience members wishing to see this are perhaps suffering the same masochistic urges as Frank in the first film.

Horror at the Video Store!

The pictures discussed so far had the advantage of actually seeing the inside of a commercial cinema. At the cheaper end of British filmmaking in this era, some horror pictures were only seen by the customers of their local video rental library, and even then, perhaps not the nicer sort of video library. *Screamtime* was a compilation of three short horror stories from the team of Michael Armstrong (last seen in Europe directing Eurosleaze classic *Mark of the Devil*) and Stanley Long, veteran British sexploitation movie producer director, here working under the pseudonym Al Beresford. The three stories contained in the film were apparently seen in some British cinemas as short supporting features, but were more widely seen in this compilation. *Screamtime* was put together in America with incredibly sleazy and dumb linking material based around two schmucks who steal the VHS tapes containing the stories from a New York video store.

The first story, 'That's the Way to Do It', is probably the best of the three. Robin Bailey plays an ageing seaside Punch and Judy man who pays more attention to his puppets than he does his fed-up wife (Ann Lynn) and horrible, aggressive stepson (Jonathon Morris). After Morris burns down his Punch and Judy tent, those who are oppressing Bailey become the target of an unseen assailant using a plank of wood. A horrified Bailey is convinced that Mr Punch has turned to murder. The second story, 'Dreamhouse', is about a couple who are given an old house by the groom's father as a wedding present, but the bride keeps having disturbing visions of a knife-wielding attacker and blood. 'Dreamhouse' suffers from not really having enough story even for its short length, which is rather odd as the film has a very clever twist at the end and should really be better than it is. The third film, 'Do You Believe in Fairies?', stars the charmless David Van Day, who went on to pop stardom soon after as half of the pop duo Dollar. He plays a trials bike rider who needs some extra money to fix his bike, so answers an advert to become handyman at the home of two eccentric old ladies (Dora Bryan and Jean Anderson). The greedy Van Day learns that the house is filled with valuables and burgles the house, only to discover that the old ladies' warnings that the house is protected by fairies is murderously true.

Both the saving grace and most frustrating element of *Screamtime* is that it has some good ideas and it is clear that nobody involved with it actually wanted to make a bad film. The people responsible for the film clearly have some ambition, just not enough money or talent to bring their ideas to anything like a satisfying fruition.

Don't Open Till Christmas was released in 1984, but was a highly troubled production, which took two years to make—director-star Edmund Purdom quitting the project at least once. Purdom was English, but had spent most of his career abroad and was, in the 1950s, being groomed as a star leading man by MGM. Subsequently, Purdom worked extensively in Italy, and the influence of the Italian *giallo* horror-mystery genre can be clearly seen here in a plot about a mysterious unseen killer who is targeting people in Santa Claus outfits in the run up to Christmas. The crimes are investigated by Purdom's police inspector and subsequently by a witness who is suspected of the murders.

This latter role is played by Gerry Sundquist, a promising young leading man of the 1970s whose career trajectory can be judged by the very fact that he is appearing in this film. This was to be Sundquist's final film appearance before he died by his own hand in 1993. Tragically, by the time *Don't Open Till Christmas* was finally released in December 1984, one of the other stars of the film, Alan Lake, had also committed suicide some two months previously. Lake is actually very good in the film, putting in an effectively creepy and intense performance. The film itself is, objectively speaking, absolutely terrible. It is, however, never dull for a moment, and in the final analysis it can only be described as highly entertaining.

17
The 1990s: New Blood, New Mediums

If the rise of home video in the 1980s revolutionised how film was distributed and consumed, the 1990s saw video and the newly emerging digital technology starting to affect how films were produced. The emergence of affordable camcorders (a somewhat redundant term today, this originally referred to the fact that older generations of video technology had the recording mechanism is a separate unit to the camera) and editing equipment had two important effects. In the professional filmmaking sphere, it was now possible to experiment much more easily and cheaply with editing techniques, which was a boon to directors and editors alike. The other effect was potentially even more interesting: such equipment began to reach a price and quality level that the process of film production was, to an extent, democratised. This meant that horror fans were able to produce films of their own, which aspired to professional quality.

An early entry in what we might term a horror sub-species was *Zombie Genocide*, made in 1993 in Craigavon, County Armagh, Northern Ireland, thus counting both as a British film and as Ireland's first ever zombie movie. Directed by Andrew Harrison, Khris Carville, and Darryl Sloan, no one is likely to mistake this sixty-four-minute production for a professionally made film, but the makers clearly know how to frame a shot and there are far worse-acted films out there. Remarkably, the film was entirely edited in camera, a difficult feat that negated the requirement for editing equipment. It is certainly more fun than *The Blair Witch Project*.

Around the same time, Darren Ward was making amateur action and horror films, his *Blue Fear* (1994) being a tribute to the *giallo* genre, while two years later, Manchester-based Thomas J. Moose directed *Zombie Toxin*. Fascinatingly, this was a zombie comedy, bearing the advertising slogan 'It's Monty Python meets *Dawn of the Dead*', thus treading territory that would reach the local multiplex by the time *Shaun of the Dead* was released ten years later. These early fan productions were sold on VHS tapes, outside of the traditional film distribution networks, which brings up the thorny issue of how British filmmakers got their films seen, or sometimes did not.

Directors and producers became more able to get films made than at any time since the old days of Rank and Associated British. This was especially true in the post-1997 New Labour era, when National Lottery money was poured into production in an attempt to revitalise Britain's film sector. Unfortunately, not enough strategic thought went into the choice of films, which meant that rather too many gangster dramas gained public funding. By the 1990s, cinema-going had made a comeback thanks to the emergence of the multiplex cinema, but despite each cinema having multiple screens, in most cases, the big chains preferred to book high-profile Hollywood releases than the glut of British product being offered to them. As the new millennium dawned, many British genre films made their debut on DVD, which had quickly supplanted VHS as the primary home entertainment medium, or even on late night television.

Cyberpunks and Sci-Fi Horrors

Science fiction horror remained an interesting sub-genre and demonstrated how much healthy cross-pollination between different media was happening. The British comics' scene, long mired in dated Second World War adventures and comedy publications with their roots in the 1930s, was revitalised by a new wave of talent such as Alan Moore and Brian Bolland and the phenomenally successful comic *2000AD*, which was launched in 1977 and remains in production to this day. This was followed by other titles, including the short-lived (1982–85) but hugely influential *Warrior*. These took a slew of literary and cinematic influences and gave them a SF twist, and this very British approach eventually made its way to film production.

Hardware (1990) was an SF-horror mixture directed by the South African Richard Stanley that proved to be rather too influenced by *2000AD*, the similarities to a comic strip that title had ran called 'SHOK!' The publishers sued successfully, but despite this, *Hardware* caught the spirit of *2000AD* rather better than the two official movie adaptations of the comic's star attraction *Judge Dredd*. Made on a very low budget, *Hardware* became an unexpected hit, its clearly expressed set of influences including *The Terminator*, *Mad Max*, and *Alien*; additionally, literary sources such as the work of William Gibson and Philip K. Dick saw it catch the SF zeitgeist of the time.

The story saw a former soldier in an irradiated, post-apocalyptic America (Dylan McDermott) buy some scrap robot parts from a scavenger for his artist girlfriend (Stacey Travis). These turn out to be from a self-powering, self-repairing, virtually indestructible prototype military killer robot, which repairs itself using other items of scrap in her apartment and goes on the rampage. Seen today, *Hardware* is a little disappointing, not really having enough plot to sustain itself. When they come, however, the deaths are amusingly graphic, especially that of Travis's sleazy voyeur neighbour, played by the brilliant William Hootkins.

Hardware was picked up by the Miramax Studios pair Bob and Harvey Weinstein, who seemed uniquely able to spot interesting new talent, and the film went on to make a big profit. Richard Stanley went on to make his masterpiece, *Dust Devil*, first released in 1992. Mainly British financed, this unique supernatural horror film was shot in Namibia and is a very South African-themed work. Stanley's original cut of *Dust Devil* was 110 minutes long, but the film's British backers had the film reduced to a mere eighty-seven minutes, while Miramax released its own shortened edit of the film in the US market. Eventually, Stanley financed his own director's cut of *Dust Devil*, which thankfully remains the standard version of the film seen today.

Stanley did not have a lot of luck as a mainstream film director. His next project was a big budget remake of H. G. Wells' *The Island of Dr Moreau*, which he wrote himself and spent four years developing, only to be fired during the first week of shooting after a series of disasters. Most of these were not his fault and the film that was eventually released, directed by John Frankenheimer and starring Marlon Brando and Val Kilmer, had very little to do with Stanley's vision for the project. So traumatised was Richard Stanley by the experience that he has largely turned his back on feature film production ever since, which can only be regarded as the terrible waste of a potentially great talent.

Split Second (1992) had very little attention payed to it during the film's very brief 1992 cinema release, most people who were interested seeing it on its VHS release, which I recall being quite a grotty looking transfer. In many ways, this cartoonish action SF-horror mixture is very good fun, all concerned appearing quite clearly aware of the absurdity of the whole enterprise. It was directed by Tony Maylam, who had directed *The Burning* in 1980, which somehow made its way onto the Video Nasties list and was incidentally the first production of Miramax. What had originally been a serious script about a serial killer influenced by astrological predictions somehow mutated into a futuristic action-horror piece heavily influenced by *Alien* (especially in its creature design) and *Blade Runner*. The latter influence could be seen in the setting of a shabby London suffering from constant flooding thanks to global warming. *Blade Runner* star Rutger Hauer plays tough, half-crazed cop Harley Stone, who is hunting for a serial killer who turns out to be a bizarre, mutated monster who tears out its victim's hearts. It is a guilty pleasure, but a genuine one.

Stephen Norrington was an effects technician on both *Hardware* and *Split Second*, as well as larger-scale productions including *Aliens*. He got a chance to write and direct his own SF horror with *Death Machine* (1994). This looked like it had a fair amount of money spent on it by its backers, Entertainment Film Distributors and Victor Company of Japan, not much of which was earned back. A project to create cyborg super soldiers is causing its subjects to go dangerously insane. The technology has been created by annoying Goth man-child Brad Dourif, a surly teenage computer hacker in the body of a forty-four-year-old man. Pursued by his own new boss (Ely Pouget) and a set of eco warriors trying to bring the company down, Dourif unleashes his lethal creation, the Warbeast, in the company's own headquarters.

Death Machine looks good but is terribly disappointing, dragging on for a very dull half hour before the Warbeast makes an appearance, and suffers from being way too hip for its own good. Stephen Norrington did manage a big hit with his next movie though, the 1998 comic book vampire movie *Blade* (1998), but his 2003 feature *The League of Extraordinary Gentlemen* was such a bad experience for both director and the film's star Sean Connery that neither has completed a feature film since.

At least *Death Machine* had a professional sheen to it, which is more than can be said for 1995 SF-horror *Proteus*, based on a novel by Harry Adam Knight (aka the writer and film critic John Brosnan). This was part of the post-*Cliffhanger* attempt to turn Craig Fairbrass into a kind of British Sylvester Stallone. On the plus side, the brawny Fairbrass could not look more like Stallone if he tried (which he probably did). On the minus side is almost everything else about the film. Fairbrass plays one of a group of heroin smugglers adrift in a dinghy on the high seas who drift into contact with an abandoned oil rig. The rig is really a secret biological testing laboratory in which experiments have taken place that produced a shape-shifting monster.

This shameless *Aliens/The Thing* rip-off is fatally compromised by the script's decision to make Fairbrass and his crew heroin smugglers, which means if the monster wants to do away with this bunch of low-lifes, great. The film never really recovers from this lack of a point of audience identification, nor its own low budget, but most horror fans will have seen much cheaper and much better films than this.

The SF-horror sub-genre did produce one near-classic in the '90s, 1997's *Event Horizon*. Although a Paramount production, the director and crew were entirely British and the film was shot at Pinewood. In the year 2047, a rescue mission is sent to the missing spacecraft Event Horizon, and the mission finds that the crew have been massacred. In some ways, the film is a space-bound version of *Hellraiser*, as the experimental engines of the Event Horizon tear a hole in space and time and unleash hell itself on-board the ship, which begins to affect the rescue crew.

Event Horizon was directed by Paul W. S. Anderson, who agreed to take on the project despite Paramount giving him an extremely short time to deliver the film. Paramount and Fox were relying on James Cameron to deliver the *Titanic* movie they were co-producing, but extreme delays on this film left Paramount without a summer blockbuster for 1995. The gap was to be filled by the expensive, but hastily filmed *Event Horizon*, complete with a starry cast including Sam Neill, Laurence Fishburne, and Joely Richardson. Problems emerged when test audiences reacted badly to Anderson's rough cut of the film, disliking the extreme violence it contained. Getting a bad case of cold feet, Paramount had Anderson cut almost half an hour from the film's length and drastically reduce the gore content.

The end result was one of the major financial film disappointments of 1995, but the film itself is actually pretty near superb. *Event Horizon* was discovered by audiences on its home video release, resulting in it being widely regarded one of the cult classic horror films of the 1990s.

Return of the Gothic

The traditional gothic horror film made another comeback during the 1990s, spurred on by the major financial success in 1992 of the Francis Ford Coppola directed *Bram Stoker's Dracula*, starring Londoner Gary Oldman in the title role. Prior to this, Tony Richardson had directed a two-part mini-series of *The Phantom of the Opera* starring Charles Dance and Burt Lancaster in England and Paris for the American NBC television network. Also for television—this time Turner Network Television—was producer David Wickes' 1992 version of *Frankenstein*, an excellent production starring Patrick Bergin as the Baron and Randy Quaid as his creation. This was a natural follow on from Wickes' previous two television productions, filmed versions of *Jack the Ripper* (1988) and *Jekyll and Hyde* (1990), both of which starred Michael Caine. Tragically, *Frankenstein* was the last production actor Michael Gothard (as seen in *Scream and Scream Again* and *The Devils*) made before his death by suicide on 2 December 1992.

In 1992, audiences were also treated to a new version of *The Turn of the Screw*, previously adapted as *The Innocents* (1961) and expanded upon in Michael Winner's 1972 prequel *The Nightcomers*. This time, Patsy Kensit played the governess with two haunted children in her charge, while Julian Sands played their neglectful, drugged-up guardian, the latter detail a clue that this version is set, for some reason, in the mid-1960s. The whole thing tries for atmosphere but has an underfunded look and is landed with both some barely adequate performances and a strange framing device featuring Marianne Faithful relating the whole tale to her encounter group.

A lack of funding certainly was not a problem for *Mary Shelley's Frankenstein*, Francis Coppola's 1994 follow-up to *Bram Stoker's Dracula*. This time, Coppola chose not to direct, handing over the reins instead to Kenneth Branagh, heir to the acting throne of Laurence Olivier and developing into a successful film director. Branagh also starred as Victor Frankenstein, opposite Robert De Niro as The Creature and Tom Hulse, who had not been much heard from in major roles since his breakthrough part as Mozart in *Amadeus* in 1984. The result was a big, fun, in-your-face, downright operatic version of the old Mary Shelley tale, which for some reason was torn to shreds by the critics on its release. Despite the fact that the film actually made money worldwide, the reputation of Branagh's *Frankenstein* was so poor that it somewhat derailed his reputation as a director of non-Shakespearean properties for a while.

Mary Reilly, on the other hand, gained both very mixed reviews and proved a very expensive box office flop from Hollywood major TriStar Pictures, shot at Pinewood and released in 1996. A new version of the Jekyll and Hyde story told from the point of view of an Irish maid in the Jekyll household, this was originally to be directed by Tim Burton. After he left the project, Stephen Frears stepped in, reassembling the major players from his 1988 hit *Dangerous Liaisons*: writer Christopher Hampton and stars John Malkovich and Glenn Close. The result was a big, expensive-looking film that seemed to be too subtle and low key for a wide audience. Malkovich's Jekyll/Hyde and Julia Roberts' maid fail to spark romantic sparks off each other, but Glenn Close livens things up considerably as a Liverpudlian (I think) brothel-keeper. Despite the film being a notorious financial disappointment for the studio, there is actually quite a bit to enjoy about *Mary Reilly*—it is certainly a more thoughtful and subtle experience than the average Hollywood blockbuster.

An American Werewolf in Paris was a rather late in the day semi-sequel, coming some sixteen years after the John Landis hit *An American Werewolf in London*. Although there was some British money involved, it was an international co-production that managed not to lose money but otherwise was rather disappointing. The project had been doing the rounds for some years before funding could finally be put together, with the result that the fresh, improvisational feel of the first film was ground out of this follow up. So misjudged is *An American Werewolf in Paris* that perhaps for the purposes of this book we can regard it as an American-French co-production and draw a veil over the whole thing.

Sleepy Hollow saw director Tim Burton, whose gothic sensibilities were there for all to see with the two films with which he made his name, *Beetlejuice* (1988) and *Batman* (1999), return to Britain, albeit for a tale set in turn of the eighteenth-century New York state. This is a loose adaptation of Washington Irving's 1820 short story *The Legend of Sleepy Hollow*, which had an odd journey to the screen, originally being planned as a cheap slasher movie until Burton came on board. Under his guidance, the film became his tribute to the British and European horror pictures he grew up watching.

The film is production designed to within an inch of its life, as is typical of most Burton movies (here the designer is Rick Heinrichs) and looks stunning. *Sleepy Hollow* is a riot of low-light photography, restricted colour palates, and an atmosphere of cold, mud and fog to help create an authentic country hamlet in 1799. In the small town of Sleepy Hollow, New York Police Constable Ichabod Crane is sent by his superiors to use his scientific detection methods to investigate a series of beheadings. Crane is regarded as a nuisance to his bosses, and they have largely sent him to get him out of their way. Crane is shocked to discover that the murders are being committed by a sword-wielding horseman who is himself without a head.

Crane is played by Johnny Depp in an interesting performance as a softly spoken, nervous, and fussy character. Crane is trying to act in a commanding manner as he tries to use science to investigate what is incontrovertibly magic, but it is clear that it does not come naturally to him. The film is excellently cast with American names such as Christina Ricci and Christopher Walken appearing alongside the cream of British character actors such as Richard Griffiths, Michael Gambon, and Miranda Richardson.

Art Horror and Moody Vampires

The going for anyone wanting to make a nuts-and-bolts, low-budget horror film in Britain had become increasingly rough, their products having little chance of a cinema release in the UK. However, a strain of art horror found a niche during the 1990s, some examples of which threw an interesting light on the future of the genre.

English artist, novelist, and playwright Philip Ridley broke into mainstream filmmaking in a big way in 1990 with his screenplay for Peter Medak's film biography *The Krays*. In the same year, he wrote and directed a more personal, but far less British project. *The Reflecting Skin* was a product of Ridley's fascination for Americana and the southern gothic literary genre. Only tangentially a horror film, this was a British-Canadian co-production shot in Alberta, Canada, but set in a mythic 1950s rural America seen through the eyes of a young boy (Jeremy Cooper). With a difficult, hostile mother and a father who disappears into reading pulp novels, the boy is largely left to his own devices. Influenced by reading a vampire novel of his father's, he imagines their lonely English widow neighbour (Lindsay Duncan) is a vampire.

The film is a portrait of a child who sees glimpses of an adult world he does not understand, imagining supernatural horrors and not seeing the real-world horrors all around. His elder brother (a young Viggo Mortensen) returns from the military, suffering from radiation poisoning, his father is implicated in a child murder and commits suicide in front of him, while a gang is kidnapping local children. *The Reflecting Skin* is endlessly fascinating and looks wonderful thanks to Ridley's painterly eye and cinematography by Dick Pope. Though many have referred to the film within the horror genre, it is hard to regard it as a true horror film instead of a very stylishly shot, often surreal drama.

Ridley's next film, *The Passion of Darkly Noon* (1995), was an even riper slice of southern gothic in which the title character, played by Brendan Fraser, is found wandering disoriented by Jude, who delivers coffins for a living. Physically and mentally traumatised by his experiences, Darkly is nursed back to health by Jude's friend Callie (Ashley Judd). He is ever more conflicted and dangerously conflicted by the clash between his religious passion and his increasing passion for Callie. Both this and *The Reflecting Skin* have grown into cult films over the years, finding their audience after commercial cinema found them downright bewildering. Ridley was to return to horror cinema some fourteen years later with *Heartless* in 2010. At this point, the very limited releases his first two films as director received were replaced by a simultaneous cinema and home entertainment release, a development that offered hope for artists making less obviously commercial forms of cinema.

Rather more directly connected to the traditional gothic horror is a pair of art-vampire films made in England in the 1990s, curiously both by oriental directors. *The Tale of a Vampire* (1992) was co-written (with Jane Corbett) and directed by Shimako Sato, whose background was unusual for a filmmaker working in Britain. Not only is Sato female, but she is Japanese-born, having studied filmmaking in London. *The Wisdom of Crocodiles* was released in 1998 and directed by Po-Chih Leong, an Anglo-Chinese director who had worked in a variety of genres in Hong Kong and would later direct action movies in America starring the likes of Steven Seagal.

The vampires in these films, played by Julian Sands and Jude Law respectively, were intensely romantic figures, placing these films as interesting staging posts in the development of vampire imagery. In *The Tale of a Vampire*, Sands plays Alex, an ancient vampire, lovelorn for the loss of his love Virginia, who stalks trainee librarian Suzanna Hamilton who just happens to be the double of his missing paramour. Sands in this period was not always the most convincingly naturalistic of actors, but there is something about Sato's heightened style that suits the stylised delivery of both Sands and Kenneth Cranham (playing the film's equivalent of a Van Helsing figure). Both seem to be channelling the style of a previous generation of actors of the ilk of James Mason and Peter O'Toole, but somehow it works.

The floppy haired, impossibly handsome Alex seems terribly lost and vulnerable, making it difficult to truly dislike the character, even though we see him drinking the blood of tramps. *The Wisdom of Crocodile*'s Steven Griscz is similarly just absurdly handsome, a quality that he uses to stay alive. Griscz kills single women and drinks their blood, but now (in a new twist on vampire lore) must make a woman fall in love with him in order that her blood can fully revitalise him. These films show how much the vampire mythos was changing, the traditional middle-European aristocrat established by Lugosi and Lee being replaced by a more modern image.

In some ways, this change was more a return to a previous vision of the vampire. It is easy to forget that Bela Lugosi was a very handsome man back in 1930, while Christopher Lee in his first appearance as Dracula was specifically sold to audiences as 'The Terrifying Lover'. No matter how handsome a figure Lee cut, we always knew that the monster was never too far from the surface. By the 1990s, actors like Julian Sands and Jude Law looked like they had stepped from the cover of a Mills and Boon romance novel. The defining feature of Sands' Alex is not his need for blood, but instead his loneliness, while Law's Griscz needs to be loved as a part of the plot, while at the same time suffering artfully from 'despair' and 'disappointment'—we can tell because he writes the words in his notebook. We can see quite clearly here the direction of travel of the vampire genre, which was eventually to arrive at the phenomenal success of the *Twilight* saga on both page and screen in the 2000s.

The key influence of this development of the vampire mythos is Anne Rice's *The Vampire Chronicles*, an ongoing series of novels that began with *Interview with the Vampire* in 1976. Rice established the image of the vampire as a beautiful, doomed, flawed romantic figure, itself taken in part from cinematic sources of the past. Poppy Z. Brite's *Lost Souls*, published in 1992, can be seen as a highly influential updating of Rice's themes with huge appeal to a younger, hipper readership than Rice. The vampire was often seen in the 1990s as an AIDS metaphor, which not only replaced the rather tired idea that they represented a decaying aristocracy, but was also in interesting reversion to earlier vampire imagery: some of Bram Stoker's original ideas back in 1897 were based around the vampire as an invading disease.

18

The 2000s: Homemade Horrors and Zombies on the Run

The coming of the new millennium brought with it a strange, wonderful, and wholly unexpected phenomenon: not only did horror movies become popular again, but Britain once more became a centre for their production. A group of talented, fairly young film directors emerged who gravitated towards the horror genre as a way of showcasing their skills.

This tells us a few interesting things about the state of the horror genre at this stage. The classic period of British horror from the late 1950s to the mid-1970s had cast a long shadow across the form and had created something of a stigma. Along with a group of outdated tropes that were no longer found to be scary by most audiences (it is interesting to note that when Universal mounted a new version of *The Mummy* in 1999, it was more in the action-adventure tradition of *Indiana Jones* than as a horror film), the rise of American slasher movies and Italian *gialli* in the 1970s gave horror films an occasionally deserved reputation for misogyny. New writers and directors took on board horror's past but found ways to make the genre relevant to the times in which they were being made.

By the 2000s, finance could be raised for low- to medium-budget horror films, which had a reliable international market as opposed to the somewhat parochial rash of London-based gangster movies that sprang up in the 1990s after the success of Guy Ritchie's *Lock, Stock and Two Smoking Barrels*. Some of the new wave of British horror managed to gain cinema releases, but there were other options: home video, dedicated horror television channels thanks to the rise of multi-channel TV, and newly emerging streaming video services. Often, the finance was raised from multi-national sources, which more than ever raised questions over what precisely was a British horror film.

Welsh director Marc Evans had an international success with *My Little Eye* on its release in 2002, a film from a British production company with a largely British crew that was shot in Canada and did everything possible to disguise its British origins. On the other hand, Christopher Smith's *Black Death* (2010) looked and felt British, but was entirely financed by German interests and was filmed in that country. That film's medieval British setting was shared by the previous year's *Solomon Kane*, which had an even more complex parentage. It was based on a series of pulp stories by 1920s and 1930s American pulp author Robert E. Howard, and it had a mainly British cast, but was a UK-France-Czech co-production using largely Czech locations and studio facilities.

Most importantly of all, the new British horror film was producing work that actually reflected the reality of modern Britain. Geneviève Jolliffe's *Urban Ghost Story* (1998) was an interesting example of this made at the end of the previous decade. Story-wise, this offered very little that was new, being a fairly standard story of a teenage girl who died briefly in a car accident, only to find that her home is now the subject of poltergeist activity. Where the film differs from the norm is that she lives in a dilapidated Glasgow tower block riddled with drugs and loan sharks. The story also makes some intelligent choices about what would actually happen to a working-class single mum and her daughter faced with a terrifying supernatural menace. They become the target of a muck-raking journalist, religious fanatics, parapsychological researchers, and social services, none of whom seem to care very much what happens to the couple themselves.

Newcastle upon Tyne-born director Neil Marshall came up with a terrific pair of outdoor-set horror films that also brought a refreshingly modern spin on the genre. *Dog Soldiers* (2002) started with the brilliantly high-concept notion of soldiers *v.* werewolves, and from it was created something of a modern classic. The film is set in the Scottish Highlands, where a squadron of regular army soldiers are pitted against a Special Forces unit as part of a training exercise, only to find that their opposition has been massacred by werewolves.

Writer-director Marshall was from a military family, which gave him an ideal perspective from which to create realistic dialogue between his cast of ordinary soldiers. The relationships between the squadron are drawn with real affection and inside knowledge, and it is interesting to note that the focus of the film is very much with the regular soldiers. In a previous era, the film would follow the officers, and we might get couple of comic-relief privates played by Anthony Newly and Michael Ripper. Here, the men are led by their battle-hardened sergeant (the ever excellent Sean Pertwee) and the only officer we see is blood-thirsty martinet Liam Cunningham, complete with public school tough guy accent.

Dog Soldiers was mainly shot in the forests of Luxembourg, thanks to that country's tax breaks, which made the film financially possible to produce. Perhaps most importantly, the film obeys one of the cardinal rules of movie production: hire the best actors you can afford. This really helps the picture, with not one performance striking a false note; *Dog Soldiers'* success rests on the casing of Sean Pertwee, Kevin McKidd, and Liam Cunningham, each of whom have gone on to great success.

Neil Marshall's next move was, in effect, to produce a bigger-budgeted, female version of *Dog Soldiers* in the form of *The Descent* (2005), which made the director's name. Instead of the blokey, virtually all-male military environment of a group of squaddies, we are presented with a group of six female cavers who are searching a previously unmapped series of caves when they encounter a terrifying group of monsters that begin hunting them. A masterwork of claustrophobic terror, *The Descent* gained a lot of attention thanks to the decision to make the group of cavers all female, which, thanks to Marshall's intelligent screenwriting, completely changed the character relationships from the norm in horror films.

Despite being shot in Scotland and at Pinewood Studios, the film was set in the Appalachian Mountains of North Carolina and featured a cosmopolitan cast of virtually unknown actresses. This was yet another example of a British film disguising its origins, which proved to be a wise move. The film's UK release was disrupted by the London bombings of 2005, which had a noticeable effect on the film's box office take, despite excellent reviews. *The Descent* exported extremely well, however, and was especially popular in America, making the film into a sizeable hit.

Neil Marshall's career was also given a major boost by the success of *The Descent*, and the director found himself lumped in with a group of up-and-coming horror filmmakers from countries as diverse as America, France, and Australia who were given the label 'The Splat Pack', a term initially coined by British film journalist Alan Jones. This silly, but undeniably catchy name covered directors making films more violent by some degrees from what had come before—some of the results were dubbed by disapproving critics as torture porn. It proved ironic that, of all directors working in Britain, it should be Marshall who gained this attention, since he subsequently distanced himself not only from the horror genre, but from theatrically released films (he had no connection to 2009's *The Descent: Part 2*). Instead, he has since ridden the wave of the renaissance in American television, directing for series including *Game of Thrones*, *Black Sails*, and *Constantine*.

Bristol-born Christopher Smith directed a group of four horror pictures between 2004 and 2010, which did not always gain the critical plaudits of some other productions of the era, but nonetheless represent a very solid and varied body of work. *Creep* (2004) anticipates some of the themes of *The Descent*, albeit in an urban setting; Franka Potenta, who made her name in the low-budget 1998 German hit *Run Lola Run*, finds herself trapped in the London Underground overnight and stalked by a hideous, deformed cannibalistic killer. This is, of course, not entirely dissimilar to the plot of the 1972 film *Death Line*, but this can safely be put down to coincidence after a gap of over thirty years.

The presence of Potenta in the lead role indicates the fact that much of the funding for *Creep* came from German sources, as did some of the money behind Smith's follow-up: *Severance* (2006). The grungy, often downright nasty feel of *Creep* was replaced here by black comedy, as a group of office workers are sent on a team-building exercise in the Hungarian countryside where, one by one, the group are murdered horribly, forcing the survivors to take extreme measure in order to survive. *Severance* gained generally positive reviews, but failed to become the breakout hit it perhaps deserved to be. It gained an added degree of notoriety in 2009 when it was alleged that the murder of a teenager by three adults was inspired by one of the killings in the film.

Triangle (2009) saw Smith working with his largest budget to date in a psychological horror film set on an abandoned ocean liner discovered by a group whose boat has capsized in a storm. This might not sound like the most original plotline in the world, with and almost-identical plot being explored by films as diverse as *Ghost Ship* (an American horror from 2002), the dreadful 1995 British production *Proteus*, and even Hammer's 1968 oddity *The Lost Continent*. Writer-director Smith has, however, a few tricks up his sleeve, using the basic plot as a structure on which to hang a tale involving time-loops and *déjà vu*. Inventive and different, *Triangle* was invested in heavily by the UK Film Council, which distributed funds from the National Lottery, but struggled to turn a profit at the box office.

Black Death (2010) saw Smith brought in for the first time to direct someone else's script—that of British writer Dario Poloni. The plot saw medieval knight Ulric (Sean Bean) and a group of mercenaries on a quest to investigate a village that has mysteriously remained free of the plague that has ravaged the rest of the countryside. Ulric, who is a Christian fanatic, suspects that black magic is involved and that it is being used to bring the dead back to life. A fascinating piece of work, *Black Death* is clearly of the same lineage as the classic *Witchfinder General* (1968), an entirely honourable resemblance made more so by Smith's decision to strip the film's second half of any actual sorcery. Instead, we see a timely example of state power and religious extremism being used to crush a community that happens to be of a different faith to those who are in power.

Black Death is certainly well cast, with the brooding Sean Bean, coming off the back of his success in *Game of Thrones*, a terrific choice as Ulric, and a young Eddie Redmayne as the novice monk Osmund. Despite an interesting and well-expressed point of view, a convincingly grim and muddy air, and some enthusiastic reviews, the film was not the break-out hit it perhaps deserved to be. At any rate, it seems that Smith, at this point, had said all he wanted to within the horror genre, and he has worked since in other fields. His next production was a two-part TV adaptation of author Kate Mosse's *Labyrinth*, followed by, of all things, a made-in-Yorkshire Christmas comedy film, 2014's *Get Santa*.

The most critically feted of the new wave of British horror movie directors is undoubtedly Ben Wheatley, who has used miniscule budgets and a tendency to splice genres together to great effect. He has previously made animations and short films, gaining attention by showcasing his work online, before directing comedy series for television such as *Ideal*, starring Johnny Vegas, and *Modern Toss*. Wheatley's first feature was the low-budget 2009 crime drama *Down Terrace*, which took an idiosyncratic approach to the British gangster film, lased with a streak of black comedy. The film cost such a tiny amount to make (estimated at just over £9,000) that, as with the films Wheatley would make over the next couple of years, the director and co-writer had almost total artistic freedom. *Down Terrace* gained a raft of enthusiastic reviews and awards both for the film and its screenplay, giving Wheatley's budding directorial career instant momentum.

The follow-up to *Down Terrace* was another genre collision from Wheatley in the shape of *Kill List* (2011), which he one again directed and co-wrote. This time, a plot setup that would have, in other hands, become a perfectly serviceable crime drama takes a sharp left turn and becomes an increasingly terrifying, claustrophobic psychological horror. Established almost instantly as one of the key British horror films of the decade, *Kill List* features two ex-soldiers, Jay and Gal (Neil Maskell and Michael Smiley), who set up as hired killers. While Gal is relatively laid back, Jay suffers from PTSD from his disastrous final military assignment. The pair start working for a mysterious new client who wants three people killed and uses quasi-religious blood rites. As the pair work their way through the list, a murky tale emerges, told with deliberate ambiguity involving, among other things, a satanic cult, child abuse, and extreme violence. The fact that we are never sure what the satanic cult at the heart of the story actually wants makes the film even more frightening.

Ever unpredictable, Wheatley returned the following year with *Sightseers*, which once again brought disparate types of film together to unusual effect. This was a naturalistic black comedy, shot in semi-documentary style, written by its stars, Alice Lowe and Steve Oram. The pair play Tina and Chris, a couple on a caravan holiday around British tourist attractions. Eventually, it dawns on Tina that Chris is killing people who annoy him at the places they stop. If *Kill List* was British crime-horror, *Sightseers* is a Mike Leigh-style comedy of suburban embarrassment existing in the same cinematic body as a serial killer horror movie. It is not a traditional horror movie by any means, influenced as much by the writer-stars than the director, though it does play to Wheatley's background in comedy. The comedic details are extremely well-observed and the film cleverly makes the audience complicit in Chris's killings—the victims are annoying people we might meet in everyday life, like a litter lout and a smug middle-class writer.

This was followed in 2013 by *A Field in England*, written by Amy Jump, who had co-written *Kill List* and which trod the same English Civil War ground that *Witchfinder General* made its own, Michael Reeves film having seeped its way into the psyche of British filmmaking over the intervening forty-five years. In Jump's story, a ragged group of Civil War deserters fall under the psychological control of a necromancer and alchemist and, under the terrifying influence of magic mushrooms, embark on a bizarre dig for a treasure that may or may not exist. This is a film as much about its visuals (by Wheatley and his cinematographer Laurie Rose) as its plot, shot expressionistically in monochrome as if the Civil War had released such all-encompassing evil and lack of hope that the countryside has been bleached of colour. Interestingly, Wheatley casts two actors in key roles best known for their work in comedy: Julian Barratt from *The Mighty Boosh* and Reece Shearsmith from *The League of Gentlemen*, while Irish comedian and actor Michael Smiley returns after appearing in *Down Place* and *Kill List*.

For now, Wheatley has left behind his various iterations of the horror movie in favour of some of the new opportunities that opened up with his status as Britain's most critically feted new director. He next made a version of J. G. Ballard's science fiction dystopia *High Rise* (2015), which saw him deal, for the first time, not only with the weight of critical expectation, but also with a much larger budget—£6 million hardly represents a huge budget by modern standards, but it was many times larger than he had worked with before. This brought with it actual movie stars, including Tom Hiddleston, Sienna Miller, and Jeremy Irons, but Wheatley's uncompromising attitude to source material that had been thought to be unfilmable (though it had inspired the bizarre 1987 *Doctor Who* serial *Paradise Towers*) remained and proved critically divisive, though many hailed the film as a masterpiece. His last film at time of writing was *Freefire* (2017), a wild, Tarantino-esque action comedy with an all-star cast that featured Martin Scorsese as Executive Producer.

Peter Strickland had only completed one feature film, the self-financed *Katalin Varga* (2009), before he wrote and directed the remarkable art-horror *Berberian Sound Studio* (2012). Set during the mid-1970s, this featured Toby Jones as Gilderoy, a nervous sound editor hired to work on Italian horror picture *The Equine Vortex*. Strickland clearly knows the Italian *giallo* and supernatural horror pictures of the period intimately—the title and the pastiche opening credits that we see are absolutely perfect. Gilderoy, who seems under the impression that he was hired for a film about horses, is shocked to discover that he is working on a gruesomely violent satanic horror in the vein of *Mark of the Devil*. The stressful working atmosphere and the constant steam of gruesome tortures he has to provide sound effects for start to change his personality and his very sanity until we are no longer sure whether what we are seeing is real, a stress-related fantasy, or some combination of the two.

The film is both intensely nostalgic about the films of the 1970s and about the technology behind them (if you love vintage recording equipment, this really is the film for you), but very clear-eyed about the dark side of their production. The producer is manipulative and untrustworthy and the director a pseudo-artistic, sexist git who thoroughly believes his own bullshit. The actresses involved in the film's production are treated abominably, and we learn that Gilderoy has been changed for the worse by his experiences when he becomes complicit in what amounts to the torture of one of them to get the right note of terror in her voice. As much as *Berberian Sound Studio* works as a combined love letter and critique of Italian horror of the 1970s, it is also marvellously redolent of the best of 1970s art cinema. In some alternate universe, Nicolas Roeg went straight from directing *Don't Look Now* and started production on this.

Hammer Rises from the Grave

Finally, after innumerable false starts and hopeful rumours, Hammer Films gained the necessary backing to return to film production in 2007. The company name was bought by a consortium headed by Dutch media magnate Jan de Mol, head of the highly successful international television company Endemol. The new owners also bought Hammer's film library, the rights to which had always been a complex issue as Hammer had made films over the years in partnership with almost every major studio in Hollywood.

This new Hammer started small, its first production being *Beyond the Rave*, released online as a twenty-part serial and eventually as a limited edition DVD. Directed by Matthias Hoene, who would go on to make *Cockneys Vs Zombies*, *Beyond the Rave* featured a pre-stardom Jamie Dornan as Ed, a soldier about to go to Iraq with his unit who is searching for his missing girlfriend. The trail leads to a cult of vampires operating in the rave scene.

This was followed by *The Wake Wood*, a 2009 Anglo-Irish production filmed in both County Donegal and Sweden. The film boasted an impressive cast, including Timothy Spall and Aidan Gillen, but failed to secure a wide cinematic release, eventually being seen in a very limited screening in 2011, two years after its production, ahead of its DVD release. Despite this setback, Hammer actually began to achieve some traction with its next films. *Let Me In* (2011) was a very well-done and effective Americanisation of John Ajvude Lindqvist's Swedish horror novel *Let the Right One In*, which had previously been filmed in its original language in 2008 by director Tomas Alfredson to great acclaim.

Set now in Los Alamos, New Mexico, Kodi Smit-McPhee plays twelve-year-old Owen, who is the victim of horrific bullying at the school he attends. He is befriended by a mysterious new arrival, Abby (Chloë Grace Moretz), who has a very strange relationship with the late-middle-aged Thomas (Richard Jenkins), who it is initially assumed is her parent or grandparent. As Abby and Owen grow closer emotionally, she acts as his protector from the bullies and we learn that she is a vampire. Very effectively shot, mostly at night, by director Matt Reeves, *Let Me In* was a rare English-language remake of a beloved non-American film that both respected its source material and was highly effective in its own right.

Let Me In saw Hammer working in an American context, albeit an unusual one, and their next film, *The Resident*, was even more directly American, a horror-thriller released in 2011 set in New York City. Directed by the Finnish Antti Jokinen, his first feature after a career in music videos, this starred Hilary Swank as an ER surgeon who rents a New York apartment and thinks she is being stalked. *The Resident* has a special place in the history of Hammer Films, as Christopher Lee makes his final appearance in a Hammer film, his first since 1976's *To the Devil... A Daughter*. Reviews for *The Resident* were rather mixed and the film was released straight to DVD in the US, Swank's two Best Actress Oscars having failed to turn her into a major box-office attraction.

After a run of films made elsewhere, the new Hammer Films finally returned home with a major cinema release in 2012 with *The Woman in Black* and scored the biggest hit the twenty-first-century version of the company has had to date. A highly atmospheric supernatural horror picture set in the late Victorian period, this featured Daniel Radcliffe as young lawyer Arthur Kipps, widowed after his wife dies in childbirth. Heartbroken and with his career failing, Kipps is sent to handle the sale of a secluded house, discovering upon arrival that the house is haunted by the spirit of a woman in black. Her spirit is seeking vengeance, particularly on the children of the village, and Kipps must work through his grief to discover what it is the woman wants.

Based on the novel by Susan Hill, *The Woman in Black* was directed with great care and a great deal of atmosphere by director James Watkins, who had previously co-written *My Little Eye* (2002) and *The Descent: Part 2* (2009), as well as writing and directing the disturbing, sadistic 'Hoodie Horror' *Eden Lake* (2008). In the latter, a young couple (Michael Fassbender and Kelly Reilly) are terrorised by a gang of teenagers while on a camping holiday. Nothing could be further from the subtle chills of *The Woman in Black*, in which scares are achieved by shadows and sound effects, somewhat in the same manner as Jack Clayton's 1961 classic *The Innocents*.

The Woman in Black was a considerable hit and Hammer set to work on a sequel, *The Woman in Black: Angel of Death*, released early in 2015, again based on a story by Susan Hill. The new story was set during the Second World War, during which children evacuated from London are brought to the same house that featured in the first film, causing the spirit of the woman in black to return. Although the film took around half the amount of the first at the box office, this still represented a decent profit.

Between the two *Woman in Black* films, a much smaller Hammer picture, *The Quiet Ones*, was released. This reached cinemas in April 2014, though principal photography finished in July 2012. This was another English-set film, in which Jared Harris played an Oxford University professor investigating poltergeist activity.

After this burst of activity, things have gone quiet at Hammer Films with regards to new productions. At time of writing, the company is working on a TV pilot for a series based on *Let the Right One In*, an idea that shows great promise. The Hammer name is stronger than ever, and the new company has proved that there remains a strong market for old-school creepy scares. One hopes that it is not too long before we see new productions from them.

Zombie Avalanche!

In terms of quantity, if not always quality, the key sub-genre of the British horror film in the first two decades of the twenty-first century has been the zombie movie. This amounted to an absolute avalanche of zombie pictures, from the mega-budget *World War Z* (a 2013 American production of monumental scale, which filmed scenes in Glasgow and Sandwich, Kent) to semi-professional productions that achieved cinema or DVD distribution deals against the odds.

Key to the explosion of popularity of the British zombie movie was the success of two films: *28 Days Later* (2002) and *Shaun of the Dead* (2004). The former was directed by Danny Boyle, who had become the hottest director in British film after the success of his first two films, *Shallow Grave* (1994) and *Trainspotting* (1996). His next two films, *A Life Less Ordinary* (1997) and *The Beach* (2000), had done less well, but Boyle's reinvention of the zombie movie in *28 Days Later* saw the director hit peak form once more.

The film sees Cillian Murphy play Jim, a cycle courier who wakes up in hospital from a coma to find the hospital, and central London itself, apparently deserted. The city has been struck down by an outbreak of Rage, a horrifying disease unleashed when animal rights activists free monkeys infected with the disease. Infected subjects are instantly transformed into fast-moving, unthinking cannibalistic monsters—technically not zombies, as they are not the resurrected dead, but the difference is academic—the infection spreading so fast that society has completely collapsed. Finding a few other survivors, Jim tries to get out of the city along with Selena (Naomie Harris), Frank (Brendan Gleeson), and Frank's daughter, Hannah (Megan Burns).

28 Days Later was partially shot on digital video, one of the first major films to make use of this technology. Boyle uses the technology brilliantly, imbuing the early scenes of a deserted, post-apocalyptic London with a genuinely epic feel despite its relatively modest budget of around £5 million. Crucially, Boyle and his collaborator, writer Alex Garland, do not fall into the trap of making the proceedings too grim for the audience to enjoy. The result is a film that is scary and fun, grim and exciting, and even manages to end on a note of hope, even if the ending audiences saw was not the one the filmmakers originally planned. *28 Days Later* was a considerable success on both sides of the Atlantic, resulting in the creditable, but slightly less impactful sequel *28 Weeks Later* (2007), directed by the Spaniard Juan Carlos Fresnadillo.

The idea of fast-moving zombies proved to be a masterstroke, bringing something truly different to the genre, but just as important to the development of the British zombie movie was *Shaun of the Dead*. If any one film illustrated how much horror had become a cherished part of the British psyche by the early 2000s, it was director Edgar Wright and his co-writer/star Simon Pegg's film. *Shaun of the Dead* was described as a 'RomZomCom', a description that very effectively described the mixture of genres the film worked within. Pegg played Shaun, who is worried that he is headed towards middle age with his life and relationships with his parents (Penelope Wilton and Bill Nighy) and his girlfriend (Kate Ashfield) in a complete mess. Matters are complicated considerably when his home village is infected by an outbreak of zombie-ism (if that's a word).

The film mixes a romantic slacker comedy with the cosy domesticity of the television sitcom alongside some genuinely extreme violence. It helped enormously that the script was genuinely funny—a real rarity in British horror. The gold standard of British horror comedy to this point was probably *Carry on Screaming* (1966), but the general standard was more like Frankie Howerd in disappointing *The House in Nightmare Park* (1973) and the downright awful *Bloodbath at the House of Death* (1984), which proved that genius DJ Kenny Everett was no actor. It helped also that it was clear that the people behind the film genuinely loved the horror genre as much as the comedy aspects of the film.

Shaun of the Dead was a film that grew out of a TV sitcom—Wright and Pegg, plus several other cast members (in particular Nick Frost and Jessica Stevenson), having previously worked on the show *Spaced*. The film was a surprise hit, leading to two follow ups, the 2007 action movie spoof *Hot Fuzz* and 2013's SF invasion film *The World's End*—known as the Cornetto Trilogy—and major Hollywood careers for Wright and Pegg. In terms of the zombie movie, what *Shaun of the Dead* demonstrated was that the genre was far more adaptable than was previously thought. George A. Romero's American zombie films had used the form for pointed social comment, and both Danny Boyle and Wright and Pegg showed that it was possible to do this within a British context.

From this start, there followed an absolute deluge of zombie pictures. Some were straight action/gore pictures, such as the bleak, apocalyptic *The*

Zombie Diaries (2006) and director Steve Barker's made in Scotland *Outpost* (2008), which set up a mercenaries *v.* Nazi zombies plot. Sony picked up the distribution rights, resulting in the film screening at cinemas throughout Europe. *Outpost* was financially successful enough to generate a sequel, *Outpost: Black Sun* (2010), and a prequel, *Outpost: Rise of the Spetsnaz* (2013). *Devil's Playground* (2010) starred Craig Fairbrass (who had failed to become the cockney Stallone in the fifteen years following *Proteus*) and England's bloke-y star of twenty-first-century, low-budget action and horror films, Danny Dyer.

This was a much more action-oriented *28 Days Later*-inspired zombie horror than Dyer's previous encounter with the walking dead, *Dogtown* (2009). This latter film featured Dyer alongside the incredibly productive Noel Clarke, who had turned his initial success as Mickey, occasional companion to David Tennant's Doctor into a career as an actor, writer, director and producer. Dyer and Clarke play part of a group of beery, laddish types set upon by 'Zombirds' in a rural village in which all the woman have been turned into flesh-eating ghouls by one of those disastrous government biological experiments that occur in zombie flicks. This was, as the plot might suggest, a comedy zombie effort, as was the surprisingly expensive-looking and well-done *Cockneys Vs Zombies* (2012). This represented a real mishmash of styles, all thrown in the general direction of the audience, a surprisingly amount of which worked just fine. A group of young semi-criminal types attempt a disastrous bank robbery in order to gain the funds to save the old folks' home their grandparents are in from being turned into luxury apartments. Just when the raid is about to degenerate into a shootout with the police, the area is overrun with zombies. A surprising amount of mileage is gained from seeing old stagers like Honor Blackman, Dudley Sutton, Georgina Hale, and Tony Selby swearing their heads off and committing gruesome acts of violence against zombies. Without the zombies, it would be *Carry on Eastenders*, which role the film fulfils quite well. As it stands, *Cockneys Vs Zombies* is actually too good to be described as a guilty pleasure. It does not all work, but when it does, it is surprisingly enjoyable.

Other strands of comedy were also mined with zombie themes added: 2005's *Boy Eats Girl* got full marks for a nice title, but this Anglo-Irish teen romantic comedy went downhill from there. It also managed to get itself banned in some places thanks to a scene of, for want of a better phrase, accidental suicide. Another inventively titled production was 2010's *Stag Night of the Dead*, in which a group of men continue with a planned stag night despite an ongoing zombie outbreak, the shambling undead being part of the evening's entertainment on a disused military base. This was more in the laddish vein of *Dogtown*, as was 2016's *Ibiza Undead*. Newcastle and Gateshead-shot *Zombie Women of Satan* (2009) was low budget and high concept, the theme being circus freaks *v.* sex cult zombies—the title alone was apparently enough to have some stores refusing to stock the film.

While the horror comedy and gore-hound markets were well-catered for, filmmakers with other agendas found the zombie sub-genre an interesting vehicle for serious messages. *Battle of the Bone* (2008) was shot on video by writer-director George Clarke for £10,000 in Northern Ireland, and had some trenchant points to make about the Protestant/Catholic religious divide in that country. Berating the men of violence for carrying on a dispute the reasons about which are lost in history, it explicitly uses the plot device of a zombie outbreak to present a common threat so extreme that it forces both sides to work together. The film's shoestring budget and semi-professional nature show in every frame, but it gets marks for originality and sincerity.

Attack of the Herbals (2010) was a low-budget Scottish zombie comedy with a plot somewhat reminiscent of a 1950s Ealing comedy as a group of locals try to save their rural village from the encroachment of a large supermarket complex. Here, a film about what might have been a parochial issue was given much wider appeal by the addition of a zombie subplot. In a similar fashion, *The Dead* (2010) was a British production filmed entirely in Africa in extremely difficult circumstances as a white American Air Force engineer and a black African soldier gone AWOL try to get across the continent in a world overrun by zombies. The film does not strain to make social commentary, but the basic plot setup causes the audience to make connections with the history of the continent, and *The Dead* was well-received, critics making comparisons with the work of Lucio Fulci and Sergio Leone. The Ford Brothers, who directed the film, were behind a sequel-*cum*-remake that was released three years later, entitled *The Dead 2: India*. Unfortunately, this repeated the plot of the first film rather too closely, albeit on a different continent, and made rather less impact as a result.

This overview of the 2000's British zombie phenomenon does not even cover all of the productions made in this period—there was even a 2012 Cardiff-shot sequel to George A. Romero's *Night of the Living Dead*, made possible by the 1968 film having accidentally fallen out of copyright—a positive flood of movies that continues to the present day. More recent productions include *Nina Forever* (2015), a black comedy about dealing with loss and the emotional overspill from previous relationships. In this case, a man's deceased girlfriend returns from the dead as a sarcastic zombie whenever he tries to have sex with his new girlfriend. More big-budget, major studio zombie pictures have appeared, including the 2016 movie version of the literary phenomenon *Pride, Prejudice and Zombies*, which failed to achieve popularity despite a starry cast.

The Girl with All the Gifts (2016) was another all-star production, this time featuring Gemma Arterton, Paddy Considine, and Glenn Close in a post-apocalyptic story in which a fungal infection has zombified most of humanity. Written by M. R. Carey, based on his novel of the same name, this attempted to find hope amid a seemingly hopeless situation in a story that was not entirely unlike *28 Days Later*, while at the same time being fiercely independent and unusual.

The resurgence in the zombie sub-genre has lasted for the best part of two decades and has seen the form grow from cheap Italian and American imports to major budget Hollywood-funded epics. Expensive blockbusters on the cinema screen such as *World War Z* have been joined by the astonishing long-term success of *The Walking Dead*, the American television series that, at time of writing, has been running for seven years. The zombie film is clearly not about to lapse in popularity any time soon, the rude health of the form reflecting the horror genre's continued enormous popularity. The horror film, and the zombie movie in particular, reflects the turbulent and uncertain times in which we live. Old certainties in the real world can be swept away without warning, and movies that show the breakdown of a society's rule, whether it be in the form of a man with an axe or a marauding hoard of zombies and the total destruction of society, help us to deal with this.

There are other factors that can be pointed towards, which explain why the zombie movie in particular has become so popular. Zombies, it should be pointed out, are not people—at least not any more, being already dead. Violence towards them in films offers the prospect of consequence-free violence, which often takes on a slapstick element. To pick an example, *Cockneys Vs Zombies* shows a zombie baby being drop-kicked in a scene that is played for laughs. In any other form of film, this scene would have been beyond the pale, even in the lax censorship landscape of 2012 when it was made. In a lesson that has been learned by certain political groups, if you dehumanise a group, then violence towards them becomes more acceptable. Non-horror films have taken this on board, too. There is a reason why Star Wars' Imperial Stormtroopers are covered from head to toe in white armour: it reduces their humanity so violence towards them does not count and the films retain their 12A rating.

For as long as the human race retains a dark side to its character, which it must find ways to confront, and people have fears and uncertainties they are unable to express in any other way, there will be a horror genre. It will poke into the murkiest recesses of our imaginations to find what we least want to be exposed to the light and let it bloom into full, horrific life—and we will pay to see it because, despite ourselves, most of us really love to be scared and British writers and filmmakers are very, very good at scaring people.

Long may they continue.

Endnotes

Chapter 3

1. Hollywood studios also produced Gothic romantic melodramas during this period, most notably producer Samuel Goldwyn's popular adaptations of *Wuthering Heights* (1939) and *Jane Eyre* (1943).
2. Matthews, T. D., *Censored* (London: Chatto & Windus, 1994), p. 143.
3. Holland, S., *The Trials of Hank Janson* (Surrey: Telos Publishing, 2004).
4. Horne, P., and Swaab, P. (eds), *Thorold Dickinson: A World of Film* (Manchester: Manchester University Press, 2008).

Chapter 4

1. Pimlott, B., *Harold Wilson* (London: HarperCollins, 1992), pp. 118–120.
2. Broccoli, A. R., and Zec, D., *When the Snow Melts: The Autobiography of Cubby Broccoli* (London: Boxtree Books, 1998), p. 106.

Chapter 5

1. encyclopedia.rank.ork/articles/pages/2924/The-Hollywood-Studio-System-1842-1945.html.
2. Sangster, J., *Inside Hammer: Behind the Scenes at the Legendary Film Studio* (Surrey: Reynolds and Hearn, 2001), pp. 58–59.
3. telegraph.cp.uk/culture/film/7967407/Michael-Powells-Peeping-Tom-the-film-that-killed-a career.html, 27 August 2010.
4. *The Times* (London, England), Wednesday 20 April 1960, p. 8.
5. Francis, F., and Dalton, T., *Freddie Francis: The Straight Story from Moby Dick to Glory, a Memoir* (Maryland: Scarecrow Press, 2013), pp. 129–131.

Chapter 6

1. Cohn, N., *Awopbopaloobop Alopbamboom: The Golden Age of Rock* (Boston: Da Capo Press, 1996), p. 15.

2. Francis, F., and Dalton, T., *Freddie Francis: The Straight Story from Moby Dick to Glory, a Memoir* (Maryland: Scarecrow Press, 2013), p. 133.
3. Ibid., p. 139.
4. blog.loa.org/2010/09/what-robert-bloch-owes-to-h-p-lovecraft.html.

Chapter 7

1. Porter, R., *London: A Social History* (Cambridge, Massachusetts: Harvard University Press, 1994), p. 102.
2. Hollywood studios also produced Gothic romantic melodramas during this period, most notably producer Samuel Goldwyn's popular adaptations of *Wuthering Heights* (1939) and *Jane Eyre* (1943).
3. Matthews, T. D., *Censored* (London: Chatto & Windus, 1994), p. 143.
4. Hamilton, J., *Beasts in the Cellar: The Exploitation Film Career of Tony Tenser* (Surrey: FAB Press, 2005), p. 117.
5. Ibid., p. 105.
6. Ibid., pp. 181–182.
7. Hearn, M, and Barnes, A., *The Hammer Story* (London Titan Books, 1997), p. 133.

Chapter 8

1. Hogdkinson, W., 'God, What a Terrible Film', *The Guardian*, 11 March 2005.

Chapter 9

1. Email correspondence with Norman J. Warren.
2. Ibid.

Chapter 11

1. Kramp, J., *Hallo! Hier spricht Edgar Wallace* (Berlin: Schwarzkopf & Schwarzkopf, 1998), pp. 212–221.

Chapter 15

1. Hearn, M, and Barnes, A., *The Hammer Story* (London Titan Books, 1997), p. 167.

Bibliography

blog.loa.org/2010/09/what-robert-bloch-owes-to-h-p-lovecraft.html

Broccoli, A. R., and Zec, D., *When the Snow Melts: The Autobiography of Cubby Broccoli* (London: Boxtree Books, 1998)

Cohn, N., *Awopbopaloobop Alopbamboom: The Golden Age of Rock* (Boston: Da Capo Press, 1996)

encyclopedia.rank.ork/articles/pages/2924/The-Hollywood-Studio-System-1842-1945.html

Francis, F., and Dalton, T., *Freddie Francis: The Straight Story from Moby Dick to Glory, a Memoir* (Maryland: Scarecrow Press, 2013)

Hamilton, J., *Beasts in the Cellar: The Exploitation Film Career of Tony Tenser* (Surrey: FAB Press, 2005)

Hearn, M, and Barnes, A., *The Hammer Story* (London Titan Books, 1997)

Hogdkinson, W., 'God, What a Terrible Film', *The Guardian*, 11 March 2005

Holland, S., *The Trials of Hank Janson* (Surrey: Telos Publishing, 2004)

Horne, P., and Swaab, P. (eds), *Thorold Dickinson: A World of Film* (Manchester: Manchester University Press, 2008)

Kramp, J., *Hallo! Hier spricht Edgar Wallace* (Berlin: Schwarzkopf & Schwarzkopf, 1998)

Matthews, T. D., *Censored* (London: Chatto & Windus, 1994)

Pimlott, B., *Harold Wilson* (London: HarperCollins, 1992)

Porter, R., *London: A Social History* (Cambridge, Massachusetts: Harvard University Press, 1994)

Sangster, J., *Inside Hammer: Behind the Scenes at the Legendary Film Studio* (Surrey: Reynolds and Hearn, 2001)

telegraph.cp.uk/culture/film/7967407/Michael-Powells-Peeping-Tom-the-film-that-killed-a career.html

The Times, 20 April 1960